Issues in Adoption

William Dudley, *Book Editor*

Daniel Leone, *President*
Bonnie Szumski, *Publisher*
Scott Barbour, *Managing Editor*
Helen Cothran, *Senior Editor*

CURRENT CONTROVERSIES

GREENHAVEN
PRESS®

THOMSON
™
GALE

San Diego • Detroit • New York • San Francisco • Cleveland
New Haven, Conn. • Waterville, Maine • London • Munich

© 2004 by Greenhaven Press. Greenhaven Press is an imprint of The Gale Group, Inc., a division of Thomson Learning, Inc.

Greenhaven® and Thomson Learning™ are trademarks used herein under license.

For more information, contact
Greenhaven Press
27500 Drake Rd.
Farmington Hills, MI 48331-3535
Or you can visit our Internet site at http://www.gale.com

ALL RIGHTS RESERVED.
No part of this work covered by the copyright hereon may be reproduced or used in any form or by any means—graphic, electronic, or mechanical, including photocopying, recording, taping, Web distribution or information storage retrieval systems—without the written permission of the publisher.

Every effort has been made to trace the owners of copyrighted material.

Cover credit: © Carecchio Elisabeth/CORBIS SYGMA

LIBRARY OF CONGRESS CATALOGING-IN-PUBLICATION DATA

Issues in adoption / William Dudley, book editor.
    p. cm. — (Current controversies)
Includes bibliographical references and index.
ISBN 0-7377-1625-8 (lib. bdg. : alk. paper) —
ISBN 0-7377-1626-6 (pbk. : alk. paper)
    1. Adoption—United States. I. Dudley, William, 1964– . II. Series.
HV875.55.I87 2004
362.73'4'0973—dc21   2003057253

Printed in the United States of America

Contents

Chapter 1: Should Adoption Be Encouraged?

Yes: Adoption Should Be Encouraged

No: Adoption Should Not Be Encouraged

want babies than help children in need. In a perfect world, no babies would be relinquished for adoption.

Chapter 2: Does America's Adoption System Need More Government Regulation?

Yes: More Regulation Is Needed

No: More Regulation Is Not Needed

Chapter 3: Should Adoptees Be Given Open Access to Adoption and Birth Records?

Yes: Adoptees Should Be Granted Open Access to Personal Information

No: Adoptees Should Not Be Granted Open Access to Personal Information

Chapter 4: Should Adoptions by Gays and Lesbians Be Permitted?

Yes: Gay and Lesbian Adoptions Should Be Permitted

No: Gay and Lesbian Adoptions Should Be Restricted

Foreword

By definition, controversies are "discussions of questions in which opposing opinions clash" (Webster's Twentieth Century Dictionary Unabridged). Few would deny that controversies are a pervasive part of the human condition and exist on virtually every level of human enterprise. Controversies transpire between individuals and among groups, within nations and between nations. Controversies supply the grist necessary for progress by providing challenges and challengers to the status quo. They also create atmospheres where strife and warfare can flourish. A world without controversies would be a peaceful world; but it also would be, by and large, static and prosaic.

The Series' Purpose

The purpose of the Current Controversies series is to explore many of the social, political, and economic controversies dominating the national and international scenes today. Titles selected for inclusion in the series are highly focused and specific. For example, from the larger category of criminal justice, Current Controversies deals with specific topics such as police brutality, gun control, white collar crime, and others. The debates in Current Controversies also are presented in a useful, timeless fashion. Articles and book excerpts included in each title are selected if they contribute valuable, long-range ideas to the overall debate. And wherever possible, current information is enhanced with historical documents and other relevant materials. Thus, while individual titles are current in focus, every effort is made to ensure that they will not become quickly outdated. Books in the Current Controversies series will remain important resources for librarians, teachers, and students for many years.

In addition to keeping the titles focused and specific, great care is taken in the editorial format of each book in the series. Book introductions and chapter prefaces are offered to provide background material for readers. Chapters are organized around several key questions that are answered with diverse opinions representing all points on the political spectrum. Materials in each chapter include opinions in which authors clearly disagree as well as alternative opinions in which authors may agree on a broader issue but disagree on the possible solutions. In this way, the content of each volume in Current Controversies mirrors the mosaic of opinions encountered in society. Readers will quickly realize that there are many viable answers to these complex issues. By questioning each author's conclusions, students and casual readers can begin to develop the critical thinking skills so important to evaluating opinionated material.

Current Controversies is also ideal for controlled research. Each anthology in the series is composed of primary sources taken from a wide gamut of informational categories including periodicals, newspapers, books, United States and foreign government documents, and the publications of private and public organizations. Readers will find factual support for reports, debates, and research papers covering all areas of important issues. In addition, an annotated table of contents, an index, a book and periodical bibliography, and a list of organizations to contact are included in each book to expedite further research.

Perhaps more than ever before in history, people are confronted with diverse and contradictory information. During the Persian Gulf War, for example, the public was not only treated to minute-to-minute coverage of the war, it was also inundated with critiques of the coverage and countless analyses of the factors motivating U.S. involvement. Being able to sort through the plethora of opinions accompanying today's major issues, and to draw one's own conclusions, can be a complicated and frustrating struggle. It is the editors' hope that Current Controversies will help readers with this struggle.

Greenhaven Press anthologies primarily consist of previously published material taken from a variety of sources, including periodicals, books, scholarly journals, newspapers, government documents, and position papers from private and public organizations. These original sources are often edited for length and to ensure their accessibility for a young adult audience. The anthology editors also change the original titles of these works in order to clearly present the main thesis of each viewpoint and to explicitly indicate the opinion presented in the viewpoint. These alterations are made in consideration of both the reading and comprehension levels of a young adult audience. Every effort is made to ensure that Greenhaven Press accurately reflects the original intent of the authors included in this anthology.

"While adoption remains entrenched in American life, its increasing openness ensures that concerns about its effects . . . will increasingly become matters of public debate."

Introduction

Adoption can be defined as a process by which children are brought together with adults who are not their biological parents to form a family. Practiced informally throughout human history, adoption in the United States has evolved into a formalized legal procedure; its primary statutory purpose is to protect the welfare of children in cases where the birth parents are gone or unable to care for their offspring. Through adoption, the legal ties to a child's birth parents are severed. Adoptees (adopted persons) are seen in the eyes of the law as permanent members of the adoptive family with all the legal rights and privileges of biological children.

Adoption has long been an important part of America's social landscape. A survey by the Evans B. Donaldson Institute in 1997 found that six out of ten Americans have had a "personal experience" with adoption, meaning that they, a family member, or close friend had been adopted, adopted a child, or placed a child for adoption. Because no national organization or government branch keeps track of adoptions, national statistics on the prevalence of adoption in the United States are at best rough estimates. The number of adopted children under the age of eighteen in the United States has been estimated to be between 1 and 2 million. Approximately 150,000 adoptions are approved in U.S. courts every year (some of these cases involve the children's kin rather than unrelated adults).

The lack of precise data on adoption is in part a result of its historical development in the United States. For much of the twentieth century, adoption was a practice shrouded in secrecy. Under what are now called "closed" or "confidential" adoptions, the identities of the birth parents and adoptive parents were kept from each other by the adoption agencies that made the arrangements. Pregnant women who had decided to give up their children were often given as little contact as possible with their babies at birth, and in some cases were not even told of their babies' gender. Adoptees were issued new birth certificates listing only their adoptive parents and were sometimes never told by their parents that they were adopted. Such practices reflected the prevailing wisdom of the time that "adoptive families stood their best chance of thriving if they locked out all reminders of how they were formed," author Adam Pertman writes. In addition, these secretive methods were thought the best way to protect both birth parents and child from the social stigma of illegitimacy.

Introduction

The practice of closed adoption was the center of growing controversy during the last quarter of the twentieth century. Critics argued that shrouding adoption in secrecy and shame led to long-term emotional problems for children and parents. The 1978 publication of *The Adoption Triangle* by social workers Annette Baran and Reuben Pannor and child psychologist Arthur D. Sorosky marked a sea change in public and expert opinion on adoption. The authors asserted that the practice of closed adoption "can be the cause of many potential problems" because of the trauma associated with separating mother and infant—an event the authors labeled as "psychological amputation." They also contended that adopted children can suffer emotional problems due to "genealogical bewilderment" and a loss of their "true identity." The publication of that book coincided with the rise of an adoption rights movement whose goals included the promotion of reunions between birth parents and children and changes in state laws preventing adoptees from accessing their original birth certificates.

A solution the authors of *The Adoption Triangle* prescribed was "open" adoption. Under open adoptions, which in recent decades have begun to replace confidential adoptions as the American norm for domestic infant adoption, the birth parent or parents meet the prospective adoptive parents, participate in the adoption process (in some cases choosing the adoptive parents), and maintain contact with the child and adoptive family after the child is born and adopted. Birth parents in open adoptions still give up their basic parental rights, but they also enter into some type of agreement for continued communication, which could range from occasional letters to ongoing personal contact. The opening of the adoption process has been accelerated by the Internet, which has allowed birth mothers and people seeking to adopt to find and directly communicate with each other. The Internet has also proved a powerful tool for adoptees and birth parents seeking to find each other.

Proponents of open adoption argue that it benefits all members of the "adoption triad." Adoptees benefit by acquiring knowledge of their family and medical history and experiencing fewer feelings of rejection. Birth parents benefit from knowing how their children are faring, enabling them to cope better with their decision to relinquish their children. Adoptive parents, proponents of open adoption argue, also benefit because open adoption usually results in a stronger relationship with their adopted children. "All three members of the triad," Pertman contends, "become more secure when their relationships cease to be based on fear and fantasy."

The growing trend towards open adoption is not without its critics, however. Some argue that the purported benefits of openness have not been proven by clinical research and that allowing an ongoing relationship between the birth parent(s) and the adopted child's family may not be in anyone's best interests, including the child's. Family therapist Patrick F. Fagan argues that blending birth families with adoptive families may result in a "confusion of roles" that "interferes with parent and child bonding in the adoptive family and inhibits the birth parents' grieving process." Fagan and others have called for a renewed emphasis on traditional closed adoptions. Another group of critics has attacked open adoption for not being open enough, arguing that some birth mothers are being cheated by promises of continued contact with their offspring, only to find out that agreements made prior to the adoption finalization are legally unenforceable. Other critics, such as author Evelyn Burns Robinson, have called for the abolition of adoption itself in favor of a system of temporary guardianship in which the children's legal ties to their natural parents are not severed. Robinson asserts that even in cases where the mother suffers from a mental health problem that puts her children at risk, "there is no justification . . . for changing the child's identity and pretending that the child has a different mother."

Robinson's abolitionist views remain a minority opinion in the United States. A 2002 survey sponsored by the Dave Thomas Foundation for Adoption found that 63 percent of Americans had a high opinion of adoption and that nearly 40 percent of American adults had considered adopting a child. In addition, adoption has become increasingly popular among several groups that had in the past not been allowed to formally adopt children, including single people, unmarried couples, older parents, and gays and lesbians. But while adoption remains entrenched in American life, its increasing openness ensures that concerns about its effects on all members of the adoption triad—concerns that were formerly swept under the rug—will increasingly become matters of public debate. The viewpoints in *Issues in Adoption: Current Controversies* examine several of the leading controversies surrounding adoption in the early twenty-first century.

Chapter 1

Should Adoption Be Encouraged?

Chapter Preface

Adoption in America is marked by supply and demand imbalances. One exists between the shrinking number of infants (especially healthy white infants) being placed for adoption and the growing number of infertile couples and other families and individuals desiring to adopt. Would-be adoptive parents often wait for years, spend thousands of dollars, and in some cases travel to other countries in their quest to adopt a baby. However, another imbalance exists between the thousands of older American children eligible for adoption now housed in temporary foster homes and the number of families and individuals willing to adopt these children, many of whom may require special medical and educational attention. Social policy efforts to rectify these imbalances, such as encouraging pregnant women to consider adoption or placing more foster care children in adoptive homes, have themselves caused controversy, especially as regards the interests and rights of birth mothers.

Some adoption advocates believe that more pregnant women should be encouraged to make adoption relinquishment plans. The percentage of unmarried pregnant women who decide on such a course of action has declined significantly in the United States. Between 1965 and 1972 almost 20 percent of white infants born to single mothers were placed for adoption, but by the end of the century that number had dwindled to less than 2 percent. Both abortion, legalized in 1973, and single parenthood, less stigmatized now than in the past, have become far more popular among single pregnant women. This trend is worrisome to those who believe that adoption may be a better choice than abortion or single parenthood for both mother and child. Abortion is criticized by pro-life activists not only because they believe it constitutes murder, but because it is something that imposes long-term psychological and emotional costs on women. Single parenthood is also denigrated by those who believe that it hurts society. Marvin Olasky, a scholar who has written several books about the welfare system, argues that "numerous research studies show that single-parenting is socially, economically, and psychologically destructive, but adoption of infants overwhelmingly works out well for babies, birth parents, and adoptive parents." In 2000 Congress endorsed this idea by passing legislation funding adoption awareness training for mothers and counselors.

Whether or not such counseling is appropriate is a matter of debate. The idea that adoption is a panacea that helps all concerned is not shared by those who believe that women have been and continue to be unfairly coerced into relinquishing their children for the benefit of adoptive parents. "The glory days of white-baby relinquishment in the 1950s and 1960s depended on coercion," writes columnist Katha Pollitt, who belittles adoption promotion efforts as harmful "guilt and pressure tactics" aimed at vulnerable women. Some psychologists contend that adoption may cause emotional problems for mothers that may not fully erupt until years later. Some birth mothers have since regretted their decision and question the process by which they were encouraged to consider adoption.

Concern over birth parents also helps drive the debate over whether to place more foster care children in permanent adoptive homes—a goal enshrined in the 1997 Adoption and Safe Families Act, a national law that created financial inducements for states to increase the number of children being adopted. The Child Welfare League has estimated that about one-fifth of the half million children in foster care in the United States are waiting for adoption. Supporters of ASFA argue that children need permanency and that too many of them have been living in temporary foster homes for months or even years—a situation they blame in part on the goal of "family preservation" that guided most child welfare departments prior to 1997. Most children in foster care have been placed there because they have been found to be victims of child abuse or neglect at the hands of their birth families. Under the guise of family preservation, many were housed in "temporary" foster homes for months or even years waiting for their parents to be rehabilitated and designated as fit parents. Under ASFA the goal of family preservation was deemphasized in favor of finding permanent homes for foster children. But critics of ASFA continue to defend the ideal of family preservation and argue that many parents labeled as neglectful are simply poor people who should have access to greater social services, not have their children taken from them and adopted by someone else. Evelyn Burns Robinson, an adoption critic and former social worker, argues that "we must stop using the *permanent* practice of adoption to solve what are often *temporary* problems involving the biological mother."

The rights and needs of birth mothers are important concerns that animate the debate over whether adoption should be promoted as a social policy. Birth mothers are not the only people affected by adoption, of course; their interests must be balanced with those of the adoptive parents and children. The authors of the articles in this chapter present various arguments on whether adoption should be encouraged.

Adoption Should Be Encouraged as an Alternative to Abortion and Single Parenthood

by Jean Garton

About the author: *Jean Garton is cofounder and past president of Lutherans for Life and author of* Who Broke the Baby?

In a classroom of six-year olds, the teacher was discussing a picture of a family. One of the children featured had a different hair color than did the other family members. A little girl in the class said maybe that was because the boy had been adopted. "I know all about adoptions," she said, "because I was adopted." 'What does that mean if you're adopted?" asked a classmate. "It means," said the little girl, "that you grew in your mommy's heart instead of her tummy."

Yet there are whole organizations that exist for the sole purpose of aborting the adoption option. They believe that babies are better dead than with parents who are not theirs by birth.

When the founder of an anti-adoption group was asked how she would counsel a teenage daughter who became pregnant, she said she would counsel her daughter "first to keep the baby, second to have an abortion, third to commit suicide, and only fourth to put the baby up for adoption."

Why all the hostility? In a *National Review* article (6/7/1993) Dr. Marvin Olasky suggests three reasons.

1. In order for abortion to be legal and accepted, the unborn child has to be seen as the woman's property.
2. For female autonomy to be affirmed, it must not be acknowledged that it is better for a child to live in a two-parent family than with a single parent.
3. Every happy adoptee is a reminder to aborting mothers of the road not taken.

Jean Garton, "The Adoption Option," presentation at the World Congress of Families II, November 14–17, 1999. Copyright © 1999 by Jean Garton. Reproduced by permission.

Adoption may not be a new reproductive technology, but it is a tried and true family-building option. Adoption, all in all, has served women, children and society well.

- It stems the tide of poverty and misery that can flow from out-of-wedlock births;
- It places children into more stable family structures than they might have with biological or foster parents; and
- It allows childless couples to create families.

As one professional noted, "There are no unwanted children, only unfound parents."

In the United States today [1999] there are 2 million couples seeking to adopt. Unfortunately, there are only 30,000 children available for placement each year. Such numbers result from two factors.

First, the number of infertile couples in the U.S. exceeds one million, and even recent advances in reproductive technology can only help one in five. Secondly, America's annual abortion rate of 1.3 million drastically reduces the number of children available for adoption.

The desperation of childless couples is evident in ads which appear daily in newspapers across the country. The following are actual placements.

HELP! Our dream is of a small voice calling mommy and daddy. We are a warm, compassionate, financially secure and loving couple. Call us at _____.

HUGS, KISSES & DREAMS await your newborn. Your child will be part of a warm, tender and happy home. We are a loving and happily married couple who love sports and enjoy travel. Call Arlene and Jim at _____.

INFANT ADOPTION! We are two loving people waiting to love a third. We are dreaming of 2 A.M. feedings and buggy rides through the park. Your expenses paid. Call Sally and Jeff at _____.

Americans have increasingly been turning to other countries for children, with the largest numbers now coming from Asia, in particular Korea, Vietnam and China. The obvious difference in appearance that results from transracial adoption was reflected in a true story told by the mother of two young sons.

One day when they were in a store, a stranger asked if the boys were friends rather than brothers, noting that they didn't look at all alike. The child "of color" said, "that's because I'm adopted. That's when you have the same family but not the same face."

The findings from a four-year federally funded . . . study showed positive family dynamics across all types of adoptions whether transracial or same-race. Overall the children adopted from Asia have the most positive results in a very positive picture.

Especially significant is that, given the large number of minority children and babies needing to be adopted, transracially adopted adolescents are closest of all to their parents.

The History of Adoption

Adoption in the contemporary context reflects very little of its history in American culture or in its ancient past. It is so thoroughly bureaucratized it is easy to assume that adoption is a product of the 20th century. The history of adoption, however, begins much earlier.

One of the first written accounts dates back 4,000 years to the Code of Hammurabi. The Egyptians, Greeks and Romans recognized and legalized adoption. For instance, to ensure the continuation of his power, Julius Caesar adopted his nephew Octavian, who was later known as Caesar Augustus. . . .

However, the primary interest in adoption for earlier societies was to secure the continuation of power rather than in the best interests of the child. Consistent with their belief that children were property, Greeks and Romans treated children as secondary parties to the adoption contract.

The Bible provides the first view of adoption as a covenant rather than a contract. Ancient Hebrews believed that contracts governed the exchange of property but that the formation of personal relationships was by a covenant, a sacred promise that was the foundation of kinship and family.

> *"Adoption, all in all, has served women, children and society well."*

The story of Moses in the Old Testament is a classic account of the adoption covenant. When his mother feared that Moses would be killed, she placed him in a reed basket on the Nile River. He was found by the Pharaoh's daughter who rescued him and, the Bible says, Moses "became her son."

Moses' life and well-being were secured by the sacrifice of two women: his mother and Pharaoh's daughter. Their adoption covenant was a promise which ensured that Moses' life would be spared and nurtured.

For Christians, adoption is generally viewed as an honorable institution. It is even more significant in a spiritual sense for those who are not part of the "chosen people" of the Old Testament—not of the lineage of Abraham, Isaac and Jacob—in that they become members of God's family by adoption through belief in God's Son as Savior.

Adoption Is Not Presented as an Option

Because of misconceptions about adoption, many more girls and women today are either aborting their babies or raising them as single parents. Over 1 million teenagers in America become pregnant each year. Over 40 percent of them choose abortion. Only 2–3 percent place their child for adoption.

There are over 4,000 crisis pregnancy centers that offer supportive services. Yet all together they report that only 2 percent of their clients choose to place their child for adoption. Planned Parenthood, on the other hand, claims that 3 percent of their clients choose adoption. What's wrong with this picture?

The truth is that adoption is rarely presented as an option. Yet society does itself and these young women no favor when the option of adoption is not offered and encouraged.

Adoption serves all four parties well—the child, the biological mother, the adopting parents and society—because the evidence is overwhelming as to the negative effects experienced by single mothers and their children.

Comparing Outcomes

Unmarried mothers who keep their children, when compared to those who place them for adoption, are more likely:

- to have serious employment problems;
- to require public assistance;
- to live in poverty;
- to have children with health problems;
- to have children with serious behavior problems;
- to have infants who die from injuries;
- to repeat an out-of-wedlock pregnancy;
- to have children who have out-of-wedlock pregnancies;
- to be school dropouts;
- to remain unmarried.

By way of contrast, unmarried mothers who make an adoption plan for their children are more likely:

- to finish school;
- to obtain a higher education;
- to escape living in poverty;
- to not require public assistance;
- to delay marriage longer;
- to marry eventually;
- to be employed 12 months after the birth;
- to avoid a second out-of wedlock pregnancy.

Outcomes for those who choose adoption are often similar to those cited by women who choose abortion.

- Each can pursue earlier goals and plans.
- Each can live independently.
- Neither will have to parent prematurely.
- Each will be free of the financial burdens of parenting.
- Each will avoid being forced into a hasty marriage.
- If young, each can resume their youthful lifestyle.

Teenagers, in particular, who bear and keep children outside of marriage are statistically more likely to remain uneducated, unemployed and underprivileged. When compared with the general population, children placed with adoptive couples, rather than remaining with unmarried young mothers, fare much better economically and have more stable lives.

Language has played a negative role in the adoption discussion. It is difficult for a young woman to see adoption as a positive solution when terms are used such as "giving up" or "giving away" her child instead of making an adoption plan.

In adoption what a mother "gives up" are parenting responsibilities which she is unable to provide her child. That is not to ignore the physical or emotional pain involved in entrusting a child to an adopting couple. On the contrary, it means that the biological mother will be assuming immediate pain in order to spare her child the greater pain that lies ahead. Adoption is looking after the interests of the child first, while providing specialized, sensitive counseling to help the hurting mother.

> *"Because of misconceptions about adoption, many more girls and women today are either aborting their babies or raising them as single parents."*

Adopted Children Fare Well

It is a myth that adopted children do not do as well in life as do children living with a biological parent. A recent study of 700 teenagers who had been adopted as infants found them to be every bit as well-adjusted, socially skilled and intellectually able as their non-adopted peers.

Children adopted at a later age, after years in foster care, appear to have more behavioral and emotional problems and to have experienced more physical abuse. Elizabeth Bartholet of Harvard University, an adoption law expert, says, "It's abuse that hurts kids, not adoption."

A U.S. Senator, Mary Landrieu of Louisiana, tells of her husband's adoption from an orphanage in Ireland when he was five. He had a brother whom he recently met who was not adopted into a family. They are now both in their fifties. The Senator's husband is confident, successful and fulfilled. His brother is none of those and continues to be adrift. Is that just a coincidence?

Adoption is part of my own family history. My father was born into an extremely poor immigrant family with an alcoholic father. Upon his mother's death, his older siblings were placed with relatives. He and his brother were placed in an orphanage.

After a short time he was adopted and eventually enjoyed not only a long career as a high official in the New York City Police Department but a happy 65 year-long marriage to my mother. His non-adopted brother became a many-times-divorced, frequently fired bartender. Is that just a coincidence?

Adoption is currently playing a part in my daughter's family. After having four biological children, she and her husband adopted an 18-month-old little gift from Taiwan with severe facial/cranial disfigurements. A few years later, they adopted an 11-month-old little girl from Korea who was born without a right arm.

Those who think it is harder to love an adopted child than a biological child couldn't be more wrong. I know that firsthand as the grandmother of those two adopted little girls. Others know it, too.

When a young woman named Mary gave birth to her first child, her husband was on military duty so she spent the first weeks after the child's birth at her parents' home. One day Mary mentioned to her mother that she was surprised that her baby's hair was reddish when both she and her husband were blond. "Well, remember" said her mother, "that your dad's hair was once red." "But, Mom," said Mary, "that wouldn't make any difference because I'm adopted." With a surprised smile her mother said, "I always forget." (A true story!)

Finding oneself with an unexpected, unwanted pregnancy, especially if a woman is young or single, can be one of the most difficult moments she will ever face. Because abortion represents a relatively swift and supposedly "simple" resolution to an unplanned pregnancy, carrying a baby through birth and completing an adoption plan stands as an act of extraordinary courage and love. Perhaps no other gesture expresses motherhood in its most purely loving form.

The miracle of adoption is about the pain, resolution, and growth that comes when adoptive couples accept their infertility and face their fears about adoption and when a young girl and her family or a single woman face the issues of an untimely pregnancy. . . .

A Precious Gift

Adoption can be an enormously unselfish gift to a baby, not only as a way to give a child a secure, loving, stable family but to give that child the most precious gift of all—life.

Adoption isn't easy. It is one of the most complex emotional arrangements in which an individual can be involved. Yet, of the other options—aborting the child or raising the child as a single parent—adoption is the most child-centered. It is a healthy, realistic and sensible choice for all the parties involved.

Prejudice Against Adoption and Adopted Families Should Be Challenged

by Beth Hall and Gail Steinberg

About the authors: *Beth Hall and Gail Steinberg are the founders of Pact, an Adoption Alliance, a membership organization that provides teaching and support services to adoptive families and birth parents. They are also the authors of* Inside Transracial Adoption.

Racism:
- A *belief* that race is the primary determinant of human traits and capacities.
- A *belief* that racial differences produce an inherent superiority of a particular race.

Sexism:
- *Prejudice or discrimination* against someone on the basis of gender.

Adoptism:
- A *belief* that forming a family by birth is superior to forming a family by adoption.
- A *belief* that keeping a child with his/her biological parents is inherently better than placing a child for adoption.
- A *belief* that growing up as an adopted person is the primary determinant of human traits and capacities.
- A *belief* that differences in family-building structures or methods produce an inherent superiority in families of a particular structure or method.
- *Prejudice or discrimination* against members of the adoption triad.

Andrea, a birth mother, has moved on from her experience of placing her child for adoption, becoming a successful doctor and mother of two (more). We met Andrea at a workshop for adoptive parents, where she was speaking about her experience as a birth parent. She is a survivor who, faced the worst choice

Beth Hall and Gail Steinberg, "Adoptism: A Definition," www.pactadopt.org, 1998. Copyright © 1998 by Pact, an Adoption Alliance. Reproduced by permission.

she could imagine, not only made the best choice she could but lived through and with it.

> People try to be there for me, they try to understand, but it's hard to hear the words that they offer because what's behind them is the way they really feel: Knowing I wasn't ready to be a parent. . . . Disappointing my family and friends, who thought they knew me. . . . Wanting my child to be with me but knowing I'm not the best choice. . . . Perhaps the hardest of all is to hear someone say, "I think what you did was wonderful but I could never do it myself." To be set apart is one of the hardest parts of being a birth mother—not only did I lose my child, but I was wrong, out of sync with the deepest laws of nature for making a choice that no "real" parent, who truly loves her children, could make herself.

Andrea gave words to a reality and pain that isn't often perceived, **even by those who may love us best. Parents who choose adoption for their children are considered not as good or as valid as parents who parent their children.**

Ben is an adult who was adopted at birth. He is now married, and he and his wife have a two-year-old who was born to them. They are hoping to adopt a second child. He told us this story:

> I remember when I told my best friend that Lynn and I were planning to adopt. I couldn't believe his response. "Why would you even think of that?" he said. "You guys make great kids. Why would you want to take in someone else's cast-off without knowing what you're getting?" All I thought was, "Wow! You know I'm adopted and that's what you say to me? What do you say about me when I'm out of the room?"

A Hidden Bias

Ben gave words to an incredulity many adopted adults have expressed; that others hold a hidden bias about adoption and that they never know when it will pop out and cause pain. **Even those who love them best may say something unexpected, summoning up the stereotype that adopted means reject, cast-off, bad seed, etc. People who are placed for adoption are not considered to have been as valued by their birth parents as children who are raised within their original families.**

We met Sarah in the intimacy of a grief support meeting. Each person present had lost a child when a birth parent reclaimed custody. Three years before, Sarah and her husband had lost their son Greg (adopted at birth) when he was four months old. They had since adopted a little girl. Sarah spoke as a survivor, someone who had faced the worst she could have imagined and lived through it. "When Christine came and took away Greggie," she said,

> people tried to be there for us. Everyone tried, but something always seemed off when they tried to comfort me. I just couldn't shake the feeling that underneath, even our closest friends secretly felt that her reclaiming him was somehow more right than his staying with us—right, according to some higher order of things. Feeling sorry for us was something separate. I know our friends

and family did feel sorry for us but something else was at risk, something no one ever talks about. I've come to think that most people deep down believe that birth mothers and children belong together—no matter what. Nobody ever said that to us straight out, but it was there. I think even the people who love us the best had those feelings, but nobody would ever come right out and say anything. Feeling set apart from everyone was one of the hardest parts of losing Greggie for me. Not only did I lose my baby, I was wrong—out of sync with the deepest laws of nature for wanting him when she had first rights.

More than one pair of eyes welled up with tears. Sarah had given words to a hurt that isn't often spoken: that even those who love us best may not regard our families formed by adoption as valid compared to families formed by birth—*even those who love us best.* There was a long pause in the conversation after she spoke, as the hard truth sank in.

Fighting Adoptism

These are examples of adoptism at its core. Adoptism is a cultural *belief* that families formed by adoption are less truly connected than birth families; that birth families should be preserved at all costs and under all circumstances except the most severely harmful; that people who were adopted were first rejected, maybe for a reason. No matter what place you hold in the adoption triad, such judgments and discriminations feel the same. As a society, we tend to understand the dangers of bias based on race, gender or class. **Adoptism is no different. Adoptism is just as damaging.**

And we absorb the biases of our society as we grow up. As with racism and all the other "isms," it's through recognizing our deepest attitudes that we can change those that must be changed. Perhaps society's *belief* that parents must stay with their children is linked to the dark fears of childhood: "What will happen to me without Mommy and Daddy? Who will take care of me?" Maybe some of the bias against adoption is an extension of the voice of that child who can imagine no means of survival but for parents to take care of children born to them.

> *"Even those who love us best may not regard our families formed by adoption as valid compared to families formed by birth."*

Whatever adoptism's sources, the important thing is that we can change ourselves and our attitudes. Recognition allows forgiveness. We can forgive others because we share their fears. We can feel part of, instead of separate from, victims or survivors. Understanding the bias takes away its power. Adoptism is alive and well and everywhere. Let's do something about it.

International Adoptions Should Be Celebrated

by Adam Pertman

About the author: *Adam Pertman, a reporter for the* Boston Globe *for more than twenty years, is the author of* Adoption Nation: How the Adoption Revolution Is Transforming America, *from which the following viewpoint was excerpted.*

It's no accident that Americans adopt more children internationally than do the inhabitants of the rest of the planet combined. After all, nearly every one of us came to this extraordinary country from somewhere else. We don't always find it easy to accept new waves of immigrants, but we invariably succeed in weaving their facial structures, their skin tones, and their heritages into our cultural tapestry. Throughout its history, this nation has opened its doors to people who, for more reasons than anyone can count, have needed new homes. It has taken us in, given us new lives. Adopted us.

What it has not done is force us to sever our emotional, spiritual, or physical ties to our forebears or our ancestral lands. Rather, one of the genuinely noble, enriching aspects of the American sensibility—notwithstanding the intolerance of some narrow-minded people and political movements—is its celebration of people's connections to their past. We marvel at the beauty of an African-print dress, revel in the music at a Latino festival or an Irish step dance, savor the delights of Asian restaurants, incorporate the expressive words of other languages into our own.

In many essential ways, adoption is a metaphor for the society in which it is coming of age, and in which it plays an increasingly active and visible role. More and more of the parallels are revealing themselves as the domestic branch of the institution emerges from the shadows, but they have been evident for half a century to anyone who has paid attention to or participated in the adoption of children from overseas.

Adam Pertman, *Adoption Nation: How the Adoption Revolution Is Transforming America*. New York: Basic Books, 2000. Copyright © 2000 by Adam Pertman. All rights reserved. Reproduced by permission of Copyright Clearance Center, Inc.

Korean Children

The white couples who took in Korean War orphans knew that stuffing pillows under the wives' blouses wouldn't fool anybody. They couldn't even consider deceiving their sons and daughters into thinking they hadn't been adopted. And they repeatedly learned that, no matter how hard they tried to become Ozzie and Harriet, their parenting experience would be shaped by their decisions to raise children of races and cultures different than their own, children who would come home crying when classmates or teachers hurt them with racial taunts, children whose curiosity

"Americans adopt more children internationally than do the inhabitants of the rest of the planet combined."

about their backgrounds was aroused each time they passed a mirror and couldn't detect a hint of their parents' features in their reflections. Or children who avoided looking at themselves altogether.

"I have Korean friends now who used to stand in front of the mirror and try to make their eyes bigger and rounder, or wore blond wigs or even dyed their hair blond. Ridiculous things like that. My way of dealing with it was to not look in the mirror much, I guess because I knew I wouldn't like what I saw," says Crystal Lee Hyun Joo Chappell, whose white adoptive parents raised her and three other Korean children in the small town of Dimondale, Michigan, starting in the 1960s. Apart from her siblings, Crystal was the lone Korean in her elementary school; her parents' friends were white, as were their neighbors, their friends, the shoppers at their local stores. And the adoption agency had counseled her parents not to dwell on their children's past, but to immerse them in their new realities so they would "assimilate" quickly and thoroughly.

As is still the case in many adoptions by Caucasian parents of children from other races and cultures, whether born in the United States or in other nations, the absorption process sometimes works too well. "I was brought up 110 percent American," says Hyun Joo, who has used the first name given to her at birth, along with her adoptive last name, since reuniting with her biological mother in Korea several years ago. Asked what it meant to be "110 percent American," she replies: "I really thought I was white."

So she was unprepared, even shocked, when some older boys pummeled her with profanities and racial slurs on the school bus during her sixth-grade year. The little kids in the supermarket were even more cruel: They just stared. "There were constant reminders of who I was and what I really looked like, but I learned to ignore them, deny them, pretend they weren't there. It was a matter of self-preservation, I guess. But it was pretty horrible to see an infant surprised by your face, looking at you like you're an alien. You can't fault a baby because a baby's so innocent, but at the same time you feel inhuman."

This notion of coming from another planet permeates the self-descriptions of adoptees of all types and ages, most pointedly those who feel disconnected from their personal histories. That doesn't mean, as a group, that they yearn for one specific piece of their puzzle—though most want basic data about their birth parents, at a minimum, at some point in their lives. But a lopsided majority, including those who profess little interest in their genealogies, will say they feel more grounded and secure when their adoptive parents infuse their upbringings with the cultures from which they came, routinely give them information about their backgrounds and, when physical differences are apparent, expose them to other people who look like them.

Some studies, and some adoptees themselves, suggest that their inner turmoil—especially if they are deprived of background information—can lead to behavioral or ego problems. Most research, however, indicates they grow up with the same kinds of formative issues, and achieve at the same levels, as their counterparts raised in birth families. Adoption doesn't typically define adoptees' day-to-day existence, but it can play an important role in how they perceive themselves at various stages of their lives. To the extent that parents can help their children form positive self-images, giving them the resources and support to feel like earthlings simply seems like the right things to do, even when it might be emotionally or logistically difficult to accomplish.

One of the defining characteristics of the adoption revolution is the realization of that truth. As a result, a growing number of agencies and social workers are abandoning the fantasy of blind assimilation and doing a 180-degree turn: They advise prospective parents to incorporate their children's heritage into daily life. When someone white considers forming a family with children of another race, for example, whether from foster care or through a private adoption, the professionals recommend establishing role models and making friends of that race, perhaps even moving to a new neighborhood so their sons and daughters can mature among peers who look like them. And so they know their parents are comfortable with, and respect, people who share their children's traits.

> *"A growing number of agencies and social workers . . . advise prospective parents to incorporate their child's heritage into daily life."*

Prospective parents who adopt from other nations regularly receive such guidance today. Indeed, because the majority of intercountry adoptions involve social workers and other specialists employed by agencies—people educated to understand these issues as opposed to private practitioners or untrained individuals, no matter how competent, making their own arrangements—the integration of other nations' customs and histories into American families, into our social fabric, is progressing rapidly. . . .

Adoption is inculcating our society with more and more children who don't look like their parents, and by doing so, it is playing a small but important role in alleviating bias on a personal level. There are innumerable white grandparents, uncles, aunts, and cousins, for example, who have surprised themselves with the unconditional love they feel for their new black or Asian or Hispanic relatives, and who have learned critical lessons as a result. Adoption is helping to crack the walls of prejudice and intolerance on a broader scale, too: Just one family of Korean children starkly demonstrated to the white majority of Dimondale, every day, that people with different appearances could be kind, smart, accomplished, and easy to live with.

That scenario was unusual when Hyun Joo was growing up in Michigan in the 1970s, but today it is being duplicated nationwide at an escalating rate. In 1998, the last year for which statistics were available, Americans adopted almost 16,000 children from abroad, more than 10,000 of them from Asia, Central and South America, Africa, and the Caribbean. The comparable figures a decade earlier were about 8,000 total, 7,800 of whom were born in nations where the dominant skin tones and facial features aren't white-European.

These statistics reveal unmistakable trends: First, the tide of Americans adopting overseas is rising, both in sheer numbers and as a proportion of all adoptions outside the children's own families; by the latter measure, foreign adoption is up from less than 10 percent a decade ago to perhaps 20 percent today. Meanwhile, due almost entirely to the opening of Eastern Europe, an escalating number of the internationally adopted children are Caucasian; it's hard to nail down precisely how many because the former Soviet states include residents who are Asian or of mixed descent.

Some equally important, but less evident, underlying shifts are also evident from the Immigration and Naturalization Service visa counts. One is the rapid growth, on a percentage basis, of children adopted from Central America as the people there cope with endemic poverty, natural disasters, and the aftermath of devastating civil wars. From 1989 to 1998, the official annual total of adoptions from the region jumped from 595 to 976; of those, amid alarming indications that a lack of regulation had led to baby snatchings and black marketeering, Guatemala's share leaped from 202 to 911.

An even more consequential change—a revolutionary chapter in international adoption history—was unfolding at the same time, half a world away. During this ten-year period, annual adoptions from Asia rose by more than 50 percent, from 5,112 to 7,827. That explosion was significant on its own, but it wasn't the lead of the story. This was: During the final decade of the twentieth century, the number of children adopted annually from mainland China skyrocketed from thirty-three to 4,206.

Adoptions from China

Across the United States today, it's getting increasingly difficult to find a playground without at least one little girl from China, being watched lovingly by a white mother or father. Support and educational groups for adoptive families with Chinese children are proliferating, and their members are becoming vocal advocates for adoption-conscious reforms and ethnic sensitivity in schools, medical facilities, and other social institutions. For the most part, the parents also seem to be ensuring the continuous, long-term infusion of Chinese culture into our country by teaching their children about their homeland, its customs, and its traditions from the time they are infants.

"It's not that previous groups of adoptees weren't readily identifiable by the country they came from, or that the parents didn't organize and promote their interests. Those things have been true in most other groups, too— Korean adoptions for a long time, and certainly many of the parents of children from Romania, Russia, and the rest of Eastern Europe today are very proactive and very involved," says Maureen Evans, the former executive director of the Joint Council on International Children's Services, an umbrella organization of licensed, nonprofit American adoption agencies.

> *"Adoption is helping to crack the walls of prejudice and intolerance."*

"But, as a group, the parents of the Chinese girls have been more educated and more sharply focused about their children's heritage from the start. . . . And there are differences in the children themselves: We never had so many come from a single place in such a compressed period of time before, all of them very young and healthy, and all of them girls. It's the Chinese children, in their numbers and their gender, all about the same age, who have changed and will continue to change the face of adoption."

And, in the process, the face of America. Demographers already estimate that our country's population will consist of nearly as many minorities, meaning people with black, Asian, non-white Hispanic, and American Indian heritages, as Caucasians by the middle of the twenty-first century. The population specialists rarely take adoption into account when they make their calculations, however, so the pace of change will certainly be somewhat quicker and the multicultural nature of our evolving nation will be even greater because adoptees, from China and elsewhere, will integrate the traditions and customs of the places they were born with those of their adoptive nation.

Russell and Susan Correia started their multiethnic parenting the minute they brought their ten-month-old daughter home to Portland, Maine, dressing her in clothes they had bought in China and decorating her room with artwork from her homeland. They also speak enthusiastically about maintaining her ties to and associations with her roots. Their main regret is that, because Hope was abandoned, she'll never be able to meet members of her birth family or even obtain information about them.

"We'll take her back to where she was born when she's old enough to understand it all," says Susan. "We want her to know who she is and to know we're proud of that. It's something we'll celebrate and honor for her and with her." Russell nods in agreement. He says some people don't understand why he and

Susan are learning Chinese, why they belong to an organization of families with Chinese children, why it's so important to keep their daughter connected with her culture. But he feels fortunate, not put-upon.

"We've become, unwittingly, educators in adoption and tolerance, so maybe we're part of something bigger that's making America a better place, I don't know. It's certainly not why we adopted to begin with. . . . But we've also got to remember that this kind of thing has been going on a long, long time, so we're not doing something that's so unique," he adds. "My grandparents came over from Portugal two generations ago; they passed on their heritage into our country, and now, through Hope, we'll pass on both the Portuguese and the Chinese heritages. That's a good thing, isn't it?"

Testing the Limits

The unhappy reality is that many governments can't care for all their people, but that doesn't excuse the exploitation that takes place in the name of adoption. Unregulated, unscrupulous facilitators coerce or bribe poor and single women around the world to part with their babies, then charge tens of thousands of dollars to American agencies and lawyers for their "services." Agents for some U.S. adoption businesses dole out bribes to foreign judges, orphanage administrators, and other authorities to accelerate the process, to alter or create documents, even to arrange infants' adoptions over their parents' objections.

There is an extent to which, in countries like Vietnam and Russia that have functioned with underground economies for decades, payoffs are an inescapable part of doing business of any sort. Children aren't merchandise, though, and they should never be treated as such. So it's reassuring to know that only a small segment of practitioners surrender to their baser instincts. Still, there is no organized oversight of international adoption, just as there is almost none within the United States, so there are villains out there, feeling unconstrained about testing the legal and moral limits of their operations.

Sally Gillman, a senior employee at a nonprofit adoption agency in California, warns would-be parents who come to her that "everything you can imagine happens out there on Planet Adoption—the good, the bad, the exquisitely beautiful and the grotesquely ugly." Sally, not her real name, recalls a trip she took recently to Guatemala to meet with her agency's representative about an Oklahoma couple's adoption:

"Everything essentially had been done already. The home study, the visa documents, the paperwork in Guatemala City, the whole ball of wax. This couple was ready; they'd gone through years of infertility treatments, had a couple of domestic adoptions fall through when the birth mothers changed their minds, had a really hard time emotionally and spent a whole lot of money. They'd been trying to have a child, one way or another, as I recall, for nearly four years. . . .

"I told them before I left that I thought it would take just a few more days before they could fly down to see their son, a seven-month-old boy they named

Tommy, and then they could take him home a couple of weeks later or so. Well, I met our guy for coffee . . . and he told me, flat out, that he'd gone to another agency and told them he had this baby ready to go, and told them how much his costs were and they'd said yes. They paid him something like $5,000 more than we'd agreed to. I don't know if they knew what he was up to or just thought it's what this facilitator charges. Maybe he was lying, just trying to get me to up my price. I don't know. I was just revolted and walked out.

"We've obviously never used him again, but this couple I was dealing with was incredibly, absolutely devastated. It caused terrible stress between the two of them. The wife wanted to try again; the husband said he couldn't take any more disappointment. I recommended they receive counseling, which they did. I believe they finally decided to give up on having children. The whole thing was just horrible. . . . I don't even want to think about where the guy got the baby, knowing what I do about his ethics. I mean, it was bald, outright baby-selling." Asked how many children her agency had placed in the past through this same representative, Sally sighs her response: "Two. Two too many."

Sally informed the other American agency (which had agreed to pay more money) about what had happened, and received assurances that it would also cease using this facilitator. She says she did not report the man to Guatemalan authorities for the same reason that she doesn't want to be identified by name: because he

> *"Whatever faults adoption practitioners may have, on the whole they are promoting higher standards and making significant contributions to the welfare of homeless children."*

was a prominent lawyer who "had friends high up in the government." She's afraid that nothing would happen to him if she filed a complaint, but future adoptions by her agency in Guatemala could be jeopardized.

The majority of professionals avoid dilemmas of this sort by dealing only with established institutions, whatever their problems, rather than with individuals. Many concede they cut corners here and there, however, and some undoubtedly avert their eyes so they can later deny they knew about shady activities conducted on their behalf. An indeterminable number, sometimes knowingly and sometimes not, also commit errors in judgment that yield grim consequences: They don't provide parents-to-be with sufficient information, emphatically enough, about the problems and risks they might face.

Institutionalized Children

Studies have shown for decades that institutionalization, by depriving children of close emotional relationships, can badly impair their capacity to make personal connections throughout their lives. It can slow their intellectual and emotional maturation, and can erode their ability to make transitions from one developmental stage to the next. Sometimes the children's psychic disorders are so severe that, when their adoptive parents simply touch them to show affection, they scream.

In some countries, institutionalized children also have been sexually abused, beaten, shaken, and routinely handled so roughly that they sustain internal damage of every physical and psychological sort. To make matters worse, their medical records are often shoddy or deliberately falsified to camouflage the treatment they've received. And, as if all that's not complicated enough to unravel, many orphanage officials and doctors routinely report children as suffering from serious conditions that they don't really have, because their countries don't permit healthy children to be adopted by foreigners.

Most often, even the children with serious problems can be successfully dealt with through medical intervention, counseling, and other therapies. Indeed, long-term research into the lives of Romanian adoptees, who endured particularly horrid conditions, shows most making enormous strides. But many of their parents are irate that they weren't told more from the start about a host of issues—the specific environments in which their children lived, the documented repercussions of institutionalization, the warning signals of various developmental problems, the best strategies for raising children with their particular difficulties, and the resources available to help them. Some people, given that kind of input, would not have adopted; others would have been spared serious disappointments. Most would have proceeded, but with better information with which to raise their sons and daughters.

The combination of abysmal conditions in orphanages and questionable behavior by practitioners can produce excruciating outcomes. Consequently, the last several years have seen an explosion in "wrongful adoption" lawsuits, in which adoptive parents claim their agency, attorney, or facilitator lied or willfully withheld information about the mental or physical health of adoptees and/or their birth parents. The plaintiffs typically seek sizable financial settlements to compensate for the suffering they endured or to help them deal with their children's expensive medical treatments.

Wrongful adoption suits were first filed in the 1980s by Americans who adopted domestically years earlier, then discovered their children had problems their agencies had been aware of, could have determined, or should have suspected given the birth parents' medical histories. Most professionals at the time had acted in good conscience, since the accepted practice was to provide only "positive" background. In fact, it was widely believed that disclosures about mental illness or other maladies would unfairly brand the child and cause undue anxiety for adoptive parents. . . .

Agencies typically win such suits because adoptive parents' contracts explicitly state that they're aware of the risks going in. In any event, such dire scenarios constitute a tiny fraction of all adoptions abroad. But they dramatically illustrate the frightening results that institutionalization can produce, and they highlight how starkly clear professionals have to be in executing their responsibilities. The good news is that more and more countries, including those in Eastern Europe, are taking steps to revise their laws and clean up their orphanages.

At the same time, whatever faults adoption practitioners may have, on the whole they are promoting higher standards and making significant contributions to the welfare of homeless children. Nonprofit organizations in particular—but also some money-making agencies, attorneys, and facilitators—are furnishing financial and logistical support to orphanages as part of their missions. Scores of others are building new orphanages, providing their own staffing, and assisting in the training of local personnel. Their actions not only benefit the residents of the facilities receiving direct assistance, but also act as models for and apply pressure on other institutions in their areas.

The very existence of intercountry adoption serves several similarly constructive purposes. Nations that allow foreigners to assume custody of their children almost by definition invite examination by social-work and medical professionals, the media, and human-rights groups. The resulting advice can have a profound impact in places where the leaders want to do the right thing. And even minimal reporting about and monitoring in authoritarian countries like China have provoked reforms, if for no other reason than to prevent embarrassment for institution administrators and government officials.

Perhaps most pointedly, whatever its problems, intercountry adoption puts into practice the paramount principle that professionals almost universally agree should guide the process in all its forms: to provide parents for children who need them, not the other way around. That goal sometimes gets obscured or lost, particularly in the world of domestic infant adoption, where Americans yearn for the fulfillment that their fertile friends can achieve by simply tossing away their condoms or birth control pills.

Do the U.S. adoption practitioners helping other countries care for their children have a vested interest in their work, so that their well-paying clients will get continued access to younger and healthier adoptees? Sure, but only an uninformed cynic could believe that's typically their principal motivation. Nor do most people believe these countries' problems will be significantly alleviated by the adoptive parents who provide new families to a tiny proportion of their youngest, neediest citizens.

> *"The American adoption revolution is being felt around the globe."*

But it's crucial to stay focused on the children, and with few exceptions, the ones who are adopted will live better lives than they could have received, institutionalized, in their homelands. At the same time, the surge in adoptions abroad has prompted some of the affected nations to improve their laws, their orphanages, and the treatment of their own children. The progress has been painfully slow and remains wildly erratic, but it's real. In this way, at least, the American adoption revolution is being felt around the globe. . . .

Lessons from Romania

It's an intuitive truth that children mature and function better within stable, caring families than in any environment where they receive little individual attention or little sustained affection. That's why kids who bounce back and forth between their biological parents and temporary homes—no matter how nurturing or compassionate their foster parents may be—usually wind up troubled. It's also a major reason the United States and most other Western nations decided more than a half century ago that a family setting was nearly always preferable to almost any form of institutionalization.

Group facilities remain the housing of last resort for deserted children in the developing world, however, with tremendous variations in the quality of their personnel, infrastructures, and the quality of care they provide. As far as anyone can determine, though, no country any longer tolerates conditions as horrendous as the ones discovered in Romania in December 1989. [Romanian dictator Nicolae] Ceausescu and his wife, Elana, who served as his chief deputy and was executed along with her husband, believed that increasing their country's population would somehow help to alleviate its indigence. They imposed policies promoting childbirth, forbidding abortion and contraception, and financially penalizing couples who didn't produce children. The two leaders, meanwhile, were looting the nation's treasury. The predictable result was a nightmarish nation in which people lived in desperation and fear, in which poverty grew pervasive, and in which families became increasingly less able to care for their children. So they were routinely abandoned.

> *"Tens of thousands of Americans, the preponderance of those who adopt from overseas each year, do so without a hitch."*

The institutions into which they were then placed reflected the grim realities of their society at large. Children were tied onto beds. Some were found lying in their own excrement. In winter, many froze to death; the rest of the year, they atrophied away or died of malnutrition. Diseases went untreated, physical and emotional abuse seemed to be officially tolerated, and affection apparently was an emotion that these children's pathetic caretakers were too exhausted or socially brutalized to exhibit.

After Ceausescu's successor lifted a decades-old ban on entry visas and the legal prohibition on speaking to foreigners, aid agencies from the United States and Europe poured money and resources into the country. Within a short time, in response to news accounts about the plight of institutionalized children, individual Americans and other Westerners also traveled to Romania, where they picked children to adopt. The fees involved, most of which went to orphanage executives, totaled about $2,000.

Just two such adoptions by Americans were recorded in 1989; it's a bit surprising there were any, given that the revolution didn't culminate until Christmas. The following year, the number jumped to ninety, after which all hell broke loose. Hordes of facilitators, lawyers, and agencies, seeing the immense demand by white prospective parents, figured they'd discovered a human gold mine. Rather than finding homes for the kids from institutions—who were generally older and in need of help—the entrepreneurs, along with some ordinary Americans making their own arrangements, turned to local "baby brokers" for higher-priced but relatively healthy babies and toddlers.

In 1991, Americans adopted 2,594 children from Romania. A black market in babies, often bought or coerced from vulnerable families, boomed. For one year, for the first time in more than three decades, Korea was supplanted as the primary source for U.S. adoptions abroad. But the illicit enterprise in Romania was too flagrant to remain secret, and it quickly ignited an international furor.

By the middle of the year, the new leaders in Bucharest felt compelled to shut down all adoptions. They rewrote their laws to improve protections for birth parents and to give only licensed agencies in the United States and elsewhere the authority to deal directly with Romania's government on adoptions. The outflow of children from that nation's institutions into American adoptive homes fell to a few hundred annually until in June 2000, the government said corruption had again infiltrated the system—and imposed a three-month moratorium to clean it up.

Romania's experience warrants special attention not only because it represents a particularly wrenching chapter in adoption history, but also because it teaches such an explicit, unambiguous lesson about the venomous effect of money in transactions that involve human beings. The lure of big bucks draws in people who have no credentials or understanding of the sensitive issues at stake, and absent tight regulations or monitoring, it can insidiously poison the judgment of even well-meaning professionals. In Romania's case, some agencies clearly believed they were rescuing children from miserable lives and early deaths, regardless of how or from where they were obtained. But the participation by "serious" organizations fueled an inexcusable operation, provided cover for the worst offenders, and contributed to its lasting longer than it otherwise might have.

Misleading Horror Stories

When money spawns such high-profile scandals, it damages adoption itself in a comprehensive way: by undermining many Americans' confidence in a process they tend to hear about only through horror stories. Such episodes mislead some people into believing that adoption is an intrinsically dubious way to have children. And, . . . the specter of baby-selling contributes to a nebulous sense that something's somehow "wrong" with adoption—and, by subconscious implication, with its participants.

Fortunately, in practice, the positive aspects soar above the negative. Tens of thousands of Americans, the great preponderance of those who adopt from overseas each year, do so with barely a hitch. And the vast majority of their children were unambiguously homeless, genuinely needy, and truly lucky to be adopted. Most of them, as a sort of cosmic payback, become unwitting revolutionaries simply by growing up proud of their origins and comfortable with their place in the world, as adoptees.

Transracial Adoptions Can Be Beneficial

by Susan Goldsmith

About the author: *Susan Goldsmith is an award-winning journalist for* New Times Los Angeles.

On a February morning in 1994, Wayne Coombs, a Christian minister from Rancho Palos Verdes [California], drove to downtown Los Angeles with his wife, Jan, for a court hearing that would determine if they could become permanent legal guardians of a four-year-old foster child named Adam. The boy, who had been in the Coombses care since the age of six weeks, had been born addicted to cocaine and was taken away from his biological mother by L.A. County social workers because of her drug habit.

The Coombses expected no trouble in obtaining the guardianship; indeed, their attorney, Ron Stoddard, told them he had prepared little for the hearing. Stoddard said winning guardianship of Adam was a "slam dunk," given his mother's history of drug abuse and the fact that she had three other children, all of whom had been in and out of foster care because of neglect and abuse. A fifth child was living with relatives.

So the Coombses were mildly surprised to see Adam's mother, Krista, in the courtroom that day. Over the past couple of years social workers had tried to reunite her and Adam on several occasions, but each time things didn't work out and he was sent back to live with the Coombses. Despite her problems, Krista now wanted her son back.

With the hearing underway, Probate Court Commissioner Robert Blaylock reviewed the paperwork on the case, looked up from the bench, and announced he had come to a decision. Adam was to be given back to his mother—permanently—and all ties with the Coombses were to be cut. Social workers, he pointed out, believed Krista was a fit, rehabilitated parent ready to take on the responsibility of mothering Adam, and he concurred.

From her seat Krista cried out, "Thank you! Thank you, your honor!"

Susan Goldsmith, "The Color of Love," *New Times Los Angeles*, 1998. Copyright © 1998 by *New Times Los Angeles*. Reproduced by permission of the publisher and Southland Publishing, Inc.

Shocked, Stoddard tried to object, but the judge sternly pointed at him and said, "This is a done deal, as of now."

Wayne Coombs vividly remembers breaking the news to Adam. "He just looked up at me and said, 'Please, Daddy, let me speak to the judge,'" the minister recalls.

The Coombses went that afternoon to the county foster-care office where Krista was to pick up the little boy. When she arrived, Adam hid under the table and refused to come out. The Coombses videotaped the painful scene, thinking it might be the last time they'd ever see him. Unable to coax him out, Krista finally got down on her hands and knees and dragged him from under the table. "Take a good look," Wayne Coombs remembers Krista saying, "because you are never going to see this kid again."

Uncovering Facts

About two months later, the grief-stricken couple got a call from a reporter at the Christian Broadcasting Network, a conservative cable-TV operation. The reporter had heard about Adam, and since Wayne Coombs was a Christian pastor, the network wanted to do a story on his troubles with the child-welfare system in L.A. Within a week the reporter—Jennifer Robinson from Pat Robertson's The 700 Club show—was in town and poking around.

A few days of research turned up some disturbing facts. The journalist learned that the social worker who handled Adam's case had failed to tell Commissioner Blaylock that Krista had been arrested for prostitution three weeks before the guardianship hearing. She also found out Krista had been convicted for prostitution several times before—another fact Adam's social worker had kept from the court.

After Robinson's story aired on cable stations across the country, an angry Blaylock summoned all the parties back into court the next day and ordered Adam returned to Coombses.

Within 24 hours, Wayne Coombs was headed for South Central L.A. to get Adam. By court order, he was accompanied by three LAPD squad cars, in case there was trouble. "Taking a child is a very dramatic experience," says an LAPD spokesman. The pastor arrived at the designated pickup spot, a gas station, and collected Adam without incident.

A Social Worker's Testimony

Adam's social worker, Doris Brown, who was legally charged with looking out for his best interests, later testified under oath that Krista's arrest for prostitution was irrelevant to the guardianship proceeding. Brown said the L.A. County Department of Children and Family Services, which she works for, "didn't see how that information would impact on [Krista] providing adequate care and supervision for the child," Brown said during a deposition.

Not only did Brown fail to tell the court about Krista's prostitution arrest, she left out other crucial information as well. According to court records obtained by *New Times*, Brown didn't pass on anything about Krista's criminal history, which included three convictions for prostitution and two convictions for car theft.

Brown also did not mention that after Krista was reunited with Adam in 1992 and briefly lived in Richmond, Virginia, social workers in that city obtained a court order mandating that she be evaluated by child-welfare authorities because of reported drug-abuse problems and neglect of her children.

> *"Both federal and state law prohibit the use of race ... or culture to delay or derail a child's adoption."*

Krista skipped four appointments for the court-ordered evaluation in Richmond, records show. Soon after, she returned to Los Angeles with Adam and three of his siblings. Virginia officials notified the L.A. County Department of Children and Family Services about her problems on the East Coast, but social workers here never followed up, Brown testified. When asked why she never called Richmond to find out what had happened there, Brown said, "At the time, I didn't see how that was important."

So instead of relaying any of this information to the court, Brown endorsed Krista as a fit and able parent. Brown's report said her department "found no evidence that minor Adam and siblings were being abused or neglected by mother. It is mother's desire to raise minors together. Therefore, it is in the best interest of minor Adam to return to the care of his mother."

The Race Issue

But Krista's competence as a mother wasn't the only issue in the case. The players' races were important as well. Krista is African-American, as is Doris Brown. Adam is half black and half white. Wayne and Jan Coombs are white. And in the L.A. County Department of Children and Family Services [DCFS], that color combination is a highly volatile one.

"Black social workers in the department believe African-American children are disproportionately going into foster care, which is true, and that the black family is being systematically torn apart by the child-welfare system," says Bruce Rubenstein, a former deputy director of the department who resigned last year.

The controversy is not just a local one.

Many black child-welfare workers across the country see transracial adoptions and foster-care placements as "racial and cultural genocide" for the African-American community. "We view the placement of black children in white homes as a hostile act against our community," William Merritt, president of the National Association of Black Social Workers, said in testimony before the U.S. Senate in 1985. "We are, therefore, legally justified in our efforts to protect the rights of black children, black families, and the black community."

Doris Brown refused to be interviewed by *New Times*, as did Peter Digre, director of the Department of Children and Family Services. But Hal Brown (no relation to Doris Brown), a former chairman of the L.A. County Commission for Children and Families who investigated the Coombs case, was eager to talk about it.

He says Doris Brown's actions were consistent with an unofficial and illegal policy within the DCFS office on Alameda Street in South Central L.A. That office, where Doris Brown works, is known for its pro-black family stance and vehement opposition to placing African-American children in white homes. "They just see a black child and think this child has to stay with a black family," says Brown, who stepped down from the children's commission last month after 14 years. "The department is totally violating the law."

Indeed, both federal and state law prohibit the use of race, ethnic heritage, or culture to delay or derail a child's adoption or placement with foster parents. When Adam's case was before Blaylock in 1994, social workers had 90 days to try and find a same-race family for an abused or neglected child in L.A. County's foster-care system. If such a match could not be found within the allotted time, social workers were barred from further delaying or blocking a transracial foster-home placement or adoption.

The law, though, made little difference for Adam.

A Campaign Against White Parents

Six months after he was returned to the Coombses, another black social worker from DCFS, Carol Lee, visited the family for a court-mandated home check. Her assessment after watching Adam play with some friends in his backyard pool in Rancho Palos Verdes was that he was out of control and needed to be put somewhere else. "Minor Adam appears to be hyperactive, unruly and completely undisciplined in the care of these caretakers," Lee wrote in a confidential report obtained by *New Times*.

But at a court hearing in August, 1994, in which Lee was to present her findings, Hal Brown, who had been investigating the case since the Coombses lost their guardianship bid in February, showed up with a big surprise.

Brown had uncovered a disturbing campaign by the DCFS social workers to wrestle Adam away from the Coombses because they were white.

That effort included attempts by Ray LaMotte, a black supervisor at the Alameda Street DCFS office, to get the Coombses state-foster-care license revoked. In a letter to the regional director of the foster-care agency, LaMotte wrote that DCFS had "some concerns" about the Coombses and asked agency officials to investigate whether Wayne Coombs was trying to conceive a child with Krista, as she had alleged.

"There was a total lack of honesty on the part of DCFS," Brown told *New Times*. "DCFS was suggesting Wayne Coombs was having an affair with Adam's mother so he could steal the child, and they alleged he had her arrested for prostitution to get her out of the picture."

Those allegations, Brown says, were untrue. Furthermore, he adds, "I was made aware, by looking at the social worker's report, [that] they intended to remove Adam, once again, from the Coombses care that day in court."

Marilyn Martinez, the Juvenile Dependency Court commissioner hearing the second guardianship matter, was so outraged by Brown's findings that she awarded the couple permanent guardianship, which would make adopting Adam, something they had recently begun to consider, much easier. Martinez then asked the Coombses if they were willing to take in Adam's older sister, Ebony, who was then 6 and in need of a foster home. They agreed and Martinez ordered DCFS to find the girl and immediately give her to Wayne and Jan Coombs.

When social workers finally found Ebony three months later, instead of giving her to the Coombses as ordered, they put her into Maclaren Children's Center—a temporary holding facility for abused and neglected kids in El Monte—where she sat for a month, uncertain what was going to happen to her.

"They wanted to screw us and showed absolutely no concern for Ebony," Wayne Coombs says.

Ebony was turned over to the couple in October, 1994, after Hal Brown discovered she was at Maclaren. "I thought it was appalling," Brown says. "I raised hell with the department and got her out."

Two years later, Wayne and Jan Coombs officially adopted Adam and Ebony. But the joy of bringing the children into their home for good was mixed with anger at DCFS. They had spent about $60,000 of their own money fighting the department and were furious about the way both they and the children had been treated.

Unwilling to turn the other cheek, the couple filed a civil rights lawsuit in federal court against DCFS, charging they were discriminated against as adoptive parents on account of their skin color. [In 1998] the L.A. County Board of Supervisors approved settling the suit out of court for $300,000.

In a memo urging the payment, county attorneys warned that if a jury got hold of the case, the Coombses would probably be awarded up to $1.75 million.

> *"Polls show that a large majority of both black and white Americans support transracial adoptions."*

The memo says the Coombses "always provided a loving, stable environment" for Adam and Ebony, and that the children suffered emotionally as a result of being repeatedly yanked from their home. Although DCFS officials strongly denied discriminating against the Coombses, county attorneys said they believe the couple was "improperly impeded" from obtaining legal guardianship of Adam and Ebony because the Coombses "were not of the same race."

"This case was particularly outrageous because damage was done to the children to fulfill a political agenda," says Patrick McNicholas, the Coombses attorney. "And the agenda was to preclude minority children from being placed with white care givers."

A Raging Debate

The Coombses are not alone in their experiences. They are part of a debate raging across the nation over what role race should play in the adoption and foster placements of minority children whose parents cannot or will not properly care for them.

Ironically, polls show that a large majority of both black and white Americans support transracial adoptions. A 1991 survey of 975 adults conducted by CBS This Morning, for instance, found that 70 percent of whites favored them, along with 71 percent of blacks.

Such widespread public support helped persuade Congress in 1994 to pass the Multi-Ethnic Placement Act, which prohibits using race, culture, or ethnic identity to block or delay transracial foster-care placements and adoptions. For many years, it was common practice for social workers in government child-welfare agencies to hold back on adoptions and long-term foster-care placements until a same-race family could be found. The Multi-Ethnic Placement Act applies to public child-welfare agencies, which handle abused and neglected children, and to private adoption agencies that receive federal funds. (Private agencies that don't get government money are allowed to show racial and ethnic preference in placements. There are African-American, Catholic, and Jewish adoption agencies that do use such criteria, but generally they handle very small numbers of children.)

> *"The practical reasons for expediting transracial adoptions remain compelling."*

The federal act was intended to shorten the length of time children spend in foster homes and orphanages by facilitating transracial adoptions. According to Sen. Carol Moseley-Braun (D-Ill.), an African American who was one of the bill's sponsors, it was passed for practical, not political reasons.

"Today, children wait an average of two-and-a-half years to be adopted. There are half a million children in the foster care system, almost twice as many as in the mid-1980s. These children need to be adopted," Moseley-Braun wrote in the ABA Journal, a publication of the American Bar Association, in 1995. "Racial or ethnic matters should never be the determining factor in adoption or foster care placement, especially if it would leave a child without a family. Love, after all, is color-blind."

The practical reasons for expediting transracial adoptions remain compelling. Nationwide, there still are about 500,000 children in foster care. About half are black or of mixed black-white parentage, and roughly 75,000 to 100,000 are available for adoption. Minority children spend twice as long in foster care as whites, according to federal statistics; African-American children are only one-fourth as likely as white or Latino children to ever be adopted. A 1997 study by the nonprofit Stuart Foundation said that one in three children in the child-protective system will never be reunited with their natural parents. The picture is similarly grim in California, according to state figures.

While many of the kids in California's protective-care system are African-American, those who adopt or provide foster care are overwhelmingly white—85 percent, according to state figures. That means almost all of the black children in the system who are not sent back to their biological parents wind up, temporarily or permanently, in white homes. Between 1990 and 1993, 1,941 black, biracial, and Latino children were adopted in California and nearly all were taken in by whites, the Stuart report found.

Opponents of Transracial Adoption

The National Association of Black Social Workers and other opponents of transracial adoption view such statistics with alarm and outrage. And they continue to oppose black-to-white adoptions despite passage of the federal Multi-Ethnic Placement Act.

Their strongly held beliefs notwithstanding, several NABSW spokespersons refused to be interviewed by *New Times* and did not return more than a dozen phone calls.

Pelonomi Khumoestile-Taylor, an African-American doctoral candidate at Brandeis University in Waltham, Massachusetts, who is studying the politics of transracial adoption, says association members are tired of having their views distorted in the media.

"Black social workers have come under attack for their position," Khumoestile-Taylor says. "It is increasingly easy to isolate black social workers, vilify them, and make them look like bad guys and say they're nationalists. That is probably why they don't want to talk."

Although they refused to be interviewed, association members have written numerous position papers outlining why they object to transracial adoptions and placements. Those papers usually characterize the foster-care system in the U.S. as anti-black and a threat to the future of the African-American community.

"Very little effort has been put forth by the child-welfare system to keep [African-American] families together or to return children in foster care to their relatives," Leora Neal, NABSW's New York regional director, wrote recently. "Child welfare workers have historically undertaken little effort to rehabilitate African-American parents. Further, black families and other families of color who tried to adopt waiting children were often met with discrimination or discouragement."

In L.A., efforts have been made to reach out to potential African-American foster-care and adoptive parents, but how successful those attempts have been is unclear. . . .

Many black child-development experts also argue that public adoption agencies were long dominated by middle-class whites and thus tended to discriminate against potential black adoptive parents, especially low-income ones.

"The adoption system in this country was established to provide white children to white families," said Evelyn Moore, executive director of the National Black Child Development Institute, in a 1984 interview. "As a result, most people who work in the system know very little about black culture or the black community."

Other experts counter that while Moore's statement may have been true 14 years ago, it is not today. Indeed, whites make up 39 percent of L.A. County social workers, while blacks represent 34 percent (Latinos comprise 25 percent).

White Parents and Racial Identity

Besides their concern for preserving the larger African-American community, opponents of transracial placements say there is an equally important issue at stake: Whether white people can prepare a child of color to deal with a racist world.

"We are still in these United States, 1998, and issues of race matter greatly," says Ruth Arlene Howe, an African-American professor at Boston College Law School. "White families often can't understand what a black child goes through with respect to race. And people who say they are color-blind don't understand the way this country works."

Children adopted across racial lines, Howe says, "often encounter a real shock when they leave home, and it can cause a major mental health or identity crisis. The identification of a healthy self is a lifelong thing, and if it's not done well you can be crippling somebody for life."

Khumoestile-Taylor agrees. She says she has met many mixed race adoptees who are troubled about their racial identity. "Transracial adoptees talk about not fitting in any world, not the black world or the white world. . . . As long as we live in a race-conscious society and we don't know where race fits into a child's hierarchy of needs, we ought to be concerned with the issue of where children should be placed."

Studying whether a white family can adequately prepare a black or biracial child for the world outside the home has been Rita J. Simon's life work. A sociology professor at American University in Washington, D.C., she has done the only long-term study on transracial adoption in the United States, tracking 366 children—the majority of whom are African-American—for 20 years. Simon has written two books on race, identity, and adoption, and was one of the leading proponents of the Multi-Ethnic Placement Act.

"We've found transracial adoption [and placement]—as have all the studies that have been done—to be in the best interests of a child," says Simon, who is white. "They do not suffer in any way because they've been adopted by parents of another race. All the major studies have found transracial adoption is a good thing and these kids have healthy self-esteem."

Simon and co-researcher Howard Altstein found the experience of transracial adoption to be a positive one for both children and parents. Such parents made significant efforts to expose their children to their racial and cultural backgrounds, and the kids thrived after leaving home. In the end, the researchers found, the issue of being raised in a different-race home made little difference in the children's lives.

Positive Aspects of Transracial Adoption

Kirsten Albrecht, a 27-year-old L.A. lawyer who is half black and half white, was raised from shortly after birth by a white couple, co-pastors at a Presbyterian church in suburban Chicago. Albrecht says most opponents of transracial adoption have never even met someone like her.

"For me and lots of people I've known, transracial adoption has been a very positive thing," Albrecht says. "I had two very dedicated parents who were consciously aware of educating me about the African-American community. I don't feel alienated from the black community, and I don't feel I've lost out on any experience or that I missed something. And my parents very much prepared me for dealing with any discrimination or racism that came my way."

In some ways, Albrecht believes, white families are well-suited to prepare a black child to cope with racism.

"If you raise a child to believe that everything they're going to do is going to be hindered by race, you extinguish their sense of self-esteem," she says. "One advantage of a white person raising a black child is that they haven't encountered racism, so they can pass on this notion that you can do anything. They aren't tainting a child's vision that the world is always out to get them."

> *"Parents made significant efforts to expose their [adopted] children to their racial and cultural backgrounds, and the kids thrived after leaving home."*

Although she endorses transracial adoption, Albrecht says being a biracial child in a white home was not always easy. "I was called an Oreo in junior high school—meaning I was black on the outside and white on the inside," she recalls. The real message behind the name, she says, was that she really couldn't have been black because she "talked like a white person and got good grades."

Disturbed by the staggering numbers of black and biracial children in foster care who are in need of adoptive homes, Albrecht last year founded the Trans-Racial Adoption Group, an L.A.-based nonprofit that advocates cross-racial placements for minority children and acts as an information clearing house on the subject.

"We are not just dealing with the issue of cultural identity," she says. "We're dealing with early development and allowing a child to be a functioning person in society. The real issue is foster care versus adoption. The average stay in foster care in the U.S. is about four years, and once kids reach the age of four or five their chances of being adopted really drop."

Even with the federal law, Albrecht says transracial foster care placements and adoptions are still being thwarted because of race. "I think the [adoptive family] evaluation process is very subjective," she says. "It's not uncommon for things to be kept out of court, out of files, and for unfair allegations to be made against white families by black social workers. . . Whether allegations are fabricated or information is withheld, those are things that are hard to find out about and difficult to correct."

Rita Simon concurs. "The National Association of Black Social Workers is very powerful and they are delaying and derailing adoptions in the public and private setting all over the country," she says. "These stories are very sad if you care about children. They are the ones getting hurt the most."

More Foster Children Should Be Placed in Adoptive Homes

by Pete du Pont

About the author: *Pete du Pont, former governor of Delaware, is policy chairman of the National Center for Policy Analysis, a Dallas, Texas–based research organization.*

People working in the nation's government-operated foster care system finally have gained permission to give a foster child's safety and well-being priority over anything else.

That may seem like common sense, but for the past 17 years [1980–1997] federal law has required emphasis on reuniting the biological family, no matter how abusive conditions were likely to be—even if a parent had killed another child.

That is one of the changes in foster care policy brought about by the new Adoption and Safe Families Act [passed in 1997]. The act makes other improvements intended to move children out of foster care and into adoptive homes more quickly.

For example, a "permanency plan"—for reuniting the foster child with the biological family, or preparing for adoption or another outcome—is required for every child within 12 months of entering foster care, down from 18 months before the new legislation. If a child has been in foster care for 15 of the most recent 22 months, a state must start the process of terminating parental rights—the first step toward making the child legally free for adoption. And if a state places more foster children in adoptive homes than it averaged placing in the last three years, it gets a $4,000 or $6,000 bonus (depending on the characteristics of the child) for each adoption that exceeds the average.

There are other provisions of the new law that are designed to give states incentives to move more children out of foster care more quickly. Unfortunately, though, there are also a host of loopholes allowing states to continue getting

Pete du Pont, "A Step Forward for Foster Care," www.ncpa.org, December 15, 1997. Copyright © 1997 by the National Center for Policy Analysis. All rights reserved. Reproduced by permission.

federal money for foster care even if they aren't doing their job well.

Conna Craig, president of the Institute for Children, evaluates the new law as "five steps forward and two steps back, which is a net gain—but federal law doesn't yet fully meet the needs of the children."

Ms. Craig's institute surveyed the nation and found that while adoptions of 22,491 foster children were finalized in the fiscal year 1996, that left 53,642 foster children who were legally free for adoption still in foster care as fiscal 1997 began. And that was a typical year, she said.

The new law still requires too little accountability on the part of the states, and there are still a host of ways states can wait years before they act aggressively to free a child for adoption. For example, even if a child has been in foster care for 15 of the most recent 22 months, a state can claim

> *"One of every ten foster children stays in foster care longer than seven years."*

that there is a compelling reason that filing to terminate parental rights would not be in the child's best interest. Or a state can simply say that it hasn't provided the biological family the necessary services that might have made it possible to return the child safely to the home. But there are hundreds of thousands of children already in foster care to whom the law doesn't apply right away.

Trapped in the System

At any one time, there are about half a million children in foster care nationwide. The great majority do return to their biological families, but a substantial minority do not—and too often they simply are trapped in the system. One of every 10 foster children stays in foster care longer than seven years. And each year about 15,000 reach the age of majority and leave foster care without a permanent family—many to join the ranks of the homeless or to commit crimes and be imprisoned.

The Child Welfare League of America complained that the new law didn't include enough additional money for all the things that foster care workers need to do for training and for services to help reunite families. Money is indeed a big part of the problem, but not in the way the Child Welfare League means. Rather, many states are dragging their feet because they get federal funds according to the number of children in foster care.

"If the states don't do the job, they shouldn't get the money," contends Ms. Craig. She has a point. Still, we should offer about two cheers for the Adoption and Safe Families Act, applauding it as the first step in desperately needed reform of a system that still fails in great part to meet its requirements to take care of children who have no place else to go.

The Infant Adoption Industry Should Be Abolished

by Darlene Gerow

About the author: *Darlene Gerow is editor of the* CUB Communicator, *a newsletter of Concerned United Birthparents (CUB).*

Adoption is perceived by society as primarily an altruistic act where a child is rescued from a dreadful fate. The child's mother is portrayed as not wanting her child and the child's father as usually being nonexistent. The adopting parents are mythically portrayed as saint-like rescuers who provide a "happily ever after." In reality, birthparents anguish over the loss of their children, adoptive families are just as dysfunctional as natural families, and adoption is a huge, profit-driven industry where babies are the commodity. As it is currently practiced in America, infant adoption by non-relatives does more to meet the needs of affluent adopters than to help children.

A Billion-Dollar U.S. Industry

Infant adoption is big business in America. Approximately 140,000 adoptions are finalized each year although it remains unclear how many are infant adoptions and how many are older children adopted by relatives or foster parents. According to an industry analysis by Marketdata Enterprises, Inc. of Tampa, Florida, adoption provider revenues in 2000 were $1.44 billion with a projected industry annual growth rate of 11.5 percent to 2004.

Ken Watson, named the 1992 Child Advocate of the Year by the North American Council on Adoptable Children, explains that the outright sale of children is illegal, but adopters are routinely charged fees to legally parent a child. Watson recounts how some agencies circulate a fee schedule with children listed in categories by race and sex with prices proportionate to their desirability. Prices can range from $25,000 to $50,000 and upwards. According to Watson, although

Darlene Gerow, "Infant Adoption Is Big Business in America," *CUB Communicator*, Fall 2002. Copyright © 2002 by Concerned United Birthparents, Inc. Reproduced by permission.

adoption providers insist that the fee is not payment for a child, but rather money to cover the cost of services provided, "Adoptive parents are not deceived. They know they are paying for a child." Adopters with the most money obtain the children considered the most desirable.

Along with the fees charged by the adoption provider, adopters routinely reimburse relinquishing parents for expenses incurred during the pregnancy. Although these expenses are paid as an act of charity and are not tax deductible, there are adoption facilitators and web site sources that coach adopters as to how much they dare pay a relinquishing mother for such things as cars, clothes, and tuition without crossing the line into baby buying.

James Gritter, open adoption practitioner with Catholic Human Services, Inc., observes, "Birthfamilies are ostensibly given money to make their experience more tolerable, but the 'relief' they receive may soon feel like blood money, ultimately producing unspeakable guilt and misery." Gritter explains that reimbursement for expenses is coercive because when adopters invest in prospective birthparents, they expect a return on their investment. The money a young mother receives during her pregnancy is coercive because it may cause her to feel indebted to the adopters and prevent her from following her heart after birth and parenting her own baby.

Baby Selling?

Since the business of adoption has become so lucrative, it has attracted many professionals never previously interested in adoption. In the last ten years, the number of attorneys involved in adoption has doubled. Gritter contends that adoption has changed from "a professional model, in which service providers hang out their shingles and aspire to suspend self-interest, to a business model that aggressively recruits consumers on a buyer-beware basis." Randolph W. Severson, director of Heart Words: an Adoptee Advocacy and Counseling Center, cautions, "The trend runs perilously close to that cliff called selling babies."

One of the more outrageous examples of the excesses surfacing in the adoption industry appeared in *Talk* magazine in an article by Jim DeFede. DeFede reports on a boutique adoption service in Florida and its elite baby broker, Richard Gitelman, who places ads nationally seeking pregnant women, and then auctions their babies to the highest bidder among the adopters on his list. His prices vary from $75,000 to $250,000 for healthy white infants. Increasingly, for-profit businesses and unlicensed facilitators promise to connect prospective adopters with the child of their dreams and charge whatever the market will bear.

Competition for Infants

There is a huge disparity in the supply-and-demand of infants, which creates desperate and intense competition among adopters. Currently, there are forty or more adopters vying for every healthy white infant that becomes available for adoption. There are fewer desirable adoptable infants because society has become more accepting of single mothers who parent their children than in the past. The stigma of bearing a child out-of-wedlock has diminished, so the vast majority of today's single mothers choose to keep their babies instead of relinquishing them to adoption. Effective birth control methods are readily available to the fertile population, and, since abortion is legal, an unplanned pregnancy can be terminated.

While the supply of desirable adoptable infants has been decreasing, infertility in America has been increasing. It is estimated that one in six couples has trouble conceiving and that there may be as many as 5.3 million infertile couples in America. Many adopters who are currently seeking babies postponed child bearing to pursue their careers, and later, when they finally wanted to conceive, found that due to age they were infertile. Unrelated to age, another cause of infertility is chlamydia. Dubbed the "silent epidemic," chlamydia is the most frequently reported infectious disease in the U.S. and often results in infertility because there are few symptoms. Many people do not realize they were ever infected with chlamydia until they later discover complications, such as infertility.

> *"Adoption is a huge, profit-driven industry where babies are the commodity."*

Although adoption does not cure infertility, and adopting a child is not the same as having a child by birth, many of the infertile eventually pursue adopting a baby. In *U.S. News & World Report*, [Kim] Clark and [Nancy] Shute relate that the majority of adopters want only healthy infants because most foster children awaiting homes are at least five years old, many have physical or emotional handicaps, and most are of mixed races.

A Scarce and Dear Commodity

With such market demand, the adoption industry is striving to increase the supply of desirable adoptable babies. Historian Rickie Solinger writes in *Beggars and Choosers: How the Politics of Choice Shapes Adoption, Abortion and Welfare in the United States* that Representative Pat Schroeder of Colorado claims there are too many single women in the U.S. having babies with too few of them giving up their babies for adoption. Schroeder labeled babies "a scarce and dear commodity." Representative Schroeder supports the adoption industry and does not see anything wrong with viewing babies as a resource to meet the needs of adults.

Domestically, efforts are underway to encourage women to relinquish their babies for adoption; however, it is the rare mother who actually wants to be separated from her child. According to the twenty-five year old national organization, Concerned United Birthparents, Inc., mothers surrender their babies due to a lack of financial resources, lack of extended family support, and pressure by social workers or other adoption facilitators. Mothers who have relinquished their children grieve for the remainder of their lives. Losing a child, whether to death or to adoption, is a tragedy from which a mother never completely recovers. Her relinquished child never recovers from the separation either.

Traditionally, most babies relinquished for adoption were born to single, unwed, teenage mothers, but that is no longer the case. According to long-time adoption reformist and co-author of *The Adoption Triangle*, Reuben Pannor, more than half of the babies relinquished today are born to impoverished married couples in the Bible Belt and other areas with high rates of poverty. Most currently, relinquishing families already have two or more children who are the brothers and sisters of the relinquished baby. Pannor explains, "These birthparents come from the poverty pockets of our country and are the primary targets of attorneys who flood their communities with enticing advertisements."

Adoptive mother Ruth Reichl's [May 2001] article in *More* tells how at thirty-nine years old she had undergone extensive infertility treatments when her doctor admitted defeat and suggested that she consider adopting. Her doctor recommended an attorney who was "sleek and handsome" and to whom "[. . .] the adoption industry had clearly been good." The attorney explained that he would target "pregnant southern women who lacked either the means or the desire to raise their babies."

> *"There is a huge disparity in the supply-and-demand of infants, which creates desperate and intense competition among adopters."*

Poor women are especially vulnerable to the high-pressured tactics of the adoption industry. Without resources or support, they want to believe that their sacrifice really will be helpful to their children. Rarely are they informed about the long-term repercussions they and their children will experience as a result of separation.

The Industry Promotes Relinquishment

In order to promote adoption and encourage the relinquishment of infants, the adoption industry employs full-time lobbyists in Washington, D.C. The National Council for Adoption is a private lobbying group whose members include twenty-eight adoption agencies and represents 3.5 percent of U.S. adoption agencies. The N.C.F.A. and three adoption agencies just received $8.6 million from the federal treasury in October 2001 to promote adoption to pregnant women at health centers and clinics. In the press release from the U.S.A. Department of Health and Human Services, Tommy G. Thompson, H.H.S. Secretary, said, "These grants are an important step in making sure that every pregnant woman who is considering her alternatives understands the benefits of adoption."

Relinquishment and adoption is considered by some to be a solution for the societal problem of illegitimacy and welfare dependency. Psychologist Lynne

Reyman contends that by viewing adoption as a cure for poverty, we deny the humanity of birthparents. By taking the children of poor families, we compound their problems; not only are they still poor, but additionally they have lost their children.

The Industry Tightens the Screws

Other lobbying and legislative efforts of the adoption industry include supporting states to legally reduce the length of time after which relinquishment becomes irrevocable. California recently reduced the time a relinquishing mother has to change her mind from ninety to thirty days.

Some states allow no time for reconsideration. Some states have enacted legislation that allows the mother to sign a binding relinquishment even before her baby is born. Before birth, a pregnant woman may think relinquishment is the best solution for her predicament. Following birth, once the mother actually meets her infant, her priorities often change drastically. A mother needs to experience motherhood and understand the full implications of relinquishment before she signs anything.

The adoption industry aggressively supports both anti-abortion legislation and the recent "baby dump" laws. Thirty-five states have passed safe haven laws in the last two years [2000–2002]. These laws allow anyone to anonymously abandon a baby at a designated safe place. Ostensibly, their intent is to reduce infanticide, but inadvertently they encourage and condone the abandonment of infants. Since the surrender is anonymous, there are no safeguards against fraud and corruption. There is no way to confirm that the person dumping the baby is the parent or legal guardian or if both parents have agreed to the abandonment. The "baby dump" laws are supported by the adoption lobby, who see the foundlings as a source of infants for adoption.

The Internet has become the tool of choice for adopters seeking pregnant women who might consider relinquishing their babies. Laura Mansnerus reported in the *New York Times* that hopeful adopters typically pay $175 to be listed in an Internet registry for three months. Their profiles in the registry include photos, family histories, and loving descriptions of their homes, pets, hobbies, and child-rearing plans. The Internet allows adopters to advertise for babies, which is illegal in other mediums in some states.

Professional Marketing

Public relations and marketing firms with very bright and likeable marketing experts have orchestrated the commercial approach to adoption, and in their effort to make relinquishment and adoption appeal to pregnant women, they have disguised the process to make it appear as though it prioritizes birthparents, Gritter explains. Watson describes the phenomena as having "spawned a host of ancillary exploiters, including public relations and marketing firms that help prospective adoptive parents prepare biographies and photographs to increase their appeal [. . .] and insurance companies who will write a policy to reimburse [prospective] adoptive parents who have paid the expenses of a [prospective] birthparent who then decides against adoption."

The National Adoption Network was one of the first national organizations dedicated to connecting pregnant women with adopters. Severson recounts how Dian Jordan brought her skills as an advertising executive to the National Adoption Network and employed high-gloss polished creativity to solicit prospective birthparents.

Foreign Infants Help Meet Demand

Foreign procurement of desirable infants for adoption helps meet the market demand and is the fastest growing area of infant adoption. David Tuller reported in the *New York Times* that more than 18,000 children were adopted from other countries in 2000. Most came from Korea, China, Russia, other Soviet Bloc nations, India, and Guatemala.

Adam Pertman, author of *Adoption Nation*, expresses the prevailing ethnocentric justification for recruiting children from other countries, "With few exceptions, the ones [children] who are adopted will live better lives than they could have in their homelands." Affluence does not make American adopters better parents, nor guarantee that the children they adopt internationally will be happier for having been removed from their families, cultures, and heritages.

"Mothers who have relinquished their children grieve for the remainder of their lives."

One of the reasons adopters cite for adopting internationally is that relinquishing foreign mothers, especially those from Third World countries, have less recourse than their American counterparts and are unlikely to contest an adoption, or have the resources to seek contact at a later date. Although countries with white populations are especially targeted, adopters indicate that race is less of an issue with babies because all babies are cute and loveable.

Exploitation Is Endemic

Exploitation of babies and their mothers by the adoption industry is endemic in adoption today. Domestically, adoption professionals use coercive tactics to procure infants.

Adoptive mother and adoption reformist, L. Anne Babb in *Ethics in American Adoption* relates that research on ethics in adoption shows that adoption is rife with conflict of interest. Most adoption facilitators who claim to offer unbiased counseling to potential birthmothers depend upon the dollars collected from adopters to support their business. Free counseling for pregnant women often is indistinguishable from a sales pitch for relinquishment. Another area of conflict is that in most adoptions, an attorney hired by the adopters purports to represent everyone involved in the adoption transaction. Rarely does an impoverished relinquishing mother retain her own legal counsel.

Lynne Reyman describes the exploitation of young mothers in her recent book, *Musings of a Ghost Mother:*

> Fraudulent crisis lines may act as fronts for attorneys who broker adoptions. In the marketplace for infants, merchandising techniques draw in unmarried pregnant girls and women. Looking in our local yellow pages under "adoption," I see pictures of smiling adoption facilitators promising birthmothers that "all the choices are yours." One adoption facilitation center promotes college scholarships for birthmothers, among other free services. The coercive nature of these services is a reminder that the system is driven by adoptive parents, the paying consumers to whom agencies and attorneys cater.

Some tactics employed by the adoption industry are more coercive than others.

Open adoption, the revolutionary practice of allowing and even encouraging full contact between adoptive families and birth families, has been embraced by the adoption industry as a tool of unparalleled seduction to potential birthmothers. Adoption facilitators have found that a mother is more inclined to proceed with an adoption plan that includes ongoing contact with her child because the prospect of never seeing her child again is unbearable. Too often, openness is the carrot that entices a mother to relinquish, and only after the adoption is finalized, does she learn that the adoptive parents did not intend to maintain the open agreement, which is not enforceable by law. Once the adoption is finalized and the adopters have the baby, they are free to have their telephones unlisted, change their addresses, change their names, move out of state, and sever contact. Birthmothers are left without legal recourse.

Allowing adopters to be present during a mother's labor and childbirth is another coercive tactic employed by the adoption industry. Babb cautions about the manipulative potential of having prospective adoptive parents participate in an expectant mother's prenatal care, childbirth, or even visit the hospital following delivery. Babb maintains that a mother who is considering relinquishment must have the opportunity to experience motherhood without "[. . . .] the onus of anxiety or guilt about the feelings of the prospective adoptive parents. The potential heartache of prospective adoptive parents with whom [the mother] has developed a pre-delivery relationship should not be used as a coercive means of obtaining the relinquishment of an infant." If the mother does decide to relinquish, the

> *"Poor women are especially vulnerable to the high-pressure tactics of the adoption industry."*

time immediately following birth is the only time she and her child will ever have as a family. If the mother decides to not relinquish, then her baby does not need an adoptive home. Adoption is for children who need homes. Either way, the presence of adopters in the delivery room or at the hospital is inappropriate.

Foreign adoption is also plagued with abuse. Pertman describes the exploitation occurring in foreign adoption, "Unregulated, unscrupulous facilitators coerce or bribe the poor and single women around the world to part with their babies." Thousands of Americans travel to foreign countries every year to get babies with tens of thousands of dollars hidden in their clothes because, as Pertman explains, "they have decided they want a child more than they want to deliberate the ethics of their actions or of their advisors." Pertman continues, "Some agencies hire bounty hunters to locate babies for adoption, paying as much as $10,000 per find, which is a huge sum in the poor areas of the world where this is a routine practice."

> *"Most adoption facilitators who claim to offer unbiased counseling to potential birthmothers depend upon the dollars collected from adopters to support their business."*

Baby stealing is a burgeoning problem in international adoption. Michael Riley, writing about Guatemalan infants fueling the adoption industry in the *Dallas Morning News*, reports that with such high demand for infants, adoption brokers are enticed to use tactics of intimidation and manipulation. They target poor single mothers who are often isolated from their families and support systems and scour poor neighborhoods looking for pregnant women, sometimes pretending to befriend them. Riley writes, "Brothel owners sell the babies of prostitutes to help offset the downtime of the pregnant employees. Middle and upper class housewives hire expectant mothers as servants, help arrange an adoption, and then pocket the [baby broker] fee."

Mothers whose babies were taken without their understanding or consent have filed dozens of complaints with the Guatemalan attorney's office. In response to the report of baby stealing, Britain and Canada, among other countries, have instituted a mandatory DNA test for adoptions from Guatemala, but the United States tests only sporadically. Out of the twenty-nine babies tested by the U.S. last year [2001], three tests revealed that it was not the genetic mother relinquishing the baby for adoption.

Sally Stoecker, writing for the Russian magazine, *Demokratizatsiya*, reports that corruption and fraud plague Russian adoption. Demand from infertile couples in the West provide substantial profits and entice criminal elements. According to the Main Directorate of Internal Affairs in Moscow, several cases of missing children are reported daily. Kidnapping has become a frequent crime associated primarily with foreign adoption. Underprivileged women whose babies have disappeared rarely find legal recourse.

A Perfect World

The business of infant adoption is out of control. The affluent can buy any commodity they desire, including babies, while at the same time, poverty is the leading cause of relinquishment. Describing a perfect world where no babies would ever be relinquished for adoption, Barbara Eck Manning, founder of Re-solve, an organization for infertile people, explains that the fact babies are available reflects society's failure to provide education, family planning, medi-cal services and support for at-risk families. Every adoption represents a tragic breakdown of a family where a mother and child have been separated.

A glimmer of hope for that perfect world described by Manning was offered by adoption reformer, Evelyn Burns Robinson, author of *Adoption and Loss—the Hidden Grief*, during her presentation at the 23rd Annual American Adop-tion Congress Conference in Anaheim, California in April 2001. Robinson said that many people simply accept adoption as a part of our culture, but that adop-tion is a social construction. She said that adoption has not always existed, and it does not exist everywhere. She said that adoption occurs mostly in affluent, Western societies and is a fairly recent historical phenomenon. Robinson pointed out that in just over a hundred years, we have seen the end of slavery and the triumph of suffrage, and that the reason these changes occurred was be-cause someone drew attention to the injustice. Robinson's examples of the changes that occurred to slavery and suffrage make it seem possible that the in-stitution of adoption might also change, no matter how firmly entrenched in so-ciety it is, nor how much money it generates. Perhaps, with continued dili-gence, the business of infant adoption can be eliminated, and we can move a little closer to that perfect world.

Pregnant Women Should Not Be Coerced into Placing Their Children Up for Adoption

by Heather Lowe

About the author: *Heather Lowe, a writer, is an activist with Concerned United Birthparents, an organization dedicated to preventing unnecessary adoptions and protecting birth parents' rights.*

When my son made his entrance into the world . . . , a second birth took place. There on the delivery table, soaked in sweat and blood, I was reborn as a birthmother. In the long days since that double birth, I have grieved a grief of a severity I didn't think possible. I have reached new depths of suffering, and I have lived the meaning of regret. For a person who despises victimhood and espouses personal responsibility, this has been a hard role to accept—but the truth remains . . . I was hurt by bad laws.

The Birthmother Status

No little girl grows up dreaming of becoming a birthmother; a role that is generally either ignored or despised. Yet millions of women carry the badge. Increasingly we are more forthright about our aborted chance at motherhood, and some of us are even militant. But birthmothers from an earlier era still stumble upon one another, often after long acquaintance. "You too?" they say. "I had no idea. . . ."

For even if a birthmother did summon her courage to speak, the shameful, inhumane practice of closed adoption ensured that no one wanted to listen. More frequently, mothers who surrendered children didn't even try, having bought into the big lie that they would "get over it and move on." How many women have we lost to the aftereffects of this evil untruth? The terrible pain of our

Heather Lowe, "A Birthmother's View of Adoption: Suggestions for Reform," www.adopting.org, 1999. Copyright © 1999 by Heather Lowe. Reproduced by permission.

older birthmothers (those from the era of maternity homes and secretive births) is living proof that "you will forget" is a fabrication so wicked that Satan himself may have been its creator. Birthmothers never forget.

Open adoption, in which adoptive families maintain ongoing, lifelong relationships with the birthfamily, has elevated birthmother status in important ways, but injustice in adoption remains rampant, and prejudices still abound. Would-be adopters and social workers alike have an image of the "typical" birthmother, and they look down on her in smug condescension. They think they are rescuing the poor confused dear, and ex-

> *"Adoption used to be about finding homes for children, but now it's about finding children to fill the homes of infertile couples."*

pect her to be grateful to their charity in "saving" her child from a life that is not solidly middle class, or a home that is not two-parent.

Even after two decades of progress toward open adoption, birthmothers still pay. We pay every time someone tells us our child is so lucky to have found a good family (i.e., to be away from us?). We pay when coworkers (usually the same ones who told us during our pregnancies that it would be selfish to keep our children) go on to ask in disbelief, "How could you have given away your baby?" We pay dearly on Mother's Day, and we pay each time we are asked, "Do you have any children?"

I am not anti-adoption. Many cases really do call for a good adoptive family, and many children benefit from growing up outside their biological homes. But adoption as it is practiced today is a disgrace. It's become an industry geared not toward "the best interests of the child" (itself a worn out catchphrase with little real meaning) but toward serving people who think they have a God-given right to add a child to their home. Adoption used to be about finding homes for children, but now it's about finding children to fill the homes of infertile couples. To save the institution of adoption, I propose a list of nine reforms.

Personal Background

To understand why I make them, however, it's first necessary to have some background on me. For starters, I fit none of the birthmother stereotypes. Aged 27 when I gave birth, I was hardly a teen mother. I am not poor or unstable: I have a good job with a major corporation. I am not uneducated; I have a sharp mind and an undying love of learning. My child was unplanned, but not unwanted. My family and I had much to offer my son, save the one thing we could not give him: a father who stuck around.

Research into the effects of adoption on infants shows that the psychological cost of infant-maternal separation is so high that an adoption should only be done as a last resort. It is a well-documented fact that infants do suffer lifelong consequences as a result of separation from their first family, regardless of how joyous and successful their adoption eventually turns out to be. Experts in the field caution, therefore, that adoption should be done only if there is no other way for mother and baby to stay together. Unfortunately, this is not how adoption is commonly practiced. Agencies and private adoption "facilitators," which profit based on how many adoptions they can arrange, don't ask too many questions about why a potential birthmother is considering adoption.

So despite the red flags that the demographic indicators ought to have raised in my case, the adoption industry forged ahead, desperate to get one more healthy, white newborn. No one said to me, "If anyone has the resources to be a single parent, it's you." No one asked me why I was really choosing adoption, or if I was being influenced by those around me instead of going with my gut feelings. No one acknowledged that what I was actually trying to do was pay for my "sin" in getting pregnant out of wedlock—trying to make atonement by making an infertile married couple happy. The "counseling" I got was perfunctory and biased and all-around unacceptable (I'll have more to say about that in a moment). But I didn't know better. Despite attacking the potential adoption of my son as a research project, and reading a great deal of material while pregnant, I did not collect enough unbiased information to fully understand what I was doing. No one knows just how to go about becoming a birthmother until it's already too late.

> *"It is a well-documented fact that infants do suffer lifelong consequences as a result of separation from their first family."*

So, I signed the papers and they got the baby. But is this the basis for building a family—on the grief and regret of another? I often wonder how adoptive parents live with themselves, knowing how much they have taken away from my child's birthfamily. Unless, that is, it's absolutely clear that they are offering the child much more than the birthfamily could have done. My situation lacks such clarity. It is far too ambiguous. I fear that in the life of my son, I merely replaced one major loss (lack of a present father) with another (being cut out of his biological family).

Proposed Reforms

Thus, my proposed reforms:

1. Eliminate biased social workers. When I was trying to decide if I was going to surrender my child to adoption, the agency provided the prospective adopters with a counselor, as well as one for me. But that counselor was herself an adoptive mother. In our "talks," she bubbled inanely about what a wonderful gift her daughter has been (as if the girl's birthmother had searched valiantly for the perfect present and done so much better than a gift certificate). Birthmothers do not give their children as gifts to needy parents; if anything they give the parents as gifts to their children.

This phenomenon of presenting adoption as "gift-giving" is far too prevalent.

A potential birthmother does not need to be thinking about the plight of child-less couples, no matter how sad infertility may be. A woman in the midst of a crisis pregnancy has been stigmatized as a bad girl, often experiencing the dis-approval of and anger from family and friends. In order to regain her "good girl" status, she will do anything to make these people happy again, and giving away her baby to a needy couple seems like the perfect way out. The danger is that she will make an adoption decision based solely on the feelings of others.

> *"A potential birthmother does not need to be thinking about the plight of childless couples, no matter how sad infertility may be."*

My counselor's pro-adoption pro-paganda colored my thinking at a time when I desperately needed objectivity. It is unacceptable that supposedly neutral parties, offered for support and guid-ance, have such personal interest in the outcome. Adoption lawyers and social workers should never be adoptive parents themselves.

2. Mandate counseling for all potential birthmothers. Even if the expectant mother is in denial and thinks she does not need counseling, she is wrong. The law should require that she receive free counsel from an uninterested, outside party. Voluntarily losing one's child is the most serious loss most women will ever face. Being forced to do so without extensive advisement is sheer cruelty.

End Private Adoption

The need for counseling leads to another needed reform: *ending private adop-tion.* Private adoptions circumvent agencies by using lawyers as facilitators. In private adoption, there is little to no counseling. What's more, a lawyer is trained in law, not in helping expectant mothers to make painful, human deci-sions, and he will not see to it that she gets the support she needs (or that the prospective adoptive parents receive the education they need to realize all that they are taking on). Education should become mandatory for all hopeful adopters, and required reading lists should be standard.

3. Train all hospital workers in sensitive adoption practices. The horror sto-ries I have collected from other birthmoms regarding their experiences in the hospital are hair-curling, and they come from both sides of the fence. Every day I hear of nurses who think adoption is wrong and try to talk the birthmother into keeping the child in the biological family, or nurses who think adoption is glorious but that the birthmother is sinful and has no right to enjoy her own birthing. Both are equally offensive and could be cured with more education among hospital staff, who need to learn that their role is to make a mother's de-livery as pleasant and stress-free as possible, regardless of what plans she may be making for her child. Doctors, nurses, and support staff should never express their opinions on the adoption plans taking place. In the meantime, potential birthmothers must take full control of their hospital experience and not let outside ignorance alter a well-made birthing plan.

4. Keep adoptive parents out of the delivery room and away from the hospital. They don't belong anywhere near the scene. This is hard for me to say, because my child's parents were in the delivery room (at their request, not mine) and it seemed at the time to be a relatively pleasant experience, though not without a measure of awkwardness. Looking back, however, I see how it interfered with my decision-making ability. Since then I've also learned more about the pre and perinatal experience of the child. The question ought to be, "Who does the adoptee want in the delivery room?" Unfortunately, this question is almost never asked.

According to psychologists, the newborn baby recognizes its mother immediately at birth. That baby needs time to continue the bond with his first mother, whom he already knows from forty weeks of sharing her body. The prospective adoptive mother, no matter how wonderful she may be, is still a stranger to the newborn, who does not experience himself as separate from his biological mother until the age of two months. There will be time for gentle transitions into an adoptive family later, if they are in fact needed.

Adoptions are often handled as if the baby is not really present. The thinking seems to be that if the switchoff is handled quickly enough, the baby will never notice. This is patently untrue, and rushing to place a child in an adoptive home does lasting damage.

There is yet another reason prospective adopters don't belong anywhere near a delivery room. No matter how much thought has gone into a pre-birth decision, an adoption plan must be made anew after the birth, once the child has become a reality. A great majority of first-time mothers report feeling disconnected from their child while pregnant—and these are women who planned their pregnancies and intend to keep their children. For most potential birthmothers, this is their first child, and they have no idea how they will feel after the baby's actual arrival. A child that they wonder if they could love is now known to be the most precious thing on earth to them. Yet adoption laws are mostly written by men, who have no idea that motherhood is a great unknown until it actually happens. We frequently hear about the horrible birthmother who so inconsiderately changes her mind, as if a change of heart is a sin. Yes, the prospective parents will face real pain if the birthmother decides to keep her baby. But the cold truth is that no one is going to leave that hospital without pain. The potential birthmother is expected to bear the pain, and to bear it FOREVER. When she backs away from that pain, she is treated as if she has violated a contract, much as if she were selling a car, not relinquishing a child. Most states do not allow an intent to relinquish statement, but those that do must act at once to outlaw them.

> *"Adoption laws are mostly written by men, who have no idea that motherhood is a great unknown until it actually happens."*

Potential birthmothers do not *owe* anyone a child. Where the prospective adoptive parents and potential birthparents have formed a meaningful relationship, with a firm commitment to an ongoing presence in each others' lives (which in open adoption we hope they will have done), adoptive parents' presence in the delivery room may be acceptable—as long as the birthmother is the one asking for it and the emotional risks are known to her.

5. Abolish irrevocable consent. Many states allow a window of time for birthmothers to change their minds about this most immense of decisions, but many do not. In addition, many states allow consents to be taken in a hospital bed, shortly after birth, rather than in a courtroom in front of a judge—the proper place for a decision of such solemnity to be formalized.

Imagine you are given 72 hours to decide whether you will lose your child. Is that enough time? The place you are given to do it is a hospital bed, where you lie worn out from labor, hovered over by anxious adoptive parents and their guests. Their joy at the new arrival is infectious, and you might start to think that life as a birthmother will always be this saturated in gratitude and happiness. Is that the proper atmosphere to make a decision which will completely recreate you as a person and affect the rest of your days? In three months, many things can change in a birthmom's life, factors that will make her want to keep her child. Give her the time and the space to make the decision, and if her economic or social standing has not improved or if she still doubts her mothering ability, proceed with the adoption.

6. End adoption advertising. Adoptive families like to say their families were formed by God. If so, then why do they need marketing to get the job done? If God wants to form a family by adoption, then prospective adoptive parents need to sit back, shut up and let Him do it. They shouldn't sell themselves with saccharine ads and gooey posters, troll for babies on the Internet, or omit crucial facts in those "Dear Birthmother" letters. (And while they're at it, they should never refer to a pregnant woman as a "birthmother" at all. A woman is not a birthmother until she has signed away her legal rights to her child, so an expectant mother can never be a birthmother. Calling her one denies reality, forces her to think of herself as something she may not want to become, and is coercive in the extreme.)

Prospective adopters who paint themselves as the Cleavers of the nineties are hawking the family for gain. Thankfully, a lot of potential birthmothers see through it—but many of the younger, more naive ones do not. Babyselling is rightfully despised in our culture, yet somehow baby soliciting is not. There are plenty of noncoercive, dignified ways for prospective adopters to get the word out that they hope to adopt. Let's use them. We must bring back integrity to the adoption process, or we haven't progressed much since the days of the orphan trains.

7. Let closed adoptions dwindle like the Dark Age remnant they are. I have no respect for potential adoptive families who would even consider a closed adoption. Adoptive parents in a closed adoption have only solved one thing: their own infertility. They are not acting for the sake of a child but for the sake of their own need to "play family." Closed adoption parents certainly do not have the child's well-being in mind, since as a result of their own fears and insecurities they only trade one set of problems (a single parent home) for another (genealogical bewilderment).

Those who adopt overseas to make things easier on themselves are also suspect. It's one thing to save an orphaned child from a group home. It's quite another to purchase a baby overseas because you don't want to deal with the child's biologic roots, or because you feel you need a perfect white baby. Going halfway around the world to avoid the birthfamily is cowardly and wrong, but somehow society views these dogooders in a positive light. There are plenty of adoptable kids right here in the U.S. The question is, is the adoptive family up to the challenge?

8. Open records for adult adoptees. Unfortunately, we have not yet reached the point where all adoptions are open, so we have an additional problem, that of closed records. How can we say we have the best interests of a child at heart when we tell her she has no right to her original identity? Why are adoptees the only class of people deemed not trustworthy enough to know of their origins? This seems so obvious as to defy further explanation, yet only three states understand it so far. If you believe in basic human rights, you must grant adoptees the right to know. Don't let the Oregon Seven[1] fool you. The vast majority of birthmothers (some 98%) are for open records—for they are mothers first, who care about their children's psychological well-being. Closed records damage the adoptee, by keeping him forever a child. Adoptees grow up, but adoption laws do not reflect that obvious fact. They are never trusted with their heritage. This perpetual infantilization of adoptees is demeaning to all involved, and violates basic constitutional (and property) rights.

> *"The sugarcoating of adoption has got to stop. It is not a win-win situation."*

9. Make open adoption agreements legally enforceable. Only one state allows birthmothers the protection of open adoption contracts, which help to hold adoptive parents to their promises. In all other states, such agreements are actually illegal. It's a sad fact that a large percentage of adoptive parents break their promises for continued contact once they have the baby in their home. It happens more than you would think, and is especially tragic when the only reason a birthmother agreed to adoption in the first place was the promise of ongoing contact with her child. Such agreements must have the protection given to other serious agreements—the protection of law.

---

1. The Oregon Seven were seven birthmothers who were the plaintiffs in a failed lawsuit seeking an injunction to an Oregon law mandating the opening of birth records.

No More Sugarcoating

Birthmothers don't ask to be created. We become, without wanting to become. We are, without wanting to be. Our mistake? Struggling through an unplanned pregnancy in order to give life, sticking to a strong value system, refusing to care what others think of our choice. We are told over and over again during pregnancy, by people who want our oh-so-valuable babies, that we are doing the honorable thing, making a beautiful choice, loving our child completely. Then, as soon as the placement is secure, we are told to be ashamed of what we have done. We are asked how we could give away blood. We are shunned and scorned as somehow less than the "real" adoptive mothers. We hear that "good" birthparents ought to ride away into the sunset, leaving their children in the past, leaving the adoptive parents to answer the tough questions and soothe the child's losses. But fifty years of closed adoption in the United States has proven that it doesn't work. If you doubt it, turn to the Internet to see the number of adoptees in immense pain. The sugarcoating of adoption has got to stop. It is not a win-win situation. The biggest losses of all come to the one who tried heroically to find the best solution to an unplanned pregnancy. In reality, there is never a solution. All three options have severe effects on a mother's life, and when a mother chooses the very hardest road for the sake of her precious child, society ought to scrape its collective knees as it bows down to honor her sacrifice. And yet the very word is ugly . . . birthmother. As if the word "mother" is not big enough to encompass more than one type of love. I prefer the term used by some enlightened adoptive parents: first mother.

Perhaps I seem to be hard on adoptive parents. This is not because I dislike them, but because they have all the power in adoptive relationships, and therefore far greater responsibilities. The child has no say in what happens to him, and the birthparents lose all rights once the papers are signed. Adoptive parents function as the gods in the adoption triad, and like the gods of mythology they can be either benevolent or terrible. I urge both present and prospective adoptive parents to try to truly feel the enormity of birthmother and adoptee loss. Then, if you still feel the adoption is necessary and good, go ahead with it . . . but do it in a dignified way that honors your child-to-be and the family from which he comes. Then adoption is allowed to be a blessed event, not a disgraceful one.

International Adoption Is Harmful and Exploitive

by Tobias Hübinette

About the author: *Tobias Hübinette (Korean name Lee Sam-dol), a Korean who was adopted by a Swedish family, is a graduate student in Korean studies at Stockholm University, Sweden.*

What is fundamentally wrong with intercountry adoption is that white Westerners adopt children, while non-whites in non-Western countries relinquish and supply those children. Intercountry adoption is in other words a one-way traffic and not an equal exchange of children in need between countries. Since its beginning after World War II when the supply of working-class children for domestic adoption started to run short, intercountry adoption has been the last resort to have a child for infertile couples belonging to the elite who feel a strong social pressure to fulfill the standard of the nuclear family. Intercountry adoption is widely perceived as a progressive and anti-racist act of rescuing a non-white child from the miseries of the Third World, something which legitimizes the practice in the first place. Besides, the bizarre situation is loaded with demands of loyalty, guilt and gratefulness as the wealthiest of the rich in the receiving countries adopt the most shunned and unwanted in the Third World.

Historical Prerequisites

Before World War II, no Westerner thought about adopting a non-white child. Racism was the order of the day of the colonial world order in a time when the West ruled the world. Before the war, different humanitarian organizations actually tried to place Jewish refugee children from Central Europe as a part of the *Kindertransport* into Swedish homes. Today we can read about the difficulties in placing those children through letters preserved at the National Archive of Sweden: "We don't want Jewish children. Aren't there any Aryan children?"

How could Westerners be prepared to adopt "non-Aryan" children from Korea already at the beginning of the 1950s? The answers are the Holocaust and de-

Tobias Hübinette, "A Critique of Intercountry Adoption," www.transracialabductees.org, 2003. Copyright © 2003 by Tobias Hübinette. Reproduced by permission.

colonization. The scope of the Holocaust created such a shock that the West was forced to change its worldview. The West realized that the Holocaust couldn't just be a German deed, and that instead all Western countries were "guilty" after 2,000 years of Anti-Semitism. The West went from open racism to the idea of equality for all races, at least theoretically. This idea destroyed the world order having dominated the last 500 years: that the West had the right to conquer, exterminate and rule over non-white people. De-colonization was followed by violent conflicts, and the first intercountry adoptees soon started to arrive.

The Korean and Swedish Cases

The [1950–1953] Korean War was not just a Korean war. It was a cynical and dirty war between the super powers that happened to take place on the Korean peninsula as two Korean states were dominated by two Western powers as pawns in the game. 3.5 million Koreans were killed on both sides representing over 10 percent of the population. The Korean War is considered one of the bloodiest in history considering the limitation in time and in geography, and the losses correspond to one fifth of the global war casualties since World War II.

During the years of war, soldiers from the UN-army started to adopt children. The UN-army contained most of the countries which would adopt the majority of the Korean children: Australia, Canada, Luxembourg, United States, Belgium, the Netherlands, France, Sweden, Norway and Denmark. Witnesses describe the Korean War as something close to genocide. The UN-soldiers killed tens of thousands of Koreans on both sides indiscriminately, and it is also important to bear in mind that almost all of the first Korean adoptees were products of unequal relations between UN-soldiers and Korean women.

The same pattern followed in other countries. De-colonized countries like India and Ethiopia became supplying countries as a consequence of international aid efforts. Especially in East Asia, dominating intercountry adoption as a region, the Korean situation became the standard. Wars and catastrophes in countries like Vietnam and Thailand resulted in intercountry adoption from those countries. Worth noting is also that many leading supplying countries in the field of intercountry adoption fall under America's sphere of influence or have been subjected to American warfare: Korea, Vietnam, Thailand and the Philippines in Asia, and Colombia, Chile and Guatemala in South America.

"Intercountry adoption is . . . not an equal exchange of children in need between countries."

Sweden played an important role everywhere. The result is that Sweden has brought in the largest number of adoptees among all Western countries in relation to the native population: almost 45,000 from 130 different countries. After a pro-Nazi war history and a long tradition of race thinking, self-righteous Sweden after 1945 wanted to be the paradise for human rights, democracy and anti-racism. Another less idealistic motive worth mentioning was the sudden disappearance of adoptable Swedish children during the decade as a result of rapid economic growth and a high participation of women in the labor force, as well as the development of an advanced social welfare system. Even more important is Sweden's self-image as the world's most democratic country, a self-image recently challenged by the sudden appearance of a vigorous National Socialist movement and racism towards non-Western immigrants including adoptees. Intercountry adoption is in Sweden nothing else but a national project to uphold the country's self-image.

For countries like Korea, the almost insatiable demand for children has created huge social problems. Intercountry adoption has destroyed all attempts to develop an internal social welfare system, and the position of the Korean woman has remained unchanged. The Swedes have been forced to accept unwed mothers for a long time, but in Korea the children born out-of-wedlock instead disappeared abroad. In the 1970s, during the golden days of Korean adoption when Korean children like pets and mascots became status symbols among progressive whites, the pressure was enormous on Korea to find adoptable children. Temporarily relinquished children at institutions and those who simply got lost from their parents on the streets disappeared forever from the country. Intercountry adoption was also linked to the amount of money Western organizations gave to the institutions. . . .

> *"Intercountry adoption has always worked for the interests of adoptive parents and receiving countries, never for the interests of adopted children or supplying countries."*

The consequences of intercountry adoption for supplying countries in terms of a national trauma and destroyed lives for the biological parents are today obvious in a country like Korea, the country in the world which has sent away the largest number of children: more than 150,000 in 15 Western countries. Interestingly, Swedish documentaries on intercountry adoption are always focusing on the "positive" side, while the equivalents in Korea always focus on "negative" aspects.

The expression "in the best interest of the child" is used as a mantra by intercountry adoption proponents. It is a fact that intercountry adoption has always worked for the interests of adoptive parents and receiving countries, never for the interests of adopted children or supplying countries. If it would have been "in the best interest of the child", then siblings would never have been separated, and every adoptive parent would have been forced to travel to the supplying country and pick up the child and at least tried to learn something of the child's language and culture. . . .

Parallels to the Slave Trade

The West has a long tradition of uprooting non-whites and transporting them involuntarily to their own countries and for their own purposes. Hundreds of thousands of non-whites, especially Africans, were transported to the Americas to satisfy the need for manpower. Nowadays hundreds of thousands of non-whites, especially East Asians, are transported to the West to satisfy the needs of infertile white middle-class couples. The message of intercountry adoption ideology is clearly that life in the West is the best, and that the West has the right to adopt children from non-Western countries in the name of paternalistic humanism and

> *"There are indeed numerous striking similarities between the slave trade and intercountry adoption."*

materialistic superiority, something which reminds [one] of the pro-slavery arguments from the 19th century—by leaving war-stricken and impoverished West Africa the slaves were considered given a better life in the New World.

Contemporary intercountry adoption having flown in close to half a million Third World children to the West during a period of half a century has many parallels to the Atlantic slave trade which between 1440 and 1870 shipped 11 million Africans to America, and to indentured labor dispatching 12 million Indians and Chinese to the European empires between 1834 and 1922. However, a crucial difference is of course that slave trade and indentured labor belong to history and are today almost universally condemned, while intercountry adoption is still continuing, perfectly accepted by Western societies and legalized through various international conventions.

There are indeed numerous striking similarities between the slave trade and intercountry adoption. Both practices are demand driven, utilizing a highly advanced system of pricing and commodification of human beings with the young and healthy as the most valued, as well as being dependent on the existence of intermediaries in the forms of slave hunters and adoption agencies and a reliable transportation system of ships and planes. Both the African slaves and the Third World children are stripped of their identities as they are separated from their parents and siblings, baptized and Christianized, losing their language and culture and in the end only retaining a fetishized non-white body that has been branded or given a case number. . . .

Cultural Genocide and Racism

When we arrive to Sweden, we have to give up our Korean identity, and it doesn't matter whether we are five weeks or seven years old. We are emptied of our Koreanness including name and language, and are filled up with Swedishness. One effect is that few adoptees remember their childhood in their birth country. Everything un-Swedish is considered "forbidden": we are here on the Swedes' conditions. Everything linked to Korea is taboo or slandered. Korea is contemptuously considered to be a "bad" and "poor" country. Many adoptive parents have strange fantasies about Korea with strong sexual undertones: "your mother was a prostitute", "you are an incest child" and "if you had been in Korea today, either you would have been dead or a prostitute."

The adoptive parents want the adopted children to feel "chosen", but in reality adoption is nothing else but a grim lottery. Behind this is the demand from the adoptive parents to feel eternally grateful, loyal, satisfied and happy. The truth is that we would never have been here in the West without a colonial history of 500 years, without today's unequal world order, and without the dominating ideal of the middle-class nuclear family.

When the adoptee leaves the adoptive family to become an adult, the immigrant identity is waiting. From a privileged adopted child with adoptive parents who fight to make their adopted children believe that they are "special", not immigrants, the adult adoptee becomes just one of many other non-white immigrants. That is the African-Americans' strongest opinion against interracial adoption: white parents can never teach their non-white children strategies how to survive in a racist society. A similar argument was heard from some African countries refusing to use intercountry adoption already in the 1970s: "You don't treat our children with respect and dignity."

However, these arguments have oddly enough rarely reached the world of intercountry adoption. Instead it is assumed that there are no special problems, emotional or psychological costs being a non-white adoptee in a white adoptive family and living in a predominantly white surrounding. Consequently, assimilation becomes the ideal as the adoptee is stripped of name, language, religion and culture, while the bonds to the biological family and the country of origin are cut off. . . .

Outcomes of Intercountry Adoption

Studies on adoptees have been conducted ever since the first children arrived in their host countries in the 1950s, and the majority have been qualitative works based on small groups of children or adolescents with adoptive parents as informants and focusing on issues of attachment, adjustment and self-esteem. In the leading adopting regions of North America, Scandinavia and Western Europe, the field is heavily dominated by researchers who are either adoptive parents themselves or affiliated to adoption agencies. As a result of these obvious limitations, the outcomes of studies are almost without exceptions interpreted as positive, and problems that have been identified are attributed to a combination of pre-adoption and genetic factors as it is understood that there are no difficulties at all of being racially different in a white environment. As a consequence, there are few studies on adult adoptees and few quantitative population studies, while the politically sensitive issues of race and ethnicity are mostly dealt with in a shallow way.

However, recently new research has come to light, based on thousands of adult intercountry adoptees in Sweden due to unique possibilities in the country of conducting quantitative register studies, showing a less positive picture of intercountry adoption. Antecedents to the Swedish studies were conducted in the

Netherlands already in the 1990s showing high frequencies of behavior and emotional problems among adolescent intercountry adoptees compared to equivalent non-adopted control groups. The new Swedish studies, by far the most extensive ever conducted on intercountry adoptees in any Western country up to date [2003], clearly indicate that intercountry adoption is not as unproblematic and idyllic as it generally is conceived as. Instead the Swedish studies should be seen as the most scientific way of assessing the outcomes of intercountry adoption.

The adult intercountry adoptees were checked up in population registers and compared to equivalent control groups among ethnic Swedes. The results show that the group has substantial problems to establish themselves socio-economically in terms of level of education, labor market achievement and creating a family in spite of having been adopted to couples predominantly belonging to the Swedish elite. It is estimated that 90 percent of the adoptive parents belong to the upper and middle classes. In spite of this, 6.6 percent of the intercountry adoptees had a post-secondary education of three years or more compared to 20 percent among biological children of the adoptive parents whom they grew up with as siblings. 60.2 percent of the intercountry adoptees were employed compared to 77.1 percent among ethnic Swedes, and half of the former group belong to the lowest income category compared to 28.6 percent for the latter. 29.2 percent of the intercountry adoptees were either married or co-habitants compared to 56.2 percent of the majority population. Intercountry adoptees have less often children, and those who are parents are more often living without their children if they are males or as single parents if they are females, thus sadly mimicking their biological parents' behavior. Males have more often than females indicators of social maladjustment.

Moreover, epidemiological studies show high levels of psychiatric illness, addiction, criminality and suicide compared to the control groups. The odds ratio for psychiatric hospital care was found to be 3.2, for treatment for alcohol abuse 2.6 and for drug abuse 5.2. The odds ratio for severe criminality leading to imprisonment stood at 2.6 and for suicide attempt 3.6. Females have more often than males indicators of poor mental health. The most shocking finding is a record high odds ratio of 5.0 for suicide compared to ethnic Swedes, in an international perspective only comparable to the staggering suicide rates registered among indigenous people in North America and Oceania, which makes parallels to cultural genocide ghastly topical.

In this perspective, it becomes more evident than ever that intercountry adoption is nothing else but an irresponsible social experiment of gigantic measures, from the beginning to the end.

Transracial Adoption Should Not Be Encouraged

by Dorothy Roberts

About the author: *Dorothy Roberts is the author of* Shattered Bonds: The Color of Child Welfare.

It is often said that American child welfare policy operates like a pendulum. It swings between two main objectives: keeping troubled families together on one end, and protecting children from parental harm on the other. In recent years the pendulum of child welfare philosophy has swung decisively away from preserving families. State child protection officials responded to fatal child abuse cases, like that of Elisa Izquierdo in 1995, by escalating removal of at-risk children from their homes. And in 1997, Congress passed the Adoption and Safe Families Act that encourages state agencies to "free" children in foster care for adoption by terminating their parents' rights. The emphasis on adoption to cure the ills of the foster care system mirrors the 1996 welfare reform law's emphasis on private remedies for poverty, such as marriage and low-wage jobs. The overlap of these two laws marks the first time in U.S. history that the federal government requires states to protect children from maltreatment without requiring states to provide economic support to their families.

A recent class action lawsuit brought by battered women in New York City, *Nicholson v. Scoppetta*, highlights the injustice of child welfare practice that relies on child removal. In a March 11, 2002 opinion, federal district judge Jack B. Weinstein ruled that New York City's child welfare department violated the constitutional rights of battered mothers by routinely and unnecessarily placing their children in foster care. Judge Weinstein attributed the city's child removal policy in cases of domestic violence to deeper flaws in a system that is unfairly stacked against poor families. Poor mothers threatened with losing their children lack adequate legal representation in part because the state pays their court-appointed lawyers so poorly. In addition, bureaucratic inefficiency and caution lead case workers to rake what they perceive to be the path of least re-

Dorothy Roberts, "Racial Harm," *ColorLines*, vol. 5, Fall 2002, pp. 19–20. Copyright © 2002 by ColorLines Magazine. Reproduced by permission.

sistance. Instead of devising ways to keep battered mothers and their children safely united, agencies find it easier to snatch children from their homes. Most important, child protection agents fail to consider the trauma caused to children by needlessly separating them from their mothers. After all, a child killed by parents often makes frontpage news and can ruin the careers of judges and administrators. The emotional damage to thousands of children wrongfully relegated to foster care usually goes unnoticed.

Racial Disparities

But this list of flaws overlooks another critical dimension of the child welfare system reflected in the state's excessive intervention in families. By placing children in a "forced state custody" under these conditions, Judge Weinstein wrote, the city's child removal policy constituted "a form of slavery." Judge Weinstein's reference to slavery is especially apt, given the child welfare system's staggering racial disparity. Black children make up nearly half of the national foster care population, although they represent less than one-fifth of the nation's children. Latino and Native American children are also in the system in disproportionate numbers. The system's racial imbalance is most apparent in big cities where there are sizeable minority and foster care populations. In Chicago, for example, 95 percent of children in foster care are black. Out of 42,000 children in New York City's foster care system at the end of 1997, only 1,300 were white. Black children in New York were 10 times as likely as white children to be in state protective custody. Spend a day in the courts that decide child maltreatment cases in these cities and you very well may see only black or Latino parents and children. If you came with no preconceptions about the purpose of the child welfare system, you would have to conclude that it is an institution designed to monitor, regulate, and punish poor families of color.

> *"Race . . . influences child welfare decision making through strong and deeply embedded stereotypes about black family dysfunction."*

State agencies are far more likely to place black children who come to their attention in foster care instead of offering their families less traumatic assistance. According to federal statistics, black children in the child welfare system are placed in foster care at twice the rate for white children. A national study of child protective services by the U.S. Department of Health and Human Services reported that "[m]inority children, and in particular African American children, are more likely to be in foster care placement than receive in-home services, *even when they have the same problems and characteristics as white children.*" Most white children who enter the system are permitted to stay with their families, avoiding the emotional damage and physical risks of foster care placement, while most black children are taken away from theirs. And once removed from their homes, black children remain in foster care longer, are moved more often, receive fewer services, and are less likely to be either returned home or adopted than any other children.

Why are black children placed in foster care at higher rates? Despite recent declines, the U.S. child poverty rate is still exceptionally high by international standards, extreme poverty is actually growing, and black children still lag far behind. State disruption of black families reflects the persistent gulf between the material welfare of black and white children in America. But racial differences in child poverty rates don't tell the whole story. Race also influences child welfare decision making through strong and deeply embedded stereotypes about black family dysfunction. Some case workers and judges view black parents as less reformable than white parents, less willing and able to respond to the treatment child protection agencies prescribe. The "predisposition toward counterproductive separation" that Judge Weinstein observed stems not only from "bureaucratic caution" but also from an indifference to the bonds between parents of color and their children. In the past several decades, the number of children receiving child welfare services has declined dramatically, while the foster care population has skyrocketed. As the child welfare system began to serve fewer white children and more children of color, state and federal governments spent more money on out-of-home care and less on in-home services.

> *"The asserted benefits of transracial adoption . . . masquerade as reasons to oppose policies that preserve black families."*

All of the cruelties inflicted by overzealous child protective agents fall disproportionately on nonwhite families. But the impact of the state's destruction of families extends beyond harm to individual parents and children. The child welfare system also inflicts damage on the communities where state disruption and supervision of families is concentrated. Placing large numbers of children in state custody interferes with a community's ability to form healthy connections among its members. Excessive state interference in family life, for example, damages people's sense of personal and community identity. Family and community disintegration weakens communities' collective ability to overcome institutionalized discrimination and to work toward greater political and economic strength. The system's racial disparity also reinforces the quintessential racist stereotype: that nonwhite people are incapable of governing themselves and need state supervision.

Why Adoption Policies Are Misguided

The racial harm caused by disproportionate state disruption of families helps to explain why current federal and state policies that emphasize adoption are misguided. The campaign to increase adoptions has hinged on the denigration of foster children's parents, the speedy destruction of their family bonds, and the rejection of family preservation as an important goal of child welfare practice. Adoption is increasingly presented not as an option for a minority of foster children who cannot be reunited with their parents, but as the preferred outcome for all children in foster care. More fundamentally, turning to adoption to fix the foster care system ignores the injustice of excessive removal of children in the first place. Placing all foster children in adoptive homes would only exacerbate the system's racial harm, not end it.

The racial politics of adoption are intensified by the promotion of transracial adoption in particular as a way of addressing the influx of black children to the foster care rolls. Although most white people seeking adoption want only a white child, many commentators and politicians support eliminating any consideration of race, along with expediting termination of parental rights, to move more black children into white adoptive homes. (It should be noted that abolishing race-matching means allowing white people to choose the race of the children they adopt, not ending the more common matching of white adoptive parents with white children or even considering the adoption of white children by blacks.) The asserted benefits of transracial adoption further obscure the system's racial bias and masquerade as reasons to oppose policies that preserve black families.

The price of a child welfare philosophy that relies on child removal rather than family support falls unjustly on minority families. The number of black and Latino children in state custody—those in foster care combined with those in juvenile detention, prisons, and other state institutions—is a national disgrace that reflects systemic injustices and that calls for radical reform. The child welfare system's racial harm is a powerful reason to replace our current child protection practices with policies that generously and non-coercively support families.

Chapter 2

Does America's Adoption System Need More Government Regulation?

CURRENT CONTROVERSIES

Chapter Preface

In 2001 a custody battle over twin baby girls made headlines in two countries and placed a spotlight on the role of the Internet in adoption proceedings. Tina Johnson, who ran an adoption website out of her California home, helped to place the twins into the home of a California couple, who paid a fee of six thousand dollars. After caring for the children for two months, the couple received a request from the birth mother for a final farewell visit. However, once the birth mother had the girls in her possession, she handed the children over to a British couple without notifying the girls' new California parents. The British couple then drove the twins to Arkansas, adopted them under that state's laws, and flew back to Great Britain. The British couple paid Johnson twelve thousand dollars for arranging the adoption.

The twins were eventually taken from the second adoptive parents, returned to the United States and placed in foster care. But the case highlighted several aspects of how adoption regulations have failed to keep pace with changing adoption practices. One notable aspect is how the Internet is enabling more and more people to bypass traditional adoption agencies and to pursue private independent adoptions. A few states, such as Connecticut and Massachusetts, as well as some nations like Great Britain, require that *all* adoptions be done through state-licensed agencies that find and match up children and adoptive homes. To be licensed, agencies must demonstrate to state regulatory agencies that they are providing adequate counseling to all involved parties and that the best interests of children are not being compromised for monetary reasons. But most states do not mandate the use of agencies in adoptions, and many have looser rules concerning private adoptions in which the parties, with the help of lawyers, negotiate their own arrangements (all adoptions, whether agency or private, require the final approval of family law judges). Even fewer regulations govern adoption websites. Johnson's business, for example, was not licensed or regulated by the state of California.

The percentage of American adoptions handled by state-licensed agencies dropped from 90 percent in 1966 to about 20 percent in 2001. Many people have turned to private adoptions after finding the agency process to be too slow and bureaucratic. But rapid growth of the private adoption industry has also spawned an increase in stories of adoption problems such as the twin girls case. Other stories range from fly-by-night adoption brokers who take thousands of dollars from prospective adoptive parents and then disappear (perhaps to reappear in another state) to babies being placed with adopted families before birth mothers have officially relinquished them. Journalist Dawn MacKeen has called private adoption "a field ripe for those trying to make fast cash since the parties involved—the adoptive parents and the birth mothers—are oftentimes highly emotional and desperate."

The twin girls case of 2001 also revealed how the Internet has enabled people to cross not only state but also national borders in attempting to arrange adoptions—often seeking locales where rules are less strict. The British couple had traveled to America in part because private adoptions were not permitted in Great Britain, and their chances of being approved for adoption in that country were slim. People seeking to adopt face a confusing patchwork of differing rules not only between state and local governments, but between nations. Many adoption advocates have called for uniform international rules to regulate the practice of adoption. In 1994 the American government signed the Convention on Protection of Children in Intercountry Adoption, negotiated by representatives of fifty-five nations in 1993. Also known as the Hague Convention, the treaty requires signatory nations to create a "Central Authority" to set adoption standards and to coordinate their efforts with other Hague nations. After some debate, the U.S. Senate finally ratified the treaty in 2000.

Although the Hague Convention has been approved, questions remain on how exactly the treaty is to be implemented and the extent to which adoptions, especially private adoptions, should be regulated. The articles in this chapter offer varying perspectives on these questions.

More Regulation Is Necessary to Protect People from International Adoption Scams

by Ann Marie Cunningham

About the author: *Ann Marie Cunningham is a writer and television producer.*

Sitting in her cozy Long Island, New York, kitchen, Millie Collica, thirty-three, keeps a watchful eye on her adopted two-year-old daughter, Arianna. "Do you have young nieces and nephews?" Millie asks. "Do you have photographs of them? If you do, you can open an adoption agency. That's all it takes."

Millie and her husband, Michael, know just how easy it is for couples desperate to become parents to be cheated by a dishonest adoption agency. In 1995, before adopting Arianna, the Collicas lost almost $20,000 to Today's Adoption Agency, based in Hawley, Pennsylvania.

Unfortunately, the Collicas are not alone. According to the U.S. Immigration and Naturalization Service (INS), international adoptions have jumped almost 40 percent in the last eleven years, from close to ten thousand in 1986 to nearly fourteen thousand in 1997. At the same time, the number of adoption scams appears to be on the rise. Although no federal agency keeps track of adoption fraud, the March 1997 issue of *Fraud Digest*, the State Department's monthly bulletin on passport and visa fraud, noted a rise in baby smuggling, citing cases in five states. The Council of Better Business Bureaus (CBBB) has received enough complaints about adoption fraud that it includes on its Web site a list of questions prospective parents should ask agencies, says Holly Cherico, vice president of communications. "Adoption represents a major investment of funds," notes Cherico, whose own brother-in-law, a policeman in New York City, was conned by an unscrupulous baby broker. "We want

Ann Marie Cunningham, "The Baby Brokers," *Ladies Home Journal*, October 1, 1998. Copyright © 1998 by the Meredith Corporation. All rights reserved. Reproduced by permission.

to alert people that they need to check out agencies."

Adoption fraud is "the worst type of rip-off," agrees New York Attorney General Dennis C. Vacco, who is investigating baby-broker scams in the state. "It combines the horrors of losing hard-earned dollars with a heartbreak that will never go away. We simply cannot allow this type of exploitation."

One Family's Pain

Millie, an administrative assistant for a small consulting firm, and Michael, a manager for a pool and spa maintenance company, spent years trying to have a child. After endless fertility treatments, they decided to try adoption. Since Millie's mother is Puerto Rican and her father Honduran, the Collicas were especially eager to adopt from Latin America.

In April 1995, they were put in touch with Today's Adoption, an agency that had successfully placed babies in the past. According to Millie, a caseworker for the agency told them that the executive director of Today's Adoption, Patricia Zuvic, was from Chile. Many of the babies they placed were from Latin America.

Millie and Michael were shown photographs of about thirty healthy children. Only two were available for adoption. Millie was drawn to a photo of a baby boy. He had dark hair and brown eyes. "He looked like he'd fit with us," she says.

The Collicas were told that if they wanted the child, they would have to act fast. "We had to make a decision by nine the next morning," recalls Millie.

The following day, the Collicas sent Zuvic $9,500. They were told they could expect their new son in about six months. Ecstatic, Millie and Michael chose a name—Steven—for the infant, and Millie decorated the nursery.

In September 1995, at the agency's suggestion, the couple decided to go to Asuncion, Paraguay, to see Steven. First, they were required to pay Today's Adoption in full. The Collicas wired the agency $10,000.

In Asuncion, they spent days with Steven, who was thirteen months old and in foster care. "We bonded immediately," Millie says. The Collicas were told that the adoption decree would be final in four weeks.

But months went by, and the couple heard nothing. When a frantic Millie called for explanations, Zuvic and her daughter, Denise, director of Today's Adoption, kept telling her, "Another two to four weeks."

> *"Adoption fraud is 'the worst type of rip-off.'"*

In March 1996, suspicious of the endless delay, Millie made a second trip to Paraguay without informing the Zuvics. She spent six weeks in Asuncion, nursing Steven through an illness. A lawyer who worked for Today's Adoption in Paraguay told her that the agency had never paid him his fee to finalize Steven's adoption. "I gave him my guarantee that I would pay him whatever he was owed," Millie says.

But what Today's Adoption had never informed the Collicas—or many of their other clients—was that on September 18, 1995, just before Michael and Millie's first trip to Paraguay, the country had declared a moratorium on all adoptions from abroad.

When the Collicas heard about the moratorium, they were stunned. In a panic, Millie phoned Today's Adoption and spoke to Denise Zuvic, who told her that Steven's adoption was already in progress and that the moratorium would not affect it. Later, Patricia Zuvic told Millie and Michael that if they "really wanted a child," they would not press so hard.

> *"Adoption fraud is notoriously difficult to prosecute."*

Devastated, the Collicas realized that they had been conned. "I was very angry," Millie says. "I felt so betrayed. It was as though Steven had died. All I could think was, How could the agency do this?"

But she was determined to take action. Millie learned that while she had been in Paraguay, the Zuvics had invited about a dozen other families who had complained about adoption delays to a meeting at their Fort Lee, New Jersey, office. One client, Mark Frankel, a writer who later chronicled his adoption experience for *New York* magazine, collected the phone numbers of the couples at the get-together and the Collicas received a copy of the phone list. "The Zuvics made a very big mistake, holding that meeting," Frankel says. "We all began to compare stories."

The Limits of the Law

The Collicas and seven other couples filed complaints about Today's Adoption with the New York State Department of Social Services. Their complaints were passed to Judith T. Kramer, an assistant attorney general of New York State. She began working on the case, and in March 1997, the New York State Supreme Court barred Today's Adoption from seeking new clients—or accepting fees from existing clients—in New York. The agency is still [in 1998] doing business in New Jersey and Pennsylvania, however, and Kramer is sharing information with the attorneys general there to try to close Today's Adoption down for good.

Efforts to recover the Collicas' and other clients' money also continue. Kramer estimates that, in total, clients of Today's Adoption lost "several hundred thousand dollars." But in order to recover the money, she needs the Zuvics' financial records. Patricia Zuvic's accountant informed Kramer that Zuvic's personal and business statements were lost in a June 1997 fire at his office. Denise Zuvic has filed for bankruptcy. (Patricia and Denise Zuvic did not return the *Journal*'s calls for an interview.)

Authorities acknowledge that adoption fraud is notoriously difficult to prosecute. In the United States, there is no federal regulation of adoption agencies, and state laws vary widely. The Joint Council on International Children's Services in Cheverly, Maryland, the oldest and largest affiliation of licensed, non-profit international adoption agencies, sets operating standards for its member adoption agencies, but not every state has laws that back up these standards. Agencies may apply for accreditation by the private Council on Accreditation of Services for Families and Children, and become licensed by their state's Department of Social Services (DSS). But many small agencies or brokers skip the lengthy accreditation process.

"We need federal statutes," says Kramer. . . . Making matters even more difficult is that "none of these agencies operates nationally," she adds. When one state closes down a dishonest agency, the agency often simply picks up and moves to another state to do business.

One state, Oklahoma, does seem to be making some progress. In March 1998, Brenda Morgan, the owner of A Chosen Angel Adoption, who was operating without a license, was arrested and jailed on thirteen felony counts for child trafficking and other related crimes. (Her husband was also later arrested and charged with the same crimes.) Seven families who were allegedly conned by Morgan plan to testify against her at the trial.[1]

Desperate People Ignore Red Flags

As the Collicas know all too well, the lack of regulations make it easy for dishonest baby brokers or agencies to prey on vulnerable couples. Most people seeking children from abroad are exhausted and frustrated by the emotional and physical toll of fertility treatments and failed attempts to adopt domestically. As a result, many are so desperate that they ignore red flags.

Unscrupulous agencies lead prospective parents to think that an adoption will be quick and easy. Brokers hold out the promise of a baby who will belong to a couple if they act fast, and entice couples to hand over a substantial payment immediately. "You're so vulnerable," explains Jackie Raguso, forty-three, a financial analyst for IBM who lives in Pound Ridge, New York. She and her husband, Matt, were also clients of Today's Adoption. "When an agency tells you they have a child waiting for you, it's like asking an alcoholic if he wants a drink."

> *"Unscrupulous agencies lead prospective parents to think that an adoption will be quick and easy."*

In truth, legitimate international adoptions can take up to eighteen months, according to the Evan B. Donaldson Adoption Institute, a nonprofit educational foundation in New York City. Nor is the process nearly as simple as baby brokers often claim. Prospective parents have to be approved by their state

---

1. Brenda Morgan eventually pleaded guilty to five criminal counts and was sentenced to ten years in prison for child trafficking. Her husband, Daniel Morgan, pleaded guilty to three counts and was sentenced to six years probation.

DSS, and the INS has to investigate to make sure both biological parents have relinquished their rights to the child before issuing him or her a visa. No legitimate agency should require a large payment until an adoption is final.

Typically, after a dishonest agency has gotten its money, the adoptive children suddenly "disappear." It's only when prospective parents decide to fight back that they learn how little recourse they have. In December 1993, Kathy Taylor, a thirty-eight-year-old finance director for a packaging distributor in Milwaukee, and her husband, Don, phoned Elena Moure-Domecq, a Cuban-born lawyer based in Miami, about adopting a child. Moure-Domecq told the couple that she had heard recently about an infant boy in Guatemala. A few days later, the Taylors sent her about $11,000. In July, after months of trying to reach Moure-Domecq by phone, the couple finally learned that the child's birth mother had "changed her mind"—but Moure-Domecq promised them another boy, and then a girl.

Finally, the Taylors and six other defrauded couples tried to sue Moure-Domecq in Florida, but not one of the families could find a lawyer in the state who considered the case worthwhile. The disgruntled clients eventually filed grievances on their own with the Florida Bar. As a result, Moure-Domecq's license to practice law was suspended for sixty days—but she was not officially ordered to stop her baby brokering. . . .

While the laws against baby brokers are limited, time served in what writer Mark Frankel calls "adoption hell" does transform many parents into international adoption activists. Since 1990, the U.S. Department of State, aided by adoptive parents groups, adoption attorneys and the Joint Council on International Children's Services, has been working to secure an international adoption treaty. Known as the Hague Convention on Intercountry Adoption, it aims to transform international adoption into a system of cooperation among countries. Each signatory nation must establish a state authority to accredit and monitor agencies and individual adoption service providers.

As of August 1998, thirty-two countries had signed the Hague Convention, including the United States. . . .

However, while international adoption can pose special risks, there are many successful adoptions every year. In fact, every couple mentioned in this article went on to find honest agencies and adopt overseas. "Even if you go through a nightmare, you have to keep fighting," says Millie Collica. "If you're determined, you can find a child. Arianna filled a huge hole in our hearts."

More Regulation of International Adoption Agencies Is Necessary

by Cindy Freidmutter

About the author: *Cindy Freidmutter is the former executive director of the Evan B. Donaldson Adoption Institute, a policy and research organization. On May 22, 2002, she testified before the House Committee on International Relations hearings on implementing regulations on international adoptions.*

Thank you for inviting me to testify about how the federal government can effectively implement the Hague Convention and the Intercountry Adoption Act (IAA)[1] to improve international adoption services for adoptive families, birth parents and adopted children and ensure a more ethical adoption environment internationally. I represent the Evan B. Donaldson Adoption Institute (Adoption Institute), a not-for-profit national policy and research organization devoted to improving the quality of adoption policy and practice, and the public's perception of adoption. Throughout the regulatory drafting process, the Adoption Institute has advocated that the State Department tailor the regulations to address the most serious problems with international adoption. Unfortunately, the current draft regulations will not fulfill a primary purpose of the IAA—"protect[ing] the rights of, and prevent[ing] abuses against children, birth families, and adoptive parents involved in adoption."

International adoption has evolved into a potentially lucrative and largely unregulated business. Over the last decade, the number of international adoptions by Americans has increased threefold from about 6,500 in 1992 to over 19,000 in 2001. Accurate information is not currently compiled by any reliable source

---

1. The Hague Convention, drafted in 1993, is an international treaty that sets minimum standards and practices governing international adoptions. The United States approved its provisions when Congress passed the Intercountry Adoption Act in 2000, with details on implementation left to be developed by the Department of State and the Immigration and Naturalization Service.

Cindy Freidmutter, testimony before the U.S. House Committee on International Relations, Washington, DC, May 22, 2002.

about the aggregate fees charged for international adoption services. One can reasonably estimate, however, that U.S. adoptive parents spent close to $200 million in 2001 for international adoption services. As the number of international adoptions has grown, there has been a corresponding sharp escalation in the number of individuals and agencies, here and abroad, involved in facilitating the adoption process. In 1989, only a handful of adoptions took place in Russia and China, but by 2001, these two countries accounted for nearly half of all international adoptions by Americans. By the end of the 1990s, there were 80 U.S.

> *"International adoption has evolved into a potentially lucrative and largely unregulated business."*

agencies active in Russia and 150 active in China. The market forces inherent in international adoption pose a potential threat to the welfare of children, as well as their birth parents and prospective adoptive parents.

Evidence and experience highlight three critical issues with international adoption services provided in the United States, which the Adoption Institute urges the State Department to address in the IAA regulations.

First, U.S. providers should be directly responsible for all financial transactions with and payments to their contractors and agents in other countries, and should be accountable to families who rely on their representations about fees.

U.S. families who adopt internationally are generally told by their agencies to carry substantial amounts of cash abroad to pay fees, a dangerous and sometimes illegal practice. [An] Adoption Institute survey of over 1,600 American families who adopted internationally through U.S. agencies found that three out of four families were required by their agencies to carry cash to their adoptive child's country of origin to pay adoption service fees, with most directed to bring $3,000 or more. And 11% of all respondents stated that when they were overseas, agency facilitators asked them to pay additional fees that were not disclosed by the agencies.

It is logical to presume that undocumented cash transactions by American adoptive families are a major factor in fostering unethical practices overseas. The current draft regulations, however, will not curb this practice by only requiring "an official and recorded means of fund transfer, whenever possible." In order to reduce financial incentives that may lead to illegal and unethical practices, financial transactions must be transparent and recorded. IAA regulations should require providers to develop an official and recorded means of fund transfer, unless the State Department issues a written determination that it is not possible to do so in a specific country.

Second, adoption service contracts between providers and prospective adoptive families should create a clear and predictable business relationship by enumerating in plain language the services to be provided, the fees to be paid, the legal responsibility of the adoption agencies for staff, agents and subcontrac-

tors, *the complaint resolution processes and other critical information.*

Currently, U.S. families adopting internationally are not afforded basic consumer legal protections. While many parents who adopt internationally sign a contract with their adoption agencies, these "contracts" too often fail to create a fair and clear business relationship with respect to services, fees and legal responsibility. Consequently, families have no recourse when agencies do not provide promised services, give them inaccurate information, or increase the fees while the adoption is in process, problems which happen to a significant minority of families.

Of the 1,600 families who responded to the Adoption Institute's survey,

- 15% reported that their agency withheld information or told them inaccurate information about the child,
- Another 15% said their agency withheld information or told them inaccurate information about the adoption process, and
- 14% said their adoption cost more than the agency told them it would cost.

The regulations should specify the type of information that must be included in adoption service contracts. Contracts protect parents and providers alike, providing clarity about the parties' respective roles and responsibilities, and guidance to courts in the event of disputes. While the draft regulations require providers to disclose "fully and in writing" their policies and practices, inexplicably they do not mandate that providers include that information in adoption service contracts. Similarly, the draft regulations require that some, but not all, fee information be disclosed in contracts.

> *"The regulations should specify the type of information that must be included in adoption service contracts."*

The bottom line is that prospective adoptive parents should not have to comb through the Code of Federal Regulations to insure that their agencies are providing legally required information and services at agreed-upon fees.

Third, prospective adoptive parents should have access to objective information to guide their choice of international adoption service providers.

One of the simplest and most effective ways of accomplishing a primary purpose of the IAA—"prevent[ing] abuses against . . . adoptive parents"—is to provide them with the information they need to make informed choices about providers. Information about service quality and provider performance would likely enhance prospective adoptive parents' ability to make educated decisions, thereby improving their satisfaction rates. Currently, a significant minority of parents who responded to the Adoption Institute survey were not happy with their agencies' performance:

- 13% were not satisfied with the services they received from adoption agencies.
- 14% would not recommend their agency to other families.

The draft regulations do not address consumer education in an effective manner. There is no requirement that an independent entity publish comparable performance information that would help prospective adoptive families make informed choices. Publication of such information would also create a strong incentive for "weaker" providers to improve service quality and performance. The regulations should mandate that service quality and outcome data generated by the accreditation process be used to educate prospective adoptive families about provider performance in the following ways:

- Publication of a consumer handbook explaining the regulation of providers, and accreditation and complaint processes,
- Creation of an annual consumer report card, available on the Internet and in print, that evaluates providers' compliance with the regulations and key quality indicators, and
- Providing access on the Internet and in print to provider-specific comparable service quality, performance and cost information.

The Adoption Institute has also recommended that the State Department adopt the following additional strategies to fundamentally improve the quality of international adoption practice. By incorporating these proposals into the regulations, the Adoption Institute believes that the federal government will dramatically improve actual experience with and public perception of international adoption.

- Identify poor quality providers in a timely manner, and create a regulatory enforcement climate where they either meet standards or lose accreditation.
- Require providers to be legally responsible to the families who contract with them for acts of their agents and contractors in the United States and abroad.
- Mandate that providers carry liability insurance that reflects the risk of work conducted by all its agents and contractors.
- Ensure prospective adoptive families receive access to the best available information about referred children.
- Guarantee adopted persons and their families access to their adoption records to the fullest extent permitted by the Hague Convention and IAA.
- Create an Ombudsman or similar independent entity that enables families engaged in international adoption to report and resolve complaints involving providers' regulatory noncompliance. An Ombudsman would also:
  - Provide consumer education about the complaint process.
  - Facilitate timely resolution of consumer complaints.
  - Routinely analyze complaint patterns and outcome data to identify providers that are in violation of regulatory standards.
  - Advise Congress and the State Department about ongoing problems, and the impact of the regulations and accreditation process on improving service quality.

The Federal Government Must Regulate Adoption

by Maureen Hogan

About the author: *Maureen Hogan is executive director of the National Adoption Foundation, a private organization that provides financial assistance and services to adoptive and prospective adoptive families.*

For years, the argument against greater regulation of adoption by the federal government has been rooted in the notion that adoption is a state law issue. The public thought adoption was a benevolent, philanthropic exercise practiced by charitable organizations donating their services to ensure better lives for orphans. In truth, adoption is big business and inherently interstate in nature. The federal government already tightly controls adoption from foster care. The truth is a powerful argument for immediate federal intervention in fee-charging adoption. By leaving regulation to the states, consumers of adoption services have been left almost entirely vulnerable to unscrupulous providers effectively shielded by distant geography from accountability. Adoption has become a multi-billion-dollar industry with some providers realizing revenues of $15 million annually. With the demand for healthy infants far in excess of the supply, American children are literally being sold to the highest bidders, often to foreign nationals living in other countries. Unfortunately, while unscrupulous facilitators trade in human beings for money, adoption effectively remains the only unregulated business in the United States.

As early as 1955, the U.S. Senate investigated abusive adoption practices. Senator Estes Kefauver of Tennessee held a series of oversight hearings in the Senate Judiciary Committee. In those hearings, Sen. Kefauver took testimony from birthparents, adoptive parents and adoptees. These witnesses detailed hundreds, if not thousands, of chilling stories which outlined a trail of unethical and deceptive business practices, including kidnaping, by adoption agencies coast to coast. The charges included the theft and sale of babies from birthparents who desperately wanted to keep them. Infants with life threatening health

Maureen Hogan, "Why the Federal Government Must Regulate Adoption," www. americanadoptioncongress.org, vol. 16, 1999. Copyright © 1999 by American Adoption Congress. Reproduced by permission.

problems were placed with unsuspecting adoptive families oblivious to the desperate need their children had for urgent medical treatment. One agency in Tennessee was responsible for the illicit placement of more than 10,000 children in more than forty states in one ten-year period.

Since Sen. Kefauver's hearings more than forty years ago some agencies he targeted are still in business and the practices he exposed have continued. The number of wrongful adoption lawsuits against agencies engaged in careless practices and deliberate fraud are skyrocketing. Unfortunately, efforts to protect the consumers of adoption services have been consistently thwarted by a multi-million-dollar lobbying effort by fee charging adoption agencies and their trade association, the National Council for Adoption (NCFA). It should come as no surprise that some NCFA members were among those targeted by Sen. Kefauver.

> *"By leaving regulation to the states, consumers of adoption services have been left almost entirely vulnerable to unscrupulous providers."*

For years, the big business interests of adoption have attempted to persuade Congress and the public that their interest in limiting openness in adoption is about privacy for birthmothers. The reality, however, may have more to do with promoting secrecy, limiting liability and preserving profits.

In 1992, NCFA charter member, the Smithlawn Maternity Center in Lubbock, Texas, was the first adoption agency in the United States to be successfully sued under federal racketeering statutes. The suit was filed by adoptive parents of two "healthy" infants. The parents alleged that agency employees concealed serious medical conditions of both children, who had different birthmothers. It was later learned from agency records that one child's mother had taken drugs before and during her pregnancy, while the other child had experienced significant trauma during delivery. The adoptive family also sued attorney George Thompson maintaining that he had a conflict of interest while representing them. While representing the family he also served on Smithlawn's board of directors. Under a subsequent settlement with the adoptive parents, Thompson, three Smithlawn officials and the agency itself were ordered to pay a settlement in excess of $1 million. (*Dallas Morning News*, 2/13/93)

Another NCFA member, LDS Social Services in Utah (whose affiliates represent over half of NCFA's membership) was sued in 1993 by a birthmother. She had been on Thorazine (a sedative) when the agency obtained her signature on the surrender, two days after the birth in 1967. When she was discharged from the hospital, she did not remember signing the surrender or being drugged. In the next few months she contacted the agency about thirty more times, expressing confusion and remorse over the loss of her son. The agency did not tell her about the drug or about her condition when she signed the surrender, and she did not ask; the agency simply said it could do nothing. In 1990 she and her son were reunited. Shortly thereafter, the agency, through a clerical mistake, gave her a copy of her medical records. After two years of further correspondence with the agency and with officials of the Mormon Church, she brought suit. The Utah courts dismissed the suit on the ground that it was started too late. (*Salt Lake Tribune*, 5/9/96) (*Safsten v. LDS Social Services, Inc.*, 942 P.2d 949; Utah 1997)

Several stories in the July/August 1998 issue of *Adoptive Families Magazine* raise concerns about other questionable practices. Consider the following scenarios:

• An adoption agency separated newborn identical twin boys and placed them in two separate adoptive homes 3,000 miles apart despite insistence by their birthmother that they be placed for adoption together. Four years later, their adoptive parents were horrified to learn that the adoption agency could charge each couple the full adoption fee for one healthy infant's adoption—doubling the fee they could collect if the twins had been placed together.

• A college freshman planned adoption for her unborn child and contacted a large Texas agency. When she later changed her mind, the agency told her that she would have to repay thousands of dollars in medical and living expenses and would be prosecuted for fraud for failing to give up her child. Several years later she learned that authorities cannot force mothers in her circumstance to give up their babies.

• An independent facilitator in Massachusetts used a South American attorney to locate and place that country's children. Eventually it was discovered that the children had been kidnapped by the attorney's employee. Though the facilitator was forced out of business, the attorney still practices adoption in his country. The parents of the kidnapped children have no idea where their babies are today.

Stories like the last one illustrate the fact that American adoption consumers are not the only ones who have reason to question some American adoption providers. Around the same time Sen. Kefauver was conducting his landmark hearings, birthmothers in Ireland and Irish officials were making a series of alarming discoveries. They learned that thousands of Irish children who had been placed for adoption in the United States, on the condition that they be placed with Catholic families, were actually auctioned off to the highest bidders by American adoption

> *"Adoption consumers are not the only ones who have reason to question some American adoption providers."*

providers. In some instances, children were placed in homes that had not even been homestudied. The Irish government was sufficiently concerned about these and other unscrupulous practices that, in 1959, they banned all adoptions of Irish children outside Ireland—a prohibition that continues to this day. (*Banished Babies* by Mike Milotte)

But Ireland is not the only country that has expressed concerns about the ethics of American adoption providers. In the February 7, 1999, issue of the

New York Times Magazine, reporter Tina Rosenberg's story "Salvador's Disappeared Children" detailed the work in El Salvador of a search and reunion organization, Pro-Busqueda. Since 1994, Pro-Busqueda has reunited children abducted and sold by Central American military juntas, in some cases to families who were aware at the time of the sale that the children were kidnapped. While Pro-Busqueda has reunited 98 disappeared children with their biological families, they have a list of 434 other families searching for children and children searching for biological families. Fourteen of the abducted children reunited with birth families had been placed for adoption in the United States.

Like Salvadoran birthmothers, poor women in Guatemala also have reason to worry about American business practices in adoption. In 1998, Public Eye, a now-canceled TV news magazine featuring Bryant Gumbal, detailed problems of NCFA member agency, Adoption Associates in Jennison, Michigan. The agency contracted with a Guatemalan attorney who they knew had been accused of stealing children from unsuspecting birthmothers. The birthmothers had been told their children were stillborn. Adoption Associates continued to accept money from American families and accept children from the attorney although the Guatemalan government was investigating him in connection with more than a dozen children and the U.S. Embassy did not recommend that Americans use him.

While human rights activists all over the world applaud the efforts of Pro-Busqueda and decry the abduction of Guatemalan children from their mothers, the silent conspiracy of American officials, desperate infertile couples, naive child welfare advocates and big business interests have combined to stall protections for children and their families. As the market for children grows, agencies short on highly marketable healthy infants have hidden medical and/or emotional problems. The children are sold to unsuspecting families ill-equipped to deal with the children's special needs. Sometimes the failure to disclose can have disastrous results for the adoptive families.

Consider the case of the Thornes of Phoenix, Arizona. You may recall that the Thornes were arrested for child abuse after a tumultuous flight from Russia during which they engaged in a physical struggle with two 4-year-old girls adopted from a Russian orphanage through a Mesa, Arizona agency. Though the agency involved knew that at least one of the children involved suffered from severe emotional problems, both children were held out to the couple as "normal." After the Thornes' arrest, the children were placed in foster care ten thousand miles from their home country. The Thornes, who paid high fees to adopt, now have criminal records and thousands of dollars in legal fees. The agency involved continues to do business with little or no liability for its failure to protect the Thornes or their daughters adequately. (*New York Times*, 11/2/97)

The Thornes' story also highlights a growing, but little known, side-effect of careless placements by unscrupulous providers. While the number of international adoptions in the United States has doubled in the past ten years, disruptions of those adoptions are increasing at a much faster rate. Previously institutionalized children with severe attachment disorder, fetal alcohol syndrome and other serious problems are entering the already-overburdened U.S. foster care system. The disrupted adoptive families are liable for the cost of foster care. When the adoptive parents cannot pay, the American taxpayers foot the bill. The agencies responsible for placing these children collect hefty fees and have no statutory liability. . . .

If adoptive parents, birthparents and adoptees band together, the first steps to greater consumer protection in adoption can be completed. In the meantime, organizations responsible for exploiting the consumers of adoption services will continue to spend millions of dollars to keep birthparents and the children they gave up for adoption from comparing notes and healing their lives.

More Federal Regulation May Displace Small International Adoption Agencies

by Laura A. Cecere

About the author: *Laura A. Cecere, an attorney, social worker, and single adoptive mother of two, is the founder and executive director of China Seas Adoption Services, an organization that provides assistance to Americans seeking to adopt children from China.*

Editor's note: The following statement was issued in response to hearings in Congress in October 1999 regarding legislation to implement the Hague Convention, a 1993 international treaty that sets standards and rules for international adoptions.

We are here today representing the thousands upon thousands of deliriously happy American parents who have adopted children abroad. We are the thousands of Americans each year who have used the current system of foreign adoption smoothly and effectively, with minimal interference by the federal government. We found the system to strike a good balance of protecting our interests without unduly burdening the process. Yet, in response to the complaints of a few, the federal government now proposes to assume a much greater role in our adoptions, so severely burdening the process, that the costs and delays that would ensue would have prevented many of us, including me, from adopting abroad at all.

How many adoptive families have experienced problems? Well, despite pages of testimony by "experts" in disrupted and troubled foreign adoptions and the eager testimony of the large agency lobbyists, no one has provided any statis-

Laura A. Cecere, statement in response to congressional testimony on implementing legislation for the Hague Convention on Intercountry Adoption, February 7, 2000.

tics. Not even estimates. . . . There's been no evidence presented that larger, accredited agencies have any more successful adoptions and less complaints than smaller, nonaccredited agencies. This, despite the fact that several organizations of those agencies have testified and could have easily presented that information. . . . Even the State Department itself testified that "[d]espite the thousands of adoptions that proceed smoothly, some come to our attention which are problematic." (Testimony of Mary Ryan, Assistant Secretary of State, Office of Consular Services, State Department) How many? What percentage of all foreign adoptions? This is left unsaid, I submit, because the numbers are so relatively low that it would be unwarranted to impose new, costly federal intervention in the foreign adoption process.

The limited research that has been done in this area so far, while not conclusive, indicates that larger, fully staffed, accredited agencies have had no better success at foreign adoptions than smaller, community-based agencies. Then, where is the justification for requiring all agencies to become accredited, a full-time, year round heavy administrative burden that would require the addition of staff and costly changes in the structure of even the smallest agency? There is none presented to the Congress by any source. No one's bothered to look. . . .

But requiring all adoption agencies handling foreign adoptions to be federally licensed can't help but impose

> *"Requiring all adoption agencies handling foreign adoptions to be federally licensed can't help but impose terrific costs on the families."*

terrific costs on the families, many of whom can barely afford their adoptions as it is. By losing families to the process, less orphans will find homes. Make no mistake about it: EACH DOLLAR THAT YOU ADD TO THIS PROCESS TRANSLATES DIRECTLY INTO LESS CHILDREN GETTING INTO HOMES.

Has the cost to an agency to prepare for and maintain federal accreditation been calculated? No. Has anyone projected how many of the current small, community-based adoption agencies (those that reach deep into their communities to recruit more homes for these orphans and who know the adoptive families personally and can serve them best, both before and after an adoption) would be eliminated from handling foreign adoptions due to the prohibitive administrative burdens and costs involved in seeking and maintaining federal accreditation? Not that I know of. How many fewer orphans will get placed and how many families will not be recruited as a result of their dropping out of the process? We don't know. No one's looked.

Has the cost of setting up the accreditation process . . . been estimated? No. . . . Has the cost of the federal government's new Central Authority . . . been estimated? No. Why are we consumers of these services given no accounting, no budget? If this new federal service were to be paid with general funds, the Department would have to explain to you how much it would cost and how it plans to cover that cost with fees for the services provided. Don't we consumers deserve the same consideration? Instead, all of these authorities ask for a blank check with which to create a complicated, extensive federal licensing procedure paid for by all adopting families, whether they need these protections (if they are indeed protections) or not. To us, this is vast federal overkill and bureaucratization with unpredicted costs and unsubstantiated, unlikely benefits.

Putting Numbers in Perspective

But let's look at what limited data the testifiers have provided to us. Dr. [Ronald S.] Federici, the psychologist who testified before the Senate [on October 5, 1999], claims to have seen 1,800 adopted children over the last 20 years from troubled families who have adopted, both domestic and international. A great number until you put it in perspective; in the same time period, there have been well over 170,000 foreign adoptions! Tressler Lutheran Services, the adoption agency that most people turn to when they need to place a child from a disrupted international adoption, in its [October 5, 1999] testimony to the Senate, reports a crisis in intercountry adoption. Over the last 5 years [1995–2000], they have been called upon to re-place out for adoption 82 children whose foreign adoptions were disrupted—ALL from certain Eastern European (high-risk) countries. This is out of the 58,295 foreign adoptions by U.S. citizens in those years!

The truth that you have yet to hear in your hearings is that foreign adoption is a fantastic, overwhelming success, with only a relatively very few complaints. Yet, ALL of us will have to pay for this elaborate scheme of federal intervention in the process. Why not require accreditation of only those agencies handling adoptions

> *"A vast, overwhelming number of international adoption agencies do foreign adoptions well."*

from certain high-risk countries already identified by the "experts"? Better yet, why not cut off all adoptions from those few high-risk countries altogether until such time as they can produce reliable, safe adoptions for U.S. citizens. The State Department certainly has enough information now to do this.

State Licensing Works

A vast, overwhelming number of international adoption agencies do foreign adoptions well and don't receive complaints or disrupted adoptions. State licensing of agencies in most states is a raging success and has worked for most of us. There is no evidence provided to you that it is not, other than a handful of anecdotal accounts. Has anyone studied the accreditation process in the states? It's not hard to do; their regulations and procedures, often voluminous, are open and available. Contrary to the comments of the State Department . . . the treaty

[Hague Convention] does not require a federal accreditation process and specifically allows for federal states to leave accreditation up to their individual states or provinces, as many other Hague countries do.

Why not have the Central Authority simply register state-licensed agencies handling foreign adoptions and collect complaints on those with agencies? It could then investigate those very few agencies with a pattern of complaints of abuse and take appropriate action to suspend them or remove them from doing foreign adoptions when necessary. Instead, this bill proposes a broad-stroke approach to penalize all agencies, imposing prohibitive costs on literally thousands of adoptive families who choose not to adopt from a high risk country. If the records at the Central Authority are transparent and open, families would then have someplace to research their choices before committing themselves, a problem that nothing in this now provides for despite the repeated cry for it by consumers.

It is worth noting that there is a rising tide of resentment among those of us who have chosen to avoid the high risk countries but who will be made to pay the price in increased federal regulation and cost nevertheless. We feel that those who are desperate for a white baby and who choose to ignore the well-known risks in some countries assume the risks associated with their adoptions. We now resent having to pay for an elaborate, costly federal licensing process and have less choices among agencies as a result of those who choose to adopt from a high risk country. It is especially disturbing when we consider the number of families who will then be financially foreclosed from adopting abroad and the number of orphans who will not get homes.

States should be left to regulate their own agencies as fits the widely varying needs of each state. Uniform strict standards nationally would leave many states with no agencies at all handling foreign adoptions. Have the ramifications of this been considered? How does this encourage more families to adopt foreign orphans? How does it better serve families to preclude their local, community-based agencies who can't afford the increased administrative burdens of a second accreditation process from serving them? . . .

There Is No Crisis

Contrary to the impression created by the industry's lobbyists and by the relative handful of complainants in these proceedings, THERE IS NO CRISIS IN FOREIGN ADOPTION. There's no indication that the current service delivery system for adopting families is seriously inadequate or in need of massive overhaul and federal regulation. We are thousands and thousands of very happy adoptive families who fear that our route to getting more orphaned children into homes will be immutably blocked by the added costs associated with federal licensing.

Government Regulations and Procedures for Adoption Are Too Cumbersome

by Jacob Sullum

About the author: *Jacob Sullum is a senior editor at the libertarian* Reason *magazine.*

On the night of Sunday, June 2, 1996, someone set a fire in the entryway of a two-story apartment building on 17th Avenue in Brooklyn. The fire spread to the walls and ceiling of the first floor, then up the staircase and into the apartment on the left. When the fire trucks arrived at 1:08 A.M., heavy black smoke was billowing from the windows.

"I can vividly remember a woman in the street screaming as we pulled up, 'There are people upstairs,'" says John Kroon, who at the time had been a firefighter for just 15 months. While his colleagues hooked up their hoses and pushed their way into the lobby, Kroon climbed a 24-foot portable ladder to a second-floor window. Breaking through it, he climbed into a darkened, smoke-filled bedroom.

The hose from Kroon's breathing equipment caught on a dresser drawer, yanking off his face mask and pulling the dresser on top of him. As he struggled to put the mask back on, he choked on the acrid smoke and felt the intense heat rise further, suggesting that the room would soon ignite. Moments later he found an unconscious woman on the floor, dragged her to the window, and handed her over to another firefighter on the ladder.

Sure that there must be a child somewhere in the room, because there had been a child guard on the window, Kroon felt around systematically, encountering one stuffed animal after another. Squeezing each object he touched, he fi-

Jacob Sullum, "Adoption Pains," *Reason*, November 1999. Copyright © 1999 by the Reason Foundation, 3415 S. Sepulveda Blvd., Suite 400, Los Angeles, CA 90034, www.reason.com. Reproduced with permission.

nally felt something human, huddled under the bed behind a row of teddy bears and dolls. He pulled out a little girl and handed her through the window.

The woman, 30-year-old Elayna Allen, was taken to Victory Memorial Hospital, where she was pronounced dead at 1:42 A.M. from cardiac arrest brought on by smoke inhalation. Her 3-year-old daughter, Francine, was taken to Jacobi Medical Center in the Bronx, where she was placed in a hyperbaric chamber, which delivers oxygen at high pressure. Both of her lungs had collapsed, and a tube was inserted into her chest to remove the gases

> *"After a few phone calls, I learned that we would need another home study, criminal background checks, and a lawyer."*

that had accumulated there. Then she was transferred to the pediatric intensive care unit at Brooklyn Hospital Center.

"Why it dark?" Francine asked when she woke up. A CT scan and an MRI indicated that her blindness was not caused by brain damage, and her vision returned eventually. A few weeks later she had recovered sufficiently to be transferred to the Rusk Institute of Rehabilitation Medicine at NYU Medical Center in Manhattan. That's where my wife met her.

Michele, then a rabbinical student at the Jewish Theological Seminary, was interning as a chaplain at the hospital. In early July, Francine's maternal grandmother, Evelyn Allen, requested a visit from a Jewish chaplain. Michele began seeing Francine a few times a week, and she started telling me about the charming, lively little girl with the pretty blue eyes.

Deciding to Adopt

One night in late July, Michele broached the possibility of adopting Francine. Evelyn, legally blind and in poor health, did not feel up to caring for her; the father's identity was unknown; and no other relative had come forward. Evelyn was looking for a nice Jewish couple to adopt Francine, and she had asked Michele if we might be interested. We were.

Evelyn said we should call Everett Wattley at the New York City Administration for Children's Services. Wattley agreed to send an ACS caseworker to do a home study, which is required by New York and most other states before a child can be placed with adoptive parents. In addition to an inspection of your home, the study involves probing questions about your family history, marital happiness, disciplinary philosophy, ability to deal with stress, and various other matters considered relevant in evaluating your qualifications for parenthood.

At least, that's what the adoption books say. Our experience was a bit different. On a Thursday morning in early August, ACS caseworker Stephen Francois arrived at our apartment on the Upper West Side of Manhattan, late, sweaty, and exhausted. He had taken the wrong subway and walked over from the East Side. We gave him some water, and he took his blood pressure pills. He sat at our dining table, right near the front door, and surveyed the immediate sur-roundings, pronouncing them clean. Although we were glad to have passed this test, we were disappointed that he didn't make a more thorough inspection, since we had been up half the night sweeping, mopping, and dusting. Francois told us apologetically that he would have to ask us some personal questions. I steeled myself for a harrowing inquisition. He asked us what we did, where we worked, and how much each of us made. He left after about 20 minutes, saying he would call his supervisor, Wattley, and tell him we had checked out.

Later that day, I talked to Wattley, who said that he had received Francois' report but that the adoption was a private matter and should be handled by a private agency. He recommended several. After a few phone calls, I learned that we would need another home study, criminal background checks, and a lawyer. Through the Jewish Child Care Association (JCCA), I arranged for an "emergency" home study and picked an attorney whose fees seemed the most reasonable.

Another Home Study

Five days later, the JCCA's social worker, Dina Rosenfeld, came to interview us. This time, it was more like the interview described in the adoption books. Rosenfeld, an experienced social worker who teaches at NYU, stayed for two and a half hours, asking detailed, searching questions. We were struck by the fact that ACS, which is supposed to be a neutral overseer, did such a lackadaisi-cal job of investigating us, while the private agency that we hired to do a home study scrutinized us much more carefully. It turns out that you get what you pay for, even if you pay to be interrogated. At the end of the interview, Rosenfeld left us with a stack of forms, saying that the background clearances, checking for criminal records and histories of child abuse, were the most important. That night we scrambled to fill out the forms and get three letters of reference.

We were in a hurry because Francine was ready to be discharged from the hospital, and if she couldn't go home with us, she would have to stay in a foster home. All of us, including the hospital staff, wanted to avoid that, since it would mean that a girl who had just lost her mother and gone from one hospital to another would have to live with strangers before finding a permanent home. Francine already knew Michele and me as the people who took her out for ice cream, brought her little presents, blew bubbles with her in the courtyard, floated bath toys with her in the fountain, and picked tomatoes with her in the hospital garden.

It was sad to see Francine, healthy and fully recovered, tied to a wheelchair with a sheet. The nurses kept her restrained that way because most of the other kids were seriously disabled and needed to use wheelchairs. It wasn't safe for a 3-year-old to wander around in all that traffic.

On Thursday, August 22, we took Francine to see our apartment for the first time. She fell asleep in the car on the way there and awoke barely in time to have milk and cookies before we had to take her back to the hospital. We weren't sure exactly what to tell her. On the one hand, we were buying bedroom furniture for her, and the psychologist at the hospital had said we should be preparing her to go home with us. On the other hand, nothing had been decided legally, and we worried about jumping the gun. The feeling of uncertainty was compounded on September 1, when we arrived at the hospital for a visit and were told that we were no longer allowed to take Francine off hospital grounds. Apparently, the administration was worried that we might abscond with Francine, pretending we were going to Baskin-Robbins when in fact we were heading to Buenos Aires.

The First Hearing

Two days later, we had our first hearing in Brooklyn's Kings County Family Court. We were asking the judge to make us Francine's guardians or, failing that, award us temporary custody, so we could take her out of the hospital. Unfortunately, the judge who had awarded temporary guardianship to Evelyn, Stephen Bogacz, was on vacation, and instead we got Judge Paula Hepner, who was inexplicably hostile and suspicious. She insisted that we could not possibly have obtained a home study and background clearances so quickly. Our lawyer, Ben Rosin, assured her that we had requested the home study in early August, with Francine in mind.

Hepner was accusing us of lying, but I couldn't imagine what she thought our motive was. Did she think that Michele had enrolled in rabbinical school so she could work as a chaplain in a hospital where she might find an orphan to adopt? Perhaps this strategy deserves a separate chapter in *The Complete Idiot's Guide to Adoption*, between "What You Should Know About Birthmothers" and "Playing the Waiting Game." In any event, there is nothing improper about commissioning a home study before you find a child. "Ideally," advises Colleen Alexander-Roberts in *The Legal Adoption Guide*, "the prospective parents have a home study completed before they locate a baby to adopt." Should this not be possible, however, a home study "can usually be accomplished quickly." Tell it to the judge.

Whatever it was that set Hepner off, it was quickly apparent that she had no intention of letting us take Francine home. She said the JCCA home study was not good enough, that we also needed another one from ACS (which had advised us that we needed a private home study). She appointed an attorney named Philip Skittone as Francine's "law guardian," yet another person who was supposed to look after her interests, to evaluate the case and make a recommendation at a hearing three and a half weeks later.

The next day I called Everett Wattley at ACS to find out what happened to Stephen Francois' home study. Wattley promised he would fax the report over to the courthouse in Brooklyn in time for the next hearing.

The Second Hearing

We arrived for our second family court hearing at 2 P.M. on Friday, September 27, and discovered that Judge Bogacz had never received the ACS report. The

ACS's courthouse liaison said the only record the agency had of any report connected with Francine's case had to do with Bogacz's order for an investigation of Evelyn, back when she was petitioning the court to become Francine's guardian. ACS had just received that (now obsolete) order, which Bogacz had issued three months before. The liaison said Wattley had told him there never was a report on Michele and me. I told Ben, our lawyer, that I had spoken to Wattley repeatedly about the report, and there was no way that there could have been a misunderstanding. Ben called Wattley, who suddenly remembered talking to me but still insisted that there was no report. Finally, we got Francois, the ACS caseworker, to scrawl out a couple of pages and fax them to the courthouse.

Skittone, Francine's law guardian, showed up two and a half hours late. I overheard him telling Evelyn's lawyer and the hospital's lawyer that he was not ready to make any recommendation regarding custody, because he didn't have enough information. It had been nearly a month since the last hearing, and all Skittone had done was talk to a social worker at the hospital on the telephone. He hadn't talked to Michele or me; he hadn't talked to Evelyn; he hadn't talked to anyone at the hospital who had treated or cared for Francine; he hadn't visited the hospital or met Francine. No wonder he didn't have enough information.

When we went into the courtroom, Skittone reiterated his firm position that he was not prepared to take a position. He asked for permission to hire a social worker, at the taxpayers' expense, to help him with the case. Judge Bogacz asked why he needed a social worker. Skittone said a social worker could interview "the child" and other people involved in the case. "Can't you do that?" Bogacz asked. "Yes," Skittone replied, "but I'm not a social worker." Perhaps sensing that his argument needed a little reinforcement, he said the case was "very unique," involving a child "who is different from every other child." He claimed the case was complex and contentious. "No, it isn't," I muttered, and Ben sternly hushed me. The lawyers are supposed to do the talking.

> *"[A] woman came running out of a courtroom, screaming that she had a headache from standing around all day for nothing. I sympathized."*

Ben noted that we had background clearances, plus a "glowing report" from the JCCA. Evelyn wanted us to have custody of Francine, and so did the hospital's social worker. He added that Francine had already been in the hospital longer than necessary (her original discharge date had been in mid-August). When it became clear that Bogacz was inclined to grant us temporary custody, the supposedly noncommittal Skittone started arguing against us. It could be confusing for Francine if she went home with us, he said, and then something came up (exactly what he had in mind wasn't clear) that disqualified us as parents. Observing that it could also be confusing for Francine if she had to stay in the hospital, Bogacz gave us temporary custody. Throwing Skittone a bone, he agreed to let him hire a social worker. He also noted that the ACS report seemed a bit sketchy—not surprising, since it had been dashed off a couple of hours before—and ordered a more complete one for the next hearing, which he scheduled for December 2.

Francine Comes Home

So Francine finally came home with us at the end of September 1996. We worried that she would have trouble adjusting, but she turned out to be remarkably resilient. "Cheer up, Francine," we used to say as she walked down the hall, smiling broadly and belting out a mangled song she had halfway learned from a CD.

From time to time, Francine would talk matter-of-factly about her "old Mommy," who "got dead." Once she was walking down Broadway with Michele when she saw the exhaust from a truck and said softly, "I don't like smoke." When Michele asked her why, she said there was a lot of smoke the night her mother died; she remembered seeing Elayna running toward her, then falling down. Michele asked her what happened next. "Look!" Francine replied. "The light changed red!" After a while, it occurred to us that when you're 3 years old you have no idea how life is supposed to be. So far as Francine knew, every little girl lives first with one mother, then with another, and in between stays in a hospital where she's tied to a wheelchair.

More Visits

About a month after we took Francine out of the hospital, we got a call from Leslie Cummins, the social worker hired by Skittone. We arranged to meet with the two of them at his office in Brooklyn. Skittone's handshake was clammy and flaccid; he talked to Francine in a squeaky voice, mispronouncing words on purpose. ("Would you like a *pwesent*?") He said he used to be an elementary school teacher; we figured his students must have hid the blackboard eraser and made faces behind his back.

While Francine drew pictures, Cummins asked us how she was doing, whether she talked about her mother, how we were getting along with Evelyn, how we handled discipline, what Francine's schedule was like. In contrast to Skittone, with his patronizing smile and gratingly cheerful demeanor, she seemed competent and genuinely nice. Skittone kept interrupting our responses to her questions with questions of his own. We left after an hour and a half, with Skittone declaring us "uniquely well qualified" as parents. He said he hoped we knew that he was just doing his job; he didn't understand why our lawyer seemed so belligerent. I shrugged and kept my mouth shut.

Two weeks later, Cummins visited our apartment for a couple of hours and asked us some more questions. We still hadn't heard from ACS, which was supposed to send another caseworker over for the home study Judge Bogacz had ordered. With a week to go before the next hearing, I called Ben to find out what was going on. He said he'd had a heated conversation with Wattley about the report, then called the judge's office and asked them to issue another order. The next day, we heard from Miguel Nunez, another ACS caseworker.

On Wednesday, November 27, Nunez came by and chatted with us for about half an hour. He was very cordial, talking about his own son, a 5-year-old, and the challenges of parenthood. He asked about Francine's medical condition, whether she talked about her mother, how she was adjusting, how our lives had changed since she came to live with us. He walked around the apartment. Nunez said he wasn't sure what the judge was looking for, since someone from ACS had already done a home study. We noted that Francois' report had been written at the last minute. Maybe the judge would prefer a report that was typed, I suggested jokingly. Nunez said handwritten ACS reports were not at all unusual. The agency's budget was tight, and they couldn't afford enough typists. Plus, the job is very depressing, what with all the abused children. "Working for the city is a joke," he said.

> *"Compared to the adoption system, the IRS is a model of efficiency."*

A Last-Minute Wrinkle

When we arrived for the next hearing, on Monday, December 2, everything seemed to be in order. Evelyn had agreed to transfer the guardianship to us. The ACS report was there. Ben gave us copies of the reports from Skittone and Cummins, which were very favorable. The rows of long wooden benches were full, so we read the reports while sitting on the linoleum floor in the waiting room, our backs against the wall. The session was scheduled to end at 1 P.M., and Skittone did not show up until 12:30. On the way to the courtroom he was buttonholed by Beverly Smith, Judge Bogacz's law secretary.

I could overhear snatches of the conversation, and after a while it became clear that they were discussing our case. They were talking about Evelyn's visitation rights. "Well, I'm not satisfied," I heard Smith say, and I got a sick feeling in my stomach. After Ben conferred with Smith, Skittone, and Evelyn's lawyer, he emerged to say, "There's a little wrinkle." Smith was insisting that a visitation agreement accompany the guardianship order, even though no one had requested one. She said Evelyn should get to visit Francine twice a week and every other Sunday. We should bring Francine out to Brooklyn half the time, and we should have Evelyn stay with us on holidays. We told Ben that we were adopting Francine, not her grandmother. We would continue twice-weekly visits, as we had agreed, and maybe we could come out to Brooklyn once in a while, but not on a regular basis. We both had full-time jobs, and it did not seem like a reasonable request.

Ben went off to negotiate with Smith. While we were waiting, an angry woman started shouting about her child. She was escorted out by a security guard but came back to make another scene. The guard asked her to leave, saying, "This is my house." Losing patience with her, he announced to the crowd, "All right, everybody, it's time for a show." Eventually, the angry woman left, nudged by an older woman who seemed to be a relative. Later another woman came running out of a courtroom, screaming that she had a headache from standing around all day for nothing. I sympathized. I wondered if that would be me after a few more hearings.

Ben came back and said the court was prepared to take Francine away and put her in a foster home if we did not sign a visitation agreement that satisfied Smith. We were shocked that she would make that sort of threat: How could taking Francine away from us possibly be good for her? Skittone walked by and smiled his goofy smile. There was an issue that needed to be resolved, he said, one he'd had in mind all along (this was news to us); our lawyer would explain it to us. We shouldn't worry.

> *"If we had known in advance how emotionally grueling the adoption process would be, I doubt that we would have started it."*

Ultimately, we agreed to twice-weekly visits, plus one Sunday or overnight visit each month. We also agreed to pay for a car service to bring Evelyn from Brooklyn. Evelyn was confused. She said she wanted to arrange visits with us privately, without a court order. She was worried that she wouldn't be able to visit as often as Smith seemed to think she should. We reassured her that she wasn't required to come that often; she just had the right to do so. Since the visitation agreement had to be drawn up and attached to the guardianship order, we had to come back for another hearing.

On Wednesday, January 15, 1997, we arrived in family court at 9:30 A.M. After last-minute wrangling over the details of the visitation agreement, with changes written into the margins and initialed by everyone, we entered the courtroom. In a hearing that took all of two minutes, Bogacz made us Francine's guardians. No one asked any questions. No one testified. We had to wait an hour or so for copies of the guardianship order, which looked like something a child might have produced on a typewriter. We realized it was a copy of Evelyn's guardianship order, with her name whited out and ours written over it in pen. This was what we'd been waiting for. We felt exhausted rather than elated.

More Steps

That December, we received papers from Ben that needed to be filled out before the adoption could be finalized, including affidavits attesting that we were in good health; Francine's medical history form, to be completed by her doctor; medical history forms for Michele and me, to be completed by our doctors; a financial disclosure affidavit (saying what, if anything, we'd paid or been paid to adopt Francine); a supplemental affidavit (regarding any changes in circumstances since the original filing); a marriage affidavit (attesting that we were, in fact, married); and a criminal background clearance form, including our addresses since 1973, when I was 8 and Michele was 5. We had already supplied much of this information, but we had to do it again because so much time had passed since we filed for adoption. We also had to submit our original marriage certificate, three more letters of reference, and our most recent tax return.

In January 1998, we went to Ben's office to be fingerprinted, which is not as easy as it looks (you have to roll your fingers just so). Three months later, we were visited by a probation officer named Renee. (I don't quite understand why, but the probation department had taken over from ACS.) Renee looked around the place and talked to Francine, who showed off some of her toys. We gave Renee a bunch of documents. She asked us about our income, our education, our occupations, our parents' education and occupations, our family histories, our childhoods, how we felt about being married, our approach to discipline. She said our file had been tagged "top priority" and we should expect to hear from the court within a month.

Not quite. In July another probation officer talked to Evelyn. In October one of Ben's paralegals called to tell us we were in the "home stretch," but the court needed a certified copy of Francine's birth certificate, an affidavit stating that her father's identity was unknown, and a report from yet another medical checkup on Francine. In November, the paralegal told us we had a court date for the final step in the adoption process: December 1, 1998.

Adoption at Last

Now that we were Francine's guardians, the venue had been switched to the New York County Family Court in Manhattan, where we lived. We were in and out of the judge's study in about five minutes. We swore to tell the truth, looked at some papers we'd already signed, confirmed that we had indeed signed them, and that was it. After more than two and a half years of jumping through hoops, it was pretty anticlimactic. "Today you are a daughter," I told Francine. The judge laughed.

After a child is adopted, a new birth certificate is issued—an odd custom that dates back to the days when you were supposed to keep adoption a secret. The birth certificate has the child's new name and lists the adoptive parents as the natural parents. Until history has been rewritten in this fashion (in Francine's case, it took more than six months), you cannot get a new Social Security card for your child, which means that the federal government does not recognize her new name. I discovered this the last time I did our taxes and foolishly tried to claim Francine as a dependent under what I'd been told was now her legal name. Once I realized the problem, I was able to clear it up with one phone call to the Internal Revenue Service. Compared to the adoption system, the IRS is a model of efficiency.

Thanks to a president and Congress bent on subsidizing all good things, I was also able to claim a tax credit for our adoption expenses. In our case, the credit did not work as social engineering, since we decided to adopt before it was approved. But we were happy to claim it, especially since our legal expenses had been much higher than we expected—and would have been higher still, had Ben not given us a steep discount because his initial cost estimate was wildly off.

A Confusing Process

Which raises the question of whether anyone really understands how this system works. Ben has completed more than 500 adoptions, and when we hired him he seemed to think our case was straightforward: There were no parental rights to sever, we had the consent of the child's guardian, and no one was contesting the adoption. I was an editor with a respectable magazine, and my wife was studying to be a rabbi. We had laudatory references and one favorable report after another. Yet it took more than two years from the day Francine came to live with us until she was officially our daughter. *The Legal Adoption Guide* says the average time in New York state is six months, and if anything our case was simpler than the typical adoption. Ben had thought Francine's adoption would be completed within a year. I still have no idea why it took so long.

I hesitate to draw lessons from our experience, since so many people who know a lot more about adoption than we do have written books about it. But the process described in these books is quite different from the one we encountered. Partly this is because the books are aimed mainly at people looking for newborn infants, rather than couples trying to adopt 3-year-old orphans. But it's also because the picture presented in the books is sanitized, perhaps so as not to discourage prospective parents. Again and again, the books say the adoption process is guided by "the child's best interests." But as we discovered, this is only one of several competing priorities motivating the people who run the system.

Two other goals—more or less universally shared—are making a living and staying out of trouble, which mean different things to different people. Not surprisingly, we found that social workers in private practice were more competent and thorough than government caseworkers, presumably because they have to compete for clients and more is expected of them. In our case, ACS's less-than-diligent approach caused nothing more serious than anxiety and frustration. But now and then, a child dies of neglect or abuse under the agency's watch, sometimes despite clear and repeated warning signs. A few cases of this sort were in the news while we were trying to adopt Francine, and we wondered how the same system that was giving us such a hard time could be so easy on parents who were obviously abusive.

A Bias Against Action

Part of the explanation, I think, is the system's bias against action. No one wants to make a decision that can later be faulted. In our case, that incentive resulted in delays that were not justified by the circumstances. But when a child is in danger, the bias against action can mean that families are kept together longer than they should be. The first sort of failure never makes the news; the second kind sometimes does, but then the blame is apt to fall on the system in general rather than the poor, harried caseworker.

Judges, who make the ultimate decisions about where children should live, are more likely to be blamed when something bad happens. They must live in dread of seeing their names in *The New York Times* because a child died after they awarded custody to the wrong people. Our first family court judge was given the choice of taking that chance or shifting the responsibility to another judge. However slight the risk that Michele and I would turn out to be the next Hedda Nussbaum and Joel Steinberg,[1] it was even less likely that newspapers would run stories about Judge Hepner's decision to leave Francine in the hospital for another month.

Skittone, the lawyer appointed as Francine's law guardian, did not have it in for us, as his favorable report demonstrated. He was just determined to do the job for which he was being paid, even if it wasn't really necessary. It would not be good for business if word got around that adoptions could be completed without the services that he and other courtroom hangers-on provide. As for the law secretary who insisted that we could not become Francine's guardians until we signed a visitation agreement that no one else thought was necessary, she seemed to be genuinely concerned that Evelyn (who was, after all, represented by a lawyer) did not correctly perceive her own interests, and so she decided to intervene. Taking Francine away from us may have been an idle threat, since she never seriously doubted that she would get her way.

We became Francine's parents long before the law recognized us as such. But because we were so powerless, we continued to worry that something would go wrong until the day the adoption was finalized. At that point, the system's bias against action started working in our favor.

Now that Francine has been living with us for three years, there's no question that being her parents was worth all the trouble. But if we had known in advance how emotionally grueling the adoption process would be, I doubt that we would have started it. We never would have found out what it was like to have Francine as a daughter.

Francine, now 6, wanders into my office from the living room, where she was watching cartoons, and tries to slip a butterfly ring that she made in summer camp onto my pinkie. It doesn't quite fit. I ask her if she remembers when Michele and I used to visit her in the hospital. "I remember when you guys took me out of the wheelchair, and they said, 'No, no, no,'" she says. "I wanted to go home, so I wouldn't have to be in a wheelchair."

I tell her that I'm writing the story of how we adopted her. I describe in gen-

---

1. Nussbaum and Steinberg were adoptive parents whose six-year-old adopted daughter was found dead of brain injuries in 1987. Steinberg was convicted in 1989 of manslaughter.

eral terms what we had to do. (Although she participated in several of the steps, I'm not sure that she understood they were all part of the same process.) "Why can't you just find a child walking around who lost its parents?" she asks. "Why can't you just take one home?"

My initial reaction is that Francine's reform proposal goes too far: There needs to be some assurance that adoptive parents are prepared to care for a child. But then again, if biological parents do not need to be certified by the government, why should there be a different standard for adoptive parents? Perhaps it is enough to have the consent of the birth mother or, in the case of an orphan, the nearest relative. The government's role would then be limited to verifying the consent and, as with any child, intervening in the event of abuse or neglect. A radical idea, perhaps. But compared to the arbitrary, unpredictable, byzantine system that we dealt with, it doesn't seem so crazy.

Infant Adoption Should Be Deregulated

by Donald J. Boudreaux

About the author: *Donald J. Boudreaux is a professor of law and economics at Clemson University in South Carolina.*

In his famous satire, Jonathan Swift "modestly" proposed slaughtering babies and feeding them to hungry Irish folk. Thanks to Swift's masterful lampoon, any proposal for modestly changing public policy affecting children risks being branded a satire. So I proclaim up front my sincerity in proposing that pregnant women, and women who have just given birth, be allowed to contract freely with adoptive parents at mutually agreeable prices for the sale of parental rights in their infants.

The proposal is not original. Richard Posner [a federal judge and author] has long championed the cause of a liberalized adoption market. But most replies to his proposal have been critical, too often failing to rise above invective. Such negative reaction belies both the modesty and the worthiness of Posner's proposal. The proposal is modest because it merely extends to birth mothers a liberty now enjoyed by many adoption agencies: the liberty to sell parental rights to adoptive parents at mutually agreeable prices. The proposal is worthwhile because it promises gains to all relevant parties to adoptions—birth mothers, couples wishing to adopt infants, and children.

Opposition to birth mothers' voluntary sales of parental rights is founded on faulty reasoning. I use basic economics to highlight the benefits of liberalized adoption and to address some of the most common objections raised by those who insist that children or society would be harmed by the free exchange of parental rights in infants.

Preliminary Clarifications

Some preliminaries are in order. First, I refer throughout to the "sale of parental rights" rather than to "baby selling." When a birth mother gives a child

Donald J. Boudreaux, "A Modest Proposal to Deregulate Infant Adoption," *Cato Journal*, vol. 15, Spring 1995. Copyright © 1995 by the Cato Institute. All rights reserved. Reproduced by permission.

up for adoption, she legally transfers her parental rights to the adoptive parents; the adoptive parents gain all those rights, but *only* those rights, that the birth mother possessed before the adoption. Such rights are those that all non-derelict parents have in their children. The rights do not include license to abuse the child or to use him or her as a slave. Parents who purchase their parental rights from birth mothers would have precisely the same rights, and only those rights, that they would have if their children were their biological offspring. Branding the sale of parental rights "baby selling" provokes people reflexively but wrongly to assume that some horror akin to slavery is being advocated.

Second, I deal here only with the sale of parental rights in infants (say, children nine months old or younger). The proposal may or may not be suitable for older children; I leave investigation of that issue for another time.

Third, I assume that only adult birth mothers have initial parental rights in children. The case I have in mind is the all-too-common one in which an unmarried woman has, or is having, an unwanted child and the father either is unknown or has ignored his parental responsibilities. Cases in which the birth mother is married or the father knows and cares about his child, or in which the birth mother herself is still a child, are more complex. Perhaps the law should give those fathers, or the parents of minor birth mothers, some say in adoption decisions. I do not, however, explore in this paper the desirable specifics of those fatherhood rights or of the rights of parents of minor birth mothers.

Fourth, I assume that the law prohibits resales of parental rights by adoptive parents. Once a final decree of adoption is issued for a particular child, that child's adoptive parents may not resell their parental rights in this child.

The Baby Shortage

All agree that adoptable healthy white infants are in short supply today. The National Committee for Adoption estimates that in the United States [in 1989] 20 couples are willing to adopt for every available infant. Various reasons are offered for the shortage. Low-cost methods of birth control and legalized abortion arguably reduce the absolute number of children born to women who do not wish to raise them. . . . In addition, the fact that women increasingly pursue professional careers before starting a family raises the demand for adoptable infants. A woman's ability to conceive and successfully carry a child to term decreases as she ages. Consequently, as more women delay having children, the number of couples suffering infertility problems rises, causing more to seek adoption.

Although medical, legal, and demographic changes affect both the supply of, and demand for, parental rights, such changes alone are insufficient to cause a baby shortage. Supplies and demands for all sorts of goods change frequently without creating lasting shortages. For a shortage to persist, prices paid to suppliers must somehow be held below market-clearing levels. And so it is with the current baby shortage. No market-clearing price for parental rights emerges because birth mothers cannot contract freely with adoptive parents.

Adoption in the United States is governed principally by state laws. Currently, birth mothers in all states and the District of Columbia are barred from selling their parental rights. Birth mothers can give the rights away, but they cannot receive monetary payments in return. Monetary compensation is allowed only for out-of-pocket medical expenses for the prenatal care and birth of children. (In some cases, these expenses include psychological counseling for birth mothers.) But the amounts are limited to ensure that birth mothers do not profit by offering their children for adoption.

> *"Opposition to birth mothers' voluntary sale of parental rights is based on faulty reasoning."*

State regulations also obstruct efforts by birth mothers and prospective adoptive parents to learn about, and to contact, each other. The most restrictive states simply ban "independent" adoptions: adoptions in which adoption agencies are not intermediaries. Other restrictions include criminal prohibitions against advertising by prospective adoptive parents, prohibitions on out-of-state couples applying for adoption within a state, and requirements that independent (though not agency) adoptions be "open"—that is, that adoptive parents give their full names and addresses to birth mothers.

Proponents of such restrictions argue that the baby shortage can be reduced by increased adoption awareness and, perhaps, by government subsidies for adoption. But even if such policies fail to alleviate the shortage, these proponents insist that birth mothers never be allowed to sell parental rights for a profit.

Let Birth Mothers Keep the Profits from the Transfer of Parental Rights

Birth mothers should be allowed to contract freely with adoptive parents for the sale of parental rights in infants at whatever prices they find mutually agreeable. Allowing such contracting does not necessitate abandonment of other regulations on adoption. Courts will still have to sign off on each adoption, allowing judges to ensure the suitability of adoptive parents. Indeed, all prospective adoptive parents could be required (as they are now) to pass home studies before being eligible to contract with birth mothers. Finally, all contracts between birth mothers and adoptive parents will be subject to the same checks on fraud, duress, and other abuses that traditionally limit contractual commitments.

The most obvious consequence of greater freedom of contract for birth mothers is that the baby shortage will end. The supply of adoptable infants will increase as birth mothers seek to sell their parental rights for a profit. The price birth mothers receive for parental rights will rise until the supply of those rights expands sufficiently to meet demand. Importantly, greater numbers of adoptable infants means that fewer couples must remain childless. That benefit is immense for those suffering the agony of unwanted childlessness.

A second effect will be greater wealth for birth mothers.

Third, there will be fewer abortions. Allowing women to sell parental rights in their infants at market prices transforms previously unwanted fetuses into valuable capital assets. If parental rights in infants can be sold profitably by birth mothers, women will be far more reluctant to abort their fetuses. Just as a car owner sells rather than destroys an automobile when he decides that he no longer wants the car, a pregnant woman with transferable parental rights is much more likely to carry her pregnancy to term and then offer the baby for adoption rather than abort the fetus. Allowing women with unwanted pregnancies to sell their parental rights for a profit will increase the cost of abortion to those women and, hence, reduce its incidence.

Fourth, the average health of infants will improve. Because parental rights in healthy infants will command higher prices than will parental rights in unhealthy ones, pregnant women will have stronger incentives to seek prenatal care of their fetuses and to avoid harmful habits such as alcohol and drug abuse.

Fifth, the incidence of child abuse will decline. Because the current [1995] welfare system rewards women for keeping their children, many children who are only marginally wanted by their birth mothers are kept by the women. Such children are surely more subject to neglect and abuse than they would be if they were adopted by loving parents. Ability to receive payment for parental rights will cause many such children to be put up for adoption.

Sixth, and relatedly, fewer children will be placed in foster care, itself a dysfunctional institution. Birth mothers who now choose not to keep their children are more likely to place those children in foster care rather than make them available for adoption.

> *"The most obvious consequence of greater freedom of contract for birth mothers is that the baby shortage will end."*

According to Conna Craig, president of the Institute for Children, 4 percent of the 35,000 children now [1995] in foster care who are eligible for adoption are infants. Birth-mother ability to keep the profits from the transfer of parental rights raises the likelihood that birth mothers will both learn about, and take advantage of, the adoption option.

Seventh, the price of infertility treatments might fall. Infertility treatments and adoption are substitute methods of securing parental rights. Thus, an increase in the supply of adoptable infants will reduce the demand for infertility treatments. The price of infertility treatments will likely fall as a consequence.

Current adoption law thus creates avoidable heartache and expense for all parties interested in infant adoptions. Liberalizing birth-mother contracting will improve adoptive-parents' chances of adopting the child (or children) of their dreams, while allowing birth mothers to acquire greater wealth. The policy change might also allow couples suffering infertility problems to pay lower costs for infertility treatments. Most important, many children who would otherwise not be born, or who would be born with birth defects, will be blessed with healthy lives. No party to the adoption process loses—save for abortion clinics as well as adoption agencies and state bureaucracies that will lose some of their business to private arrangements.

If all parties to the voluntary agreements benefit, those who morally object to such agreements are obliged to explain why their objections should trump a proposal yielding widespread benefits with little or no evident costs. . . .

Answering Objections

Justifications are offered, but none is persuasive. Here are the most commonly encountered reasons for denying freedom of contract to birth mothers.

"Economic Motives Are Inappropriate for Familial Matters Such as Adoption"

Among the most oft-repeated objection to greater contractual freedom for birth mothers is the claim that human life is not an appropriate object of economic calculation; economic motives should not intrude into such personal decisions as whether or not to adopt a child or to give a child up for adoption. According to [law professor] Martha Field, "There are some types of things that our society does not want measured in terms of money. Society may want to do what it can to help people keep these in a personal sphere that is distinct from the commercial."

This claim is laden with both emotion and vagueness. Depending on what is meant by terms such as "commercial" and expressions such as "economic motives" or "measurement in terms of money," such claims are either trivially true or factually incorrect. On one hand, if what the speaker or listener has in mind is that slavery should not be reinstated (slaves, after all, were humans whose lives were measured "in terms of money"), then no sane person disagrees. As explained above, allowing birth mothers to sell their parental rights voluntarily to adoptive parents in no way connotes a return to slavery. On the other hand, if the speaker or listener really believes that economic considerations should play no role in familial matters, then he or she has not thought through the full implications of this belief. In fact, family matters, including child-rearing and adoption, are routinely objects of economic calculation. Economic considerations are inescapable in the teeth of scarcity (although many people remain incognizant of the pervasiveness of such influences).

For example, many people—and responsible persons especially—make explicit economic decisions about whether or not to have children and, if so, when. Children are costly in monetary as well as nonmonetary ways. Raising them requires sacrifice. The things sacrificed—be they European vacations, nicer automobiles, additional education, more quiet time, or whatever—are what parents pay for children. These costs are not always out-of-pocket cash expenses, but form should not blind us to substance: they are genuine economic costs, and they are regularly considered when people make family decisions. Young newlyweds with no savings might delay starting a family to establish firmer financial grounds for raising children. Other couples might choose (say, for career reasons) never to have children. The costs and benefits of having children are inevitably weighed against each other, and decisions made accordingly. Surely such decisions are not immoral, unethical, or impersonal because they are made with economic concerns in mind. Indeed, we properly denounce people who have children without adequately considering the economic consequences of doing so.

In addition to the economic considerations mentioned above, medical treatments for fertility problems are undertaken in light of financial constraints. Those treatments are expensive, costing patients hundreds—and often several thousands—of dollars monthly. Decisions on whether or not to pursue such treatments and, if so, choosing which particular treatments to pursue and for how long, are inevitably made in the face of resource constraints. Similarly, birth mothers who put their children up for adoption under current law usually do so for economic reasons: they cannot afford to raise their children.

Those who argue that economic considerations ought not influence decisions regarding children and child bearing must, for consistency's sake, argue that unwanted babies should not be given away, and that couples and single women should not hesitate because of "mere" financial reasons to have children. Consistency also demands that opponents of a deregulated market in parental rights support bans on money payments for infertility treatments. Yet there is no widespread opposition to unregulated prices for fertility treatments, or to people making decisions to bear or to keep children in light of explicit economic concerns. These facts dispel claims that society generally disapproves of rational economic calculations in the realm of child bearing and child rearing.

"Babies Should Not Be Traded Commercially"

Some opposition to a freer market in parental rights stems not so much from the belief that it is unethical to ground family decisions on cost-benefit analysis as from the conviction that babies ought not be objects of commercial exchange.

> *"Adoption agencies rather than birth mothers reap the financial fruit of competition among prospective adoptive parents for the parental rights that are in short supply."*

This argument also proves too much; it suggests that doctors, nurses, and clinics specializing in medical treatment for people suffering fertility problems should not be allowed to sell their services for a profit. On the supply side, medical infertility specialists employ their knowledge to improve infertile couples' chances of conceiving and successfully carrying children to term. These physicians and technicians profit by selling their child-creation services. On the demand side, infertility patients spend money to purchase parental rights in infants. A couple spending $5,000 monthly for artificial insemination, in vitro fertilization, or other treatments for infertility, uses money to pursue a child no less so than does a couple who spends money to purchase parental rights in adoptive infants.

It may be countered that physicians working to improve couples' chances of having babies do not really sell parental rights in children: physicians sell skilled services that improve couples' chances of having their own biological children. Might we not, though, recast what birth mothers sell as their child-creation services? Even though the law gives birth mothers initial ownership of parental rights in whatever children they birth, why deny women the liberty to profit from their abilities to produce babies that other couples earnestly want and are willing to pay for? And why deny infertile couples the right to contract voluntarily with birth mothers? Adoption may well be less costly than infertility treatments for many couples. Not only will prices charged by birth mothers likely be lower than the costs of adopting through adoption agencies (see below), but adoption avoids the risks of medical complications that attend the use of drugs and intrusive surgery often entailed by infertility treatments. These risks include harm to infertility patients as well as to the children born as a result of these treatments.

Current Laws Do Not Prohibit Commerce

More significant, however, is the law's failure to truly prohibit commerce in parental rights. The law prevents only unlicensed, private individuals—most notably, birth mothers—from profiting from such commerce. Adoption agencies today (some of whom are for-profit firms) legally sell parental rights in infants at profitable prices. Not all states regulate the prices that adoption agencies charge for their services. Fees charged by for-profit agencies run as high as $30,000 per adoption, while fees charged by nonprofit agencies reach $25,000. And often, agency fees depend on adoptive parents' income: lower-income adoptive parents pay less than higher-income parents. In economic terms, adoption agencies price discriminate, a practice that increases their revenues.

Of course, agencies do not list "infant" or "parental rights" on itemized bills. But, again, form should not camouflage substance: adoption agencies sell parental rights at prices kept artificially high by laws prohibiting birth mothers from contracting directly with adoptive parents. . . .

The amounts that adoptive parents pay to adoption agencies as fees and expenses are bid up to reflect the artificial scarcity of parental rights. Adoption agencies rather than birth mothers reap the financial fruits of competition among prospective adoptive parents for the parental rights that are in short supply. Agencies' practice of labeling their charges "service fees" or "home study fees" does not alter the fact that the fees are determined by the forces of demand and supply, and that they reflect the artificially created scarcity of parental rights in adoptable infants. . . .

If the ban on birth-mother contracting were lifted, the full cost to adoptive parents of adopting a child would fall although payments received by birth mothers would rise.

"Only the Rich Will Benefit, while the Poor Will Be Exploited"

While studying law at the University of Virginia, I regularly proposed a free market in parental rights to fellow law students. A large majority objected by asserting that only the rich will benefit.

A valid response to this objection is "So what?" Suppose that it were in fact true that only the rich will benefit if birth mothers are allowed to sell

> *"Intentional births by profit-seeking birth mothers are a possibility, but it is difficult to see why this outcome is undesirable."*

their parental rights. This fact would not justify current restrictions on the abilities of birth mothers to contract. As long as no one is harmed by such sales, it is malice borne of envy (or, in the case of many of my fellow students, of misdirected guilt) to deny the rich opportunities to use their assets in ways that result in loving families for children. The fact that only the rich purchase Mercedes-Benz automobiles, cases of Chateau Haut Brion, and summer homes on Newport Beach is no reason to outlaw the sale of such items. (Incidentally, only the relatively wealthy can now afford infertility treatments. Should such treatments be outlawed because poor people cannot take advantage of them?)

But it is not true that only the rich will benefit. In every voluntary exchange, *both* parties are made *better* off. Moreover, the nonwealthy will be better able to adopt children when birth mothers are allowed to freely sell parental rights. First, adoption agencies under the current legal regime favor well-to-do adoptive parents: the poor tend to be discriminated against even if they are willing to spend as much as their wealthier rivals to acquire parental rights. Second, because political connections and ability to grease palms thins regulatory thickets, poor people are disadvantaged by the current system. Third, as explained above, the full price of adopting a healthy infant is today actually quite high. Not only is the wait long and agonizing, but adoption-agency fees and other out-of-pocket expenses are higher than necessary because the market is controlled. As argued earlier, allowing birth mothers to sell directly to adoptive parents will increase the quantity of adoptable infants supplied for adoption while reducing the role of adoption agencies as middlemen. Market prices paid by adoptive parents for parental rights will fall as a consequence, even as prices received by birth mothers rise. As the price of acquiring parental rights in infants falls, people of modest means are better able to adopt.

Nor will poor women be exploited by being forced into "a new oppressed and undignified occupation" [as legal scholar and author Carmel Shalev states]. No woman will be coerced into supplying parental rights. And birth mothers—most of whom, presumably, will be nonwealthy—can profit from their sales of parental rights. Given this ability to profit and the voluntary nature of the transactions, to say that greater contractual freedom for birth mothers would lead to the exploitation or "demeaning" of birth mothers is curious. In a freer market, birth mothers would continue to enjoy all the options they have now, *plus* the additional option of selling their parental rights.

Opponents of liberalized adoptions might respond that it is unseemly for the poor to be the sole supplier of adoptable infants to the nonpoor. Even granting that the suppliers of parental rights will overwhelmingly be low-income women, this is no argument to prohibit these women from contracting voluntarily with adoptive parents. Prohibiting poor women from bargaining with wealthier adoptive parents for prices that those women find profitable is a peculiar way to safeguard them from exploitation—and a selfish and harmful way to shield the sensibilities of the ethically hyperenlightened from "unseemly," if beneficial, market transactions.

Can Poor Women Make Sound Decisions?

Another argument supporting the exploitation claim is that poor women are generally unable to make sound decisions regarding the disposition of their parental rights. Their immediate need for money causes them to pursue short-term pecuniary gain at the expense of long-term woe. In the words of one commentator [Avi Katz], "financial benefits urged upon an often indigent natural mother by a baby-broker become a source of coercion to her to force her to give up her baby". Quite simply, a poor birth mother who sells her parental rights today might regret that decision a month or a year or 10 years from now.

Of course, a woman might err in her assessment of the costs and benefits of selling her parental rights, and may later regret her decision. But so, too, might a woman who under current law chooses to give her parental rights away free of charge, as might a woman who chooses abortion or who chooses never to become pregnant. Indeed, any party to any contract may later regret his or her contractual commitment. Such is the nature of uncoerced choice.

Women who, under existing law, give their children up for adoption typically do so because of their immediate financial predicaments; their need for current liquidity makes it prudent for them not to undertake—or to delay undertaking—the role of mother. It is true that the additional financial incentives under a freer adoption market to give children up for adoption will cause some women who would otherwise choose to keep their children, or to abort, to decide instead to sell their parental rights. But allowing birth mothers to bargain for profitable prices with adoptive parents does not create financial incentives for adoption where none existed before. Such incentives exist under current law.

A more fundamental question, however, is why society puts so little trust in birth mothers to make rational decisions regarding adoption of their children under a regime of voluntary contract. That paternalistic lack of trust is bizarre given that the same women are trusted to make abortion decisions, adoption decisions involving no cash payments, and decisions to keep and to rear children. If government does not assume the right to second-guess those decisions, the burden of proof is on those who advocate a policy of second-guessing women's decisions to sell their parental rights.

A Baby Industry?

"Free-Market Adoption Will Spawn a Baby Industry"

Another argument against greater freedom of birth mothers to contract with adoptive parents is that the lure of profits will induce women to become pregnant for the sole purpose of selling their parental rights to adoptive couples. While many women will still become pregnant accidentally, others will do so intentionally in search of profits. Such actions create life for all the wrong motives.

Intentional births by profit-seeking birth mothers are a possibility, but it is difficult to see why this outcome is undesirable. The market price of parental rights will reflect adoptive parents' demand for such rights. Willingness to supply parental rights (and hence willingness to become pregnant solely to sell parental rights) will vary with the market price. If demand for parental rights falls, so too will the price of these rights, leading fewer women to offer their parental rights for sale. Likewise, an increased supply of babies lowers the price of parental rights, thereby increasing the willingness of people to adopt. At market-clearing prices for parental rights, birth mothers' supply of these rights will equal adoptive parents' demand for these rights. Any excess supplies of, or demands for, parental rights will be corrected by decreases or increases in market prices. Only women who find market prices attractive will become pregnant for the purpose of profiting from the sale of their parental rights. There is no reason to suppose that the pricing mechanism will fail to keep markets cleared.

To be sure, the market will not work flawlessly, instantaneously matching demand with supply. What happens when a woman becomes pregnant believing that she can sell her baby profitably only to discover, nine months later, that the market price for parental rights has fallen? If the woman has no interest in raising the child herself, she will sell her parental rights at the lower price. Her profits will be lower than she expected when she became pregnant, but that is a risk she assumed when she chose to become pregnant. Women contemplating becoming pregnant to profit from selling their parental rights will account for the risk that the market price nine months hence might fall.

In contrast, women who decide that the current market price is too low will not sell their rights. These women keep their children. Of course, women who decide only after becoming pregnant to keep their children retain all parental rights and responsibilities, just as do today's mothers who choose to keep unplanned children. There is no reason to believe that one kind of unplanned child will be treated less well than the other.

"Liberalized Birth-Mother Contracting Will Engender Exploitation by Middlemen"

Lifting the ban on birth-mother contracting rouses fears of ruthless exploitation of birth mothers and of adoptive parents by middlemen—specialists in bringing birth mothers and adoptive parents together.

Such fears are unfounded. Although horror stories are told of how corrupt middlemen prey on vulnerable birth mothers and adoptive parents, the problems highlighted by the stories are an artifact of the law's refusal to legalize birth-mother contracting. Just as the gangsterish conduct of bootleggers during the 1920s was not indicative of the conduct of Anheuser-Busch, Seagram's, and other legitimate participants in today's legal market for alcohol, current unscrupulous actions of "baby brokers" in no way portend that legitimate participants in a legalized market for parental rights will behave unethically.

There are at least two reasons participants in a liberalized market for parental rights will perform honorably and in the best interest of all parties involved.

> *"A freer market in parental rights does promise great gains to adoptive parents, birth mothers, and children."*

First, legalized birth-mother contracting would give all market participants easy recourse to the courts for redress of untoward treatment. Liars, swindlers, and scoundrels under the current legal regime have little fear of being hauled into civil court by their victims. Second, legalized birth-mother contracting will subject to open competition all market participants. Middlemen who fleece and defraud their clients will, in addition to the threat of legal action, lose business to honest middlemen. Competition can be open only if it is legal, and—as in most markets—open competition is the best guarantee that all parties to the adoption process will behave, and be treated, properly.

In contrast, the current legal regime actually promotes exploitation by middlemen of birth mothers and adoptive parents. Adoption agencies are middlemen who profit from artificially high fees on the sale of parental rights—fees that birth mothers today are banned legally from earning. Giving birth mothers and adoptive parents the legal right to contract with each other for the sale of parental rights will end exploitation not only by illegal "baby brokers" but by adoption agencies as well.

Of course, it is not clear that liberalized birth-mother contracting will create a demand for middlemen. Legally protecting birth-mothers' options of dealing directly with adoptive parents ensures that middlemen will survive only if they perform useful services. As long as the market for the services of middlemen is competitive, their existence and their actions are to be applauded rather than feared.

Liberalize the Rules Against Birth-Mother Contracting

Giving birth mothers the legal right to contract voluntarily with adoptive parents for the sale of parental rights in infants will not solve all the problems that today afflict child care and families. The surplus of older children, disabled children, and nonwhite children will not be alleviated by a freer market in adoptions. Nor will the dysfunctional U.S. foster care system be repaired. Many infertile couples will still not wish to adopt, and many pregnant women will still choose to abort. Nevertheless, a freer market in parental rights does promise great gains to adoptive parents, birth mothers, and children. These gains ought not be forsaken merely because the market cannot cure every evil or because we are uncomfortable with use of the language of economics and of commerce to explain how a liberalized market in parental rights will function.

Implementing such a market would not entail a great legal change. All that is required is that birth mothers and adoptive parents be allowed to contract with each other for the sale of parental rights in infants at mutually agreeable prices. Laws prohibiting birth mothers from dealing directly with adoptive parents and from selling their parental rights at mutually agreeable prices would be repealed, as would restrictions on birth-mother and adoptive-parent advertising. Current government-mandated screening of adoptive parents can be retained. Courts—which still will be required to issue a final decree of adoption in each case—can ensure that no one adopts without having first passed a home study of the kind currently given to adoptive parents. Moreover, courts will keep whatever abilities they now possess to invalidate adoptions when adoptive parents turn out to be derelict or abusive. Cooling-off periods are also consistent with a freer market in parental rights: a birth mother can be given the right to reclaim her parental rights within, say, one week after initially turning her child over to the adoptive parents.

Indeed, nearly all regulations that today govern infant adoptions in the United States can be retained if birth mothers are granted freedom of contract. Reasonable people will disagree (as they do now) about which regulations are worthwhile and which are harmful. All that I propose is that birth mothers be allowed to contract freely with adoptive parents, with no restrictions on the prices paid for parental rights in infants, but subject to whatever other controls legislatures or judges deem appropriate. This modest change will yield enormous net benefits.

Chapter 3

Should Adoptees Be Given Open Access to Adoption and Birth Records?

The Open Records Controversy: An Overview

by John Cloud

About the author: *John Cloud is a correspondent for* Time *magazine.*

Cindy is shaking with fear. She tugs at her gold necklace, shifts in her seat, slams down cup after cup of black coffee. She gets this way when she has to tell a stranger why she can't sleep at night, why she and her husband have been fighting, why she can't choke down even half her meal when she goes to a nice restaurant. Two decades ago, when Cindy (a pseudonym) was in college, a man beat and raped her. Devastated and uncertain, she had the baby but surrendered the girl for adoption.

Last summer [of 1998], after soul-searching, Cindy decided to find out what had become of her child. She gave the state where the girl was born permission to contact her if the daughter asked her whereabouts. The daughter already had, and the two began exchanging letters through the adoption agency. But Cindy held back her identity and location.

A wise move, she now says. After Cindy told her daughter about the rape, the young woman wrote, in her swirly cursive, an oddly jovial response, "Hi, how's everything going?" She said she was glad to learn "about my father's situation"—the only reference to the rape—and wanted to know how to find him. Cindy was horrified. Her daughter obviously hadn't grasped her pain, the nightmares—her whole life. The daughter, with the help of her adoptive mother, persisted in trying to find her father, a man Cindy had helped send to prison. Fearing he might find her and harm her again, Cindy terminated contact.

Cindy now lives in Oregon, where voters last fall [1998] approved a two-sentence initiative called Measure 58. If it goes into effect, it will radically change traditional adoption law by allowing adoptees the unfettered right to see their birth certificate when they turn 21. Today those papers are sealed. But since the biological mother's name appears on a birth certificate, the law would mean adoptees like Cindy's daughter could easily find Mom's real name—and

John Cloud, "Tracking Down Mom," *Time*, February 22, 1999. Copyright © 1999 by Time, Inc. Reproduced by permission.

perhaps track her down. A group of birth mothers has sued Oregon, arguing that state statutes promise them confidentiality and that breaking these promises would be unconstitutional. The measure is on hold while the suit is pending. [The law went into effect on May 30, 2000.]

More than an hour south of Portland's suburbs, where Cindy has kids in school, lives another woman, Mary Inselman. Mary is angry about adoption law, but for another reason entirely. She turned 77 in December, and has never seen her birth certificate. While everyone else can see such a document without fuss, adoptees must petition a court for their records, and petitions cost money (Inselman is on a fixed income) and, more important, dignity.

> *"Several states have tried to devise workable new laws to help answer . . . [adoptees'] questions without treading on the rights of mothers."*

Inselman, who says she didn't learn she was adopted until a relative told her just six years ago, feels she should be able to discover her true backgound, but she has a more urgent reason to seek her records. She needs to find out whether any of her biological relatives has a kidney that would be suitable for her grand-daughter, who is in need of a donor. Inselman has sent letters to a local judge explaining all this, but the judge has thus far refused to release the information, offering a polite recitation of the law. Other judges across the U.S. routinely overlook the law in such cases. Adoptees cite this capriciousness as a reason for opening all records.

Two women, Cindy and Mary; two lives in turmoil because of adoption laws written in another era. Before the late '60s, states thought they were doing birth mothers a favor by confining their identities to dusty registrars' books. At the time, only "bad" girls got pregnant out of wedlock, and they were cloistered with fake names until they gave birth. Today, of course, that attitude seems quaintly outmoded. What's more, we have become sensitized to the rights of adoptees, who as they grow up want to know what everyone else already knows: who they are. "We are besieged by ghosts," says Helen Hill, a sculptor, sheep farmer and newborn political impresario, who wrote Oregon's Measure 58 in her basement and has spent part of her inheritance getting it approved. "We are haunted by questions."

Several states have tried to devise workable new laws to help answer those questions without treading on the rights of mothers. It's a tricky legislative game. In 1996, for instance, Tennessee legislators gave adoptees—except those who were the product of rape or incest—access to their birth certificate while also allowing biological mothers to tell the state they never want contact with their kids. As in Oregon, birth mothers have sued to overturn that law, saying they were promised nothing short of lifelong confidentiality (and wondering why, if adoptees can be prevented from contacting their mothers, they would have any use for the name alone). Just last month [January 1999] Delaware lawmakers said the state would give adoptees their birth certificate unless the birth mother explicitly asked to remain anonymous. Yet the moms have only 60 days to file such a request, and the state isn't planning to hunt them down to ensure that they know they can.

Predictably, the politics of adoption-law change gets very nasty very quickly. Conservative advocates of confidentiality warn that pregnant women faced with the prospect of having their records eventually opened will be more likely to choose abortion over adoption. While most adoption groups support some kind of compromise plan, the National Council for Adoption, a buttoned-up Washington coalition of agencies that arrange confidential adoptions, would require that extraordinary measures be taken by the state to find, counsel and get consent from birth parents before adoptees could even learn their names—to say nothing of meeting them. At the other extreme is the Internet-based Bastard Nation, which wants no exception whatsoever to open records and arouses activists' ire on its irreverent *bastards.org* website ("Rush for Our Records!" the site proclaims).

With such delicate positions to navigate, it's not surprising that the initiative process, which encourages simplistic laws like Oregon's Measure 58, has not provided a solution. It will take more careful legislation to let adoptees feel whole, even as the few Cindys of the nation feel safe.

Arguments Against Opening Adoption Records Are Spurious

by Kate Burke

About the author: *Kate Burke is a former president of the American Adoption Congress, a network of organizations and individuals committed to adoption reform.*

The arguments against open records haven't changed much in the past 20 years, which is both good and bad news. The good news is that if after 20 years the dedicated opposition hasn't found new reasons to keep records closed, then we can surmise that we know what we will face when an open records bill is being considered in a state legislature. The bad news is that after 20 years we haven't managed to sufficiently deal with the arguments against open records. Triad members [birth parents, adoptive parents and adoptees] have failed to take this highly emotional issue and place it firmly in the public policy arena.

Open records is a civil rights issue put forth by a "minority class" of citizen: the adoptee. One of the problems with this description is that until recently, the adoptee in question was mainly white, middle class and educated—not what society typically envisions as a "minority." As a result, it was easy for opponents of open records to brand searching adoptees as spoiled, middle class or merely curious individuals who were looking for something to occupy their time.

The arguments that the search and reunification movement have primarily used (until recently) were easily discounted by legislators and opponents alike. The advocates of open adoption records explained that we needed to search to find our identity. The opposition replied "grow up." We explained that the lack of information about birth families was emotionally disturbing to many adoptees. The opposition stated that those who held this point of view were pathological and angry adoptees, a minority. The movement talked about the positive effects of reunion, while the opposition brought forth an angry birth

Kate Burke, "The Case for Open Adoption Records," *The Decree*, vol. 13, Spring 1996. Copyright © 1996 by American Adoption Congress. Reproduced by permission.

mother who claimed her life was ruined by a telephone call from her child. If we are to ever change public policy and provide equality to adopted individuals, we must address the opposition's objections in the public policy arena. There are six main objections to open records put forth by opponents and one solution.

Opposition Statement: Opening adoption records will set the precedent of allowing anyone to obtain the records of professionals, e.g., doctors, and other private records.

Rebuttal: Opponents to open records frequently use the argument that if adoption records are opened, public policy will be setting the precedent for access to traditionally private records such as those kept by therapists, doctors, lawyers, hospitals and adoption and social service agencies to anyone who is curious. To counter this argument, we must clarify which records we want to open.

Adoption records are generally maintained on several levels by the adoption agency or attorney; the state department of social services, the court and of course, the bureau of vital statistics. If we approach open records as a civil rights issue, then we want to be the same as everyone else and not have extraordinary rights. Every state offers individuals who are not adopted access to their vital statistics, e.g., birth and marriage certificates, and access to court records about themselves.

> *"By denying adoptees access to birth certificates and court records about themselves, public policy creates a minority class of citizen whose civil rights are being violated."*

If we want to be equal to the rest of society, then we must define open records as access to original birth certificates and court records. By using this definition we overcome the argument that we are allowing adoptees access to confidential records and are setting a dangerous precedent. The precedent for U.S. citizens to have the right to copies of vital statistics and court files about themselves is already set in public policy.

By denying adoptees access to birth certificates and court records about themselves, public policy creates a minority class of citizen whose civil rights are being violated by nature of their adoptive "class" and over which they have no control.

Opposition Statement: We guaranteed birth parents confidentiality. Public policy never retroactively changes the rules. Opening records will be breaching a contract made by placing parents years ago.

Rebuttal: Opponents to open records use the "right to privacy" as their primary weapon in defeating access to records legislation. Frequently they mention the adoption contract. This contract ostensibly guaranteed the birthparent privacy. The signing of the Emancipation Proclamation by Abraham Lincoln deemed it unconstitutional to have contractual agreements concerning the ownership of human beings. Therefore, we cannot make contracts which limit or deny individual rights without the consent of all parties to the contract. In adoption, the adoptee is supposed to adhere to a verbal or implied adoption contract of which he or she was not a participant.

Certainly, we cannot deny that the civil codes have implied confidentiality for those involved in adoption. However, the precedent of retroactively negating contracts which are found to violate the civil rights of a class of people has already been set. Individuals who purchased neighborhoods in the 50's, 40's, and 30's and signed contracts which prohibited them from selling or renting to minorities found their contracts worthless in the post–civil rights era of the 1960's. In examining the adoption "contract" we must also look at the criteria birth families had to meet in order to place their children. If adoption was the path they chose or were forced to accept for their children, privacy was part of the adoption package, not an option parents could embrace or deny.

Birthparents were, by signing away their parental rights, accepting a non-negotiable condition of confidentiality. The system "assumed" that confidentiality was desired and needed to protect adoption.

Opposition Statement: Only two percent of all adoptees search; therefore, there is no need for open records as the demand is so small.

Rebuttal: Opponents to open records claim that only 2% of all adoptees want to search—a minority within a minority. Their estimate is probably correct. On a yearly basis it is estimated that between 2% and 4% of all adoptees search, but a different 2% every year. This means if 2%, or 250,000, different adoptees search each year, in 10 years the number would total 2,500,000. The tremendous growth in the number of search and support groups is further evidence that not only adoptees, but relatives and others touched by adoption, are increasingly interested in searching, so these estimates may be very conservative. And, one may also argue that 100% of adoptees search. It may not be a literal search, but it is a meaningful one none the less. It begins when the child first asks herself or others, why was I adopted?

Who are my birthparents? Where are they now? Even if estimates of 2% of all adoptees attempting searches are correct, the argument is irrelevant. Percentages and numbers don't matter when addressing civil rights issues. Statistics are not important. If only one African American wanted to attend a Mississippi University years ago, should that negate their right to do so? If only three Hispanic workers wanted humane living conditions in the grape arbors, should that negate their right? Certainly not. . . .

> *"Equal access to vital statistics and court files and searching for birthparents are two totally separate issues."*

Opposition Statement: Birthparents generally don't want to be found. Opening records will ruin lives.

Rebuttal: Equal access to vital statistics and court files and searching for birthparents are two totally separate issues. Proponents of open records hurt their cause when they confuse the two issues. An adoptee's decision to search has nothing to do with his or her right to obtain vital statistics and court files that concern him or herself. All state civil codes already provide, in statute, protection from harassment and invasion of privacy which apply to any citizen acting inappropriately. We must acknowledge that all birthparents are not thrilled at being found, but after 40 years of existence the search and reunification movement can point to a good track record of "backing off" when rejection does takes place. Open records legislation concerns adults, adults who can respect a birthparent who says, "not now" or "no thank you."

Opposition Statement: If we open records, birth mothers will abort their children rather than place them for adoption. Open records will encourage abortion, not adoptions.

Rebuttal: Recently the "far right," most notably the Right to Life movement, has been strenuously opposing access to records. Their opposition stems from the misguided notion of "adoption not abortion." "If we deny women confidentiality they will then abort their children." An article published in the May, 1991, *American Psychiatry* journal by Paul K.B. Dagg, M.D., shows just the opposite. Dr. Dagg did an overview of eight longitudinal studies of women denied abortions prior to *Roe v. Wade*. All of the studies were in agreement that approximately 5% of women denied abortions chose adoption for their children. We know from informal studies that when women who have placed a child through a confidential adoption arrangement become pregnant again, they choose abortion because they found the confidential conditions of adoption unbearable.

We must stress that an abortion is a decision not to be pregnant and adoption is a decision not to parent. Sensibly when a woman is considering an abortion, open adoption records are probably the last thing on her mind.

Opposition Statement: Open records will discourage birth parents from placing their children for adoption.

Rebuttal: In the past twenty years the "open adoption" phenomena has taken wing. The majority of infant adoptions which occur in the United States are private and open to some degree. One of the reasons open adoption has become popular is at the insistence of placing parents. Prospective adoptive parents frequently complain that most of the placing parents they meet insist on a degree of openness in their adoption. It would seem that open records and open adoption would, therefore, encourage adoption rather than discourage parents from placing their children.

Public policy must also recognize that there is a degree of responsibility to a child by a placing parent, beyond making an adoption plan. Even if confidentiality is desired at the time of placement, the child's right to information at a later date must be observed.

The Right of Adoptees to Access Their Personal Information Should Be Unconditional

by Bastard Nation

About the author: *Bastard Nation is an organization that promotes the civil rights of adoptees, including the right to obtain access to personal records.*

Conditional access legislation, which includes disclosure vetoes, contact vetoes, and intermediary systems, has often been used by adoption reformers in their efforts to try to win over legislators and pass bills. Some reformers claim that these conditional access bills serve as intermediate steps to true open records legislation. History, however, tells a different story. Once laws are passed, legislators are reluctant to revisit the issue of records legislation, which can result in future legislative changes being stalled for years, or even decades. Once they do revisit the issue, there is no indication that legislators are more inclined to openness than before the conditional access legislation passed, and in many cases that legislation itself creates an impediment in terms of legal precedent.

Unrestricted open records for adult adoptees is the norm in most of the rest of the free world, and in Alaska, Kansas, Oregon, and Alabama. Conditional access legislation is the result of reformers allowing the debate to be framed in the opposition's terms. Access to one's birth certificate is a basic civil rights issue. Veto and intermediary systems skirt the issue by framing the debate in terms of birthparent privacy. In *Doe v. Sundquist*, which challenged a TN [Tennessee] semi-open records law (it contains both contact and disclosure vetoes) on the grounds that it violated birthparent privacy, the Sixth Circuit Court of Appeals stated that "if there is a federal constitutional right of familial privacy, it does not extend as far as the plaintiffs would like." The opinion also cited a

Bastard Nation, "Conditional Access Legislation and Other Legislative Compromises," *The Basic Bastard*, Copyright © 2001 by Bastard Nation: The Adoptee Rights Organization. Reproduced by permission.

1981 decision in which the appeals court found that "the Constitution does not encompass a general right to nondisclosure of private information." If there is no right to privacy that extends to birthparent anonymity, then there is no reason why an adoptee's right to access his original birth certificate should be impeded by special governmental controls to protect birthparents. Disclosure vetoes, by which an adoptee may access his original birth certificate only if his birthparent does not object, appear to vest birthparents with such a "right to privacy," making it all the more difficult for adoptee-rights advocates to argue that the law has never guaranteed anonymity to birthparents.

> *"There is no reason why an adoptee's right to access his original birth certificate should be impeded by special government controls to protect birthparents."*

Contact vetoes, whereby the birthparent or adoptee may file a statement that they do not wish to be contacted by the other party, and by which the searching party must abide or be subject to criminal penalties, are a violation of an adoptee's right to due process and equal protection under the law. Conditional access legislation in the form of the "contact veto" implies that adoptees and birthparents are not capable of handling adult contact. If either party in an adoption does not wish contact, they can simply say no, as in any other adult situation. If they feel they are being unduly harassed, they can use the same remedies at their disposal as other citizens. Traditional no-contact orders and orders of protection are issued via court order after a person has demonstrated a pattern of threatening or abusive behavior. Even then, the person who has the order issued against him has the right to answer and face his accuser in a court of law. Contact vetoes, however, are issued based solely on the adoptive status of an individual, and are without recourse. In open records states where no contact veto exists, such as Kansas and Alaska, there are no reports of incidents that would demonstrate a necessity for special protections of the birth family.

Contact vetoes (CVs) were an experiment originating out of a law passed in New Zealand in 1986. New Zealand's [NZ] law, which calls itself a contact veto system, actually functions as a "contact preference form" (CPF) since there is nothing legally requiring the adoptee to abide by the request of the person filing their contact preference form. Since such a system does not place a condition on access or criminalize an adoptee unfairly, CPFs are an acceptable compromise to Bastard Nation and were written into Bastard Nation–supported open records laws in both Oregon and Alabama.

Interestingly, the NZ government itself has acknowledged their CPF system is a failure; adoptees often contact other members of the birth family when the birthparent has placed a "veto", thus causing the kind of exposure the birthparent wished to avoid in the first place. It can also be dangerous to write a contact preference system into proposed legislation from the beginning, as such a scheme can quickly be amended into a veto. Amending proposed open records legislation with a contact preference law should only be done when activists and their sponsor have a close and trusting relationship, and when the legislation can be assured of a better chance of passage with the sole addition of the contact preference amendment. Activists are encouraged not to include CPFs in ballot measure text, but rather once an open records measure has passed to use the CPF to head off any more dangerous legislative tinkering.

True contact veto systems, which are opposed by Bastard Nation, exist in North America in British Columbia, Colorado, and Tennessee, and sprang from similar laws originating in the Australian territories, most notably when New South Wales (NSW) passed its Adoption Information Act of 1990. Queensland has a similar veto law. Violating a contact veto in NSW carries monetary penalties as well as jail time. Similar penalties exist in the veto systems present in North America.

Age of access is another issue which activists often have to contend with in lobbying open records legislation or writing ballot measures. There are three common ages of majority used in North America upon which a person acquires all (or most of) the rights and responsibilities of being an adult. These are 18, 19, and 21. Bastard Nation therefore supports unconditional access legislation that sets the age of eligibility at any of these three levels. In other parts of the world, Bastard Nation supports setting age of access to correspond with a country's general trend in age of majority law.

Adoptees have a right to access the records of their birth in the same manner as any other citizen of this nation; any legislation that is less than access on demand, without condition, is a violation of their basic civil and human rights. Conditional access legislation is an affront to the dignity and self-respect of adoptees as well; in the case of contact vetoes, treating adopted persons as criminals, in the case of disclosure vetoes, treating them as perpetual children who must have their birthmothers' tacit permission to access their own birth certificates, and in the case of intermediary systems, treating them as incompetent to manage their own personal affairs.

> *"Conditional access legislation is an affront to the dignity and self-respect of adoptees."*

Voluntary Registries Are an Inadequate Substitute for Open Records Laws

by Melisha Mitchell with Jane Nast, Barbara Busharis, and Pam Hasegawa

About the authors: *Melisha Mitchell is the founder and executive director of the White Oak Foundation, a nonprofit organization that provides search assistance and other services for people affected by adoption. Jane Nast is past president of the American Adoption Congress (AAC). Barbara Busharis teaches law at Florida State University. Pam Hasegawa is a member of the AAC's board of directors and former public education director of the Adoptees' Liberty Movement Association registry (ALMA).*

Three years ago [1996], when I began searching for my then 28-year-old birthdaughter, a friend told me she'd heard there was some sort of adoption registry in Illinois. Maybe they could help me locate my birthdaughter? I called over half a dozen government listings before I was able to ascertain that the entity I was seeking was the Illinois Adoption Registry (IAR). I then called three more government agencies before reaching someone at the State of Illinois' main switchboard who was finally able to provide a number for the Registry's headquarters, located within the Department of Public Health. When I called the number I'd been given, a gruff-voiced civil servant answered. "I'm looking for the Illinois Adoption Registry," I explained. 'The Illinois WHAT?" I repeated my request a second time, more slowly, and heard the receiver clunk onto a desk. 'Hey," the employee barked to his colleagues, 'Does anybody know anything about an adoption registry?" About five minutes later, I heard a pair of feet shuffle to the desk. The receiver was picked up and hung up. Although this encounter alone would have probably been enough to give me second thoughts about signing up with the Illinois Adoption Registry, over the next

Melisha Mitchell with Jane Nast, Barbara Busharis, and Pam Hasegawa, "Mutual Consent Voluntary Registries; an Exercise in Patience—and Failure," *Adoptive Families Magazine*, January/February 1999. Copyright © 1999 by *Adoptive Families Magazine*®. Reproduced by permission.

few days I learned that the IAR was one of the most ineffectual registries in the country and, depending on the source, had matched either 35, 78, or 110 adoptees and birthparents in its 10 years of existence. Needless to say, I never called back again.

Underfunded. Understaffed. Underpublicized. It's a lethal combination that characterizes the majority of the less than two dozen state-level mutual consent voluntary registries (MCVRs) in the United States. Also known as passive registries, MCVRs are the cumbersome, bureaucratic band-aids that legislators began "offering' to original birth-certificate-hungry adoptees in the late 70s. They are based on the principle that, if adoptees and birthparents really want to meet each other, all we need to do is create a governmental message center where everyone can express their wishes regarding contact. Build it and they will come, they said. But most adoptees and birthparents stayed home.

To try to understand why MCVRs have encountered so much indifference in the adoption community, the American Adoption Congress (AAC) conducted a survey of 21 passive adoption registries in 1993. The survey was repeated in 1996 and again in 1998. Each time, directors of mutual consent registries from Maine to Oregon were sent a questionnaire asking them to provide statistics on the total number of registrants and matches since their registry's inception, as well as general information on cost, basic provisions, and operation. Although several registries did not participate in the 1993 and 1996 studies, all 21 states submitted responses in 1998.

What Is an MCVR?

MCVRs allow adoptees, birthparents, and in some states, birth siblings, who have been separated by adoption to register with a government agency in the state where the adoptee was born and/or adopted and then wait for a match. By registering, eligible triad members can indicate their wishes regarding contact with specified biological and adoptive relatives. At least two parties to an adoption must register independently before names or other identifying information can be released.

While the concept seemed simple, it encountered much opposition within the adoption reform movement. The same basic concept, "I'll call you, if you'll call me" had been initially introduced in the mid-50s by Jean Paton, an adoptee and social worker whose visionary non-fictional work, *The Adopted Break Silence* was published in 1955. Paton founded Orphan Voyage, the first adoptee/birthparent support group in the nation, and operated the first-of-its kind adoption registry from her home.

However, while national adoption registries (such as Adoptees' Liberty Movement Association Registry founded by Florence Fisher in New York in 1972 and the International Soundex Reunion Registry established by Emma Mae Villardi in Carson City, Nevada, in 1975) operating with a similar approach have reunited thousands of triad members and enjoyed support within the adoptee/birthparent community over the past two decades, state mutual consent registries have become increasingly unpopular with everyone.

The paradox seems to be grounded in the raison d'être for MCVRs, which historically appears NOT to have been to facilitate the reunion process but rather to stall progress of the original access-to-records bill, the Model State Adoption Act. Drafted by an HEW [Department of Health, Education and Welfare]-funded panel chaired by New Jersey Assemblyman Al Burstein during the Carter Administration, 'The Model' Act would have given adoptees aged 21 and older the right to access their original birth records.

> *"MCVRs are . . . cumbersome, bureaucratic band-aids."*

To combat this progressive piece of legislation, the National Council for Adoption (NCFA), a Washington, D.C-based adoption agency trade organization, began promoting passive mutual consent registries throughout the United States, touting MCVRs as the "only" acceptable "compromise" to the adoption reform conundrum. NCFA recommended outrageous provisions (limiting registries to adoptees over the age of 25, requiring all parties to the adoption to register annually before a match could be made), and confused enough undereducated legislators to successfully implement passive registries in many of the states which are the subject of the AAC study.

Not only was this "wait and see" approach to birthfamily reunification passed before most "adoption reform" laws were enacted, but, as the only post-adoption option offered in many states, it had a number of obvious drawbacks. Dead people may vote in Chicago, but they certainly don't apply to adoption registries! The often complicated registration procedures are impractical for elderly or seriously ill adoptees and birthparents. Registries don't work well for adoptees who are unaware they were adopted or for birthparents who have been told their child is deceased. And, to make matters worse, behind the scenes, legislators and registry administrators who, like most NCFA member agencies, were not as keen on facilitating search and reunion as those actually affected by these laws, began making the kind of budgetary and protocol decisions that would doom all but two of these state registries to single-digit reunion rates.

Understaffed, Underfunded, and Underpublicized

When AAC conducted its first survey in 1993, only one state reported both adequate funding and staffing for its MCVR. Five years later, registries in ten states continue to be plagued by underfunding and/or understaffing. A handful of states are still shuffling 5 x 8" index cards to figure out if they have a match, and have yet to computerize their registries. Others complain that archaic database programs, which can only be run on pre-Microsoft computers, make their job unnecessarily tedious. South Dakota and South Carolina both claimed that staffing and funding for their registry were "adequate" but South Dakota still has no official, or unofficial, count on the number of registrations or matches realized since its registry opened its doors in 1984, and South Carolina wrote that 30 days was "not enough time" to gather the information requested.

When staffing and funding are BOTH insufficient, even locating a phone number where interested parties may obtain further information about a given registry can be a grueling test in perseverance. Locating a staff member knowledgeable about registry operations in at least half of the 21 states surveyed required 8 to 10 phone calls. In registry offices across the country, automated voice mail systems, often used to counterbalance staffing inadequacies, also act as a barrier for those seeking to inquire anonymously about registry requirements. Oklahoma, overwhelmed by unexpected interest in their new registry-cum-confidential-intermediary program (registrants may initiate a $400 search after a six-month stint on the registry), claimed that it would take "at least another year" for them to process the estimated 6,000 applications that have poured in since the law was enacted in November 1997.

Budget restrictions are also responsible for the "lack of adequate publicity" cited by at least half of the registry coordinators we spoke with. To the question, "How does your office publicize the existence of your registry?" most respondents answered "brochures" or "newspaper article." One state indicated they were "listed in the Yellow Pages." Only three states had made any noticeable effort to actively promote their registries and had some vague semblance of a media plan. And, although six of the 21 states (Maryland, Rhode Island, Texas, Indiana, Ohio, and Illinois) purported to be "on the Internet," none of the top four Internet search engines was able to locate more than three of these state registries in [1998] (but each Web search netted hundreds of private Internet registry sites!). Once located, four of these six Web sites provided little more than sketchy information on their registry's operation, and only three included downloadable application forms.

When understaffing and underfunding aren't enough to weed out all but the most tenacious applicants, many states further fuel their poor performance records by building pernicious provisions into their registry statutes (many of them inspired by NCFA "recommendations"). New York limits registrations to adoptees who were born *and* adopted in that state, leaving those born in New York but adopted out-of-state in registry limbo. Rhode Island and Missouri require written permission from the adoptive parents before they will forward names and addresses to birthparents and adoptees who have been matched by the registry. Nebraska, too, requires adult adoptees between the ages of 21 and 25 to get signed authorizations from their adoptive parents before reuniting them with their birthfamilies. And a new law in Texas subjects

> *"With so much going against them, and so little going for them, it's a wonder passive mutual consent registries ever find anyone."*

potential matches to an hour of counseling. . . . And, as appears to have been NCFA's original plan, in 15 of the 21 states currently [in 1999] offering an MCVR, their existence seems to have stymied the introduction of more progressive legislation (such as the "search and consent" programs, also known as "active registries" currently available to interested triad members in two dozen states). Like Oklahoma, 4 of the 6 states which have averaged more than 5 matches per year since their registry's inception (LA, OR, OH, and FL), now also offer some sort of search assistance to adoptees and/or birthparents—which technically, puts them in the "active," rather than passive, registry category.

Low Success Rates

With so much going against them, and so little going for them, it's a wonder passive mutual consent registries ever find anyone. West Virginia has only made 2 matches in its 7-year history. Arkansas, which had one reunion during its first 6 years of operation, has matched up 14 times as many adoptees and birthparents since 1993, but still has a 1.5 percent success rate.

Overall, mutual consent adoption registries have made only minimal progress since the early 90s. Reunion rates in all but two of the states included in our survey are still well under 10 percent and pale in comparison to other, more active, post adoption solutions (most government and agency-sponsored search assistance programs, for example, boast an 80 percent or higher "find" rate). Even though the overall number of registrants has increased considerably in many of the states we surveyed, these improved statistics have not translated into higher reunion rates for their registries. And, even though states as diverse as Florida, Illinois, Idaho, Maine, New York, Texas, and Utah reported fractional improvements in their "reunion rates" for 1998, Maryland and Rhode Island are barely maintaining the status quo, and the Missouri, Nevada, and Ohio registries performed better, match-wise, in earlier surveys than they did in 1998. New York and Texas appear to have inexplicably lost registrants since the 1996 survey, but the lower 1998 numbers are most likely attributable to recent legislative reforms. Texas has begun centralizing its state registry and no longer includes guestimates of private agency registration numbers in their totals. New York's loss of over 500 registrants since the 1993 survey is probably due to the fact that previous statistics included adoptive parents (who were excluded from the registry five years ago).

Fee-wise, there have been few changes over the past 5 years [1993–1998]. One third of the 21 registries are still free, and the remainder charge between $10 and $75. The average cost is still $25 per registrant. Additionally, although over half of these MCVRs have opened up their rolls to birth siblings and/or adoptive parents in the past decade, this expanded access has had little impact on the number of registrants or the reunion rates in those states. Nine of the 21 registries are still reserved to birthparents and adult adopted persons.

At first glance, only two states, Louisiana and Indiana, seem to have truly separated themselves from the pack. Both states have tripled their number of applicants over the past five years. They are also the only two states with double-digit "match rates" (14 percent and 13 percent, respectively). However, since 1993, Louisiana has added on-request search assistance for adult adoptees to their palette of post-adoption options, thereby disqualifying their registry from "passive" status. Recent changes in the Indiana Adoption Medical History Registry (IAMHR) have made it difficult to accurately gauge that state's reunion rates. While some of the unique "perks" added to the Indiana registry in 1993 might be considered steps in the right direction (particularly its emphasis on the exchange of medical information and a provision that allows adoptees matched with their birthparents via the registry to access copies of their original birth certificates and other adoption files), these innovations may be skewing, rather than actually improving, the registry's reunion statistics. It appears that some adoptees and birthparents are using the IAMHR not to find one another, but to use the registry's back-door access to birth records to obtain their original birth certificates, after they've been reunited. And, too, when you consider that the focus of the Indiana registry is on the exchange of vital medical data, its 13 percent success rate is very disappointing. For someone who's dying of a mysterious, genetically-linked disease, odds this slim, combined with a total lack of search assistance, can ring like a death knell. So, even Indiana's better-than-average results (9,000 new applications and over 1500 matches since 1993) are not necessarily a sign that the times are "a changin."

"It is clearly the passive nature of mutual consent voluntary registries that is most responsible for their failure."

Even if persistent funding and staffing concerns could somehow be resolved, it is clearly the passive nature of mutual consent voluntary registries that is most responsible for their failure. When an adoptee or birthparent decides to register, they are, in most cases, really saying they have begun thinking about actively searching. Applying to a registry (or several) is usually the first leg of an often long and frustrating journey. Asking adoptees and birthparents to "sit and wait" just as they've begun to move forward is blatantly unrealistic. Unless MCVRs are proposed in tandem with more active options, signing up is about as effective as tossing an SOS into the ocean.

A Dubious Twenty-Year Milestone

States like Oregon, which recently passed a ballot initiative that would have allowed adoptees born there to begin accessing their original birth certificates by the end of 1998, and Tennessee, which passed an open records bill in 1995, have already left totally passive registries way, way behind. As adoption reform activists in Texas, Washington, New Jersey, Massachusetts, and elsewhere begin gearing up for their 1999 open records quests, many of the 21 states with the most repressive adoption laws seem to be locked in the same, unshakable apathy that characterizes passive mutual consent registries.

However, a bill introduced by Michigan Senator Carl Levin [in 1997] may supplant most of these ill-conceived state registries by creating a National Voluntary Mutual Reunion Registry. While a national registry would be far from a panacea, its higher profile and greater accessibility would at least open up the registry process to many currently excluded from state registry rolls (e.g. adoptees who were born in one state and adopted in another). [The bill did not pass.]

Although Nevada Adoption Registry, the oldest passive state registry, celebrated its 20th anniversary in 1998, there were probably no triad members rejoicing. Only 101 birthfamilies have been reunited since Nevada enacted its passive registry legislation in 1978. For two decades now, Nevada triad members, along with tens of thousands of adoptees and birth relatives from Reno to Bangor, have been stuck in the dark ages of compromise legislation. In all of the states that chose the mutual consent route back in the late 70s, 80s and early 90s, registered adoptees and birth relatives have gone from skeptical anticipation to disappointment and ultimately, resignation, as their long wait for a match has stretched out over months, then years, and now decades. Unless these triad members—or their state legislatures—seek out more pro-active solutions, fewer than 4,000 of the 65,000 adoptees, adoptive parents, and birth relatives currently enrolled with passive, mutual consent adoption registries will have any hope of ever reconstructing their family trees.

Opening Adoption and Birth Records Violates the Privacy Rights of Birth Mothers

by Marianne Means

About the author: *Marianne Means is a syndicated columnist.*

The Supreme Court this week [in May 2000] declined to block an Oregon law allowing adult adoptees access to their birth records without the prior consent of their biological parents.

This may not be the high court's last word on this emotional issue. But the action freed Oregon to go ahead with an experiment that a group of biological mothers had tried to legally stop. And it could eventually eliminate the secrecy that has traditionally protected the privacy of adoptions throughout this country.

This is a classic case of a clash of individual rights. Whose are more important?

Adults who have been adopted but have no idea of their ancestry are understandably curious about their biological roots. And knowledge about their birth parents can be useful in assessing hereditary behavioral and disease traits.

Unfair to Mothers

But the Oregon law is wickedly unfair to mothers who give up their babies for adoption. They generally do so for sad and humiliating but compelling reasons. The babies may be illegitimate, the result of horrific rape, or simply a financial and emotional burden that a poor family or teen-age mother cannot assume.

The parents have counted on the presumption—usually based on a specific promise from state officials—that the stigma of an unwanted pregnancy would not be revived years later by a forced confrontation with accusatory offspring. Illegitimacy may no longer be the devastating scandal it used to be, but the decision to make it public should be the mother's alone. Some adoptive parents may not object to their adoptee's fascination with biological roots but some

Marianne Means, "Whose Rights Rule in Adoptions?" *Liberal Opinion Week*, June 19, 2000. Copyright © 2000 by Marianne Means. Reproduced by permission.

may feel bumped to second place, with all their years of nurturing reduced to something unimportant.

Laws in Other States

Now Oregon is about to plunge into that emotional thicket while the world watches. The experiment will also challenge the sincerity of Texas Gov. George W. Bush and other conservatives opposed to abortion who have been crusading for adoption as an alternative to ending a pregnancy. If unwed, poor or mentally troubled mothers carry the fetus to term, what consequences await them later?

Will Bush and company protect their privacy? Who will adopt such children if they know they may later be forced to deal with potentially irresponsible birth parents?

Four other states allow adults who have been adopted unconditional access to their original birth certificates

"Illegitimacy may no longer be the devastating scandal it used to be, but the decision to make it public should be the mother's alone."

so they can find their biological parents whether the parents want to meet them or not. They are Kansas, Tennessee and Alaska; Alabama approved an unconditional access law last month. [May 2000]

Similar bills are also under consideration in other states, although across most of the country original birth certificates are sealed and can be opened only by court order.

Limited access is allowed in 19 states if the birth parents consent, which seems like a sensible compromise that hurts no one and can be useful to both parties.

An estimated 6 million Americans are adopted, and there is no way to know how many adult adoptees have been told about the circumstances which led to their arrival at their new family. It is an individual parental decision, and a very private one.

A few years ago open-records advocacy groups began publicly pressing for access to adoptees' pasts, claiming the right to know everything trumped the right to privacy. They have a legal and political advantage over a group of birth mothers who have been fighting them; the adoptees speak openly before the media while the mothers have of necessity remained anonymous.

An Explosive Conflict

The conflict is explosive on many levels. In some cases, there may be a happy reunion. Web sites and other commercial registries try to arrange such reunions.

But anecdotal evidence indicates that often opening old records meant to be closed creates trouble and turmoil. The mother may have a cherished civic reputation and a new family that does not know of her youthful indiscretion. There is unlikely to be any emotional or cultural bond between mother and child after all those years. In one notorious case, a black man who was the child of a rape knocked on the door of his middle-aged white birth mother and sent her into terrified shock.

Many adoptees say they simply wish to have more information and are not out to embarrass their birth mothers. But with open records they can do both.

A Portland lawyer, Franklin Hunsaker, who represented six biological mothers who fought the Oregon law, said that his clients were "scared and even angry that their rights have been ignored."

If enough women are scared about what is happening, more and more will choose abortion over adoption. The open-records movement is so young we don't have proof yet that it encourages abortion. But common sense says it will.

Removing Privacy Protections Will Threaten the Future of Infant Adoption

by William L. Pierce

About the author: *William L. Pierce is the founder and past president of the National Council for Adoption, an adoption advocacy and child welfare organization.*

On June 11, 1998, a Member of Congress, Representative Jim Oberstar (D-MN), the House Democratic Co-Chair of the Congressional Coalition on Adoption, said in a statement for the Subcommittee on Human Resources of the Committee on Ways and Means that "After Great Britain changed its adoption laws in 1975 to allow adopted individuals to view their unamended birth certificates, a significant decline took place in the number of children placed for adoption."

The Congressman's statement reflects the heated policy debate that has been taking place in the United States for at least 25 years about removing privacy from adoption. Proponents claim, among other things, that there is no negative impact on adoption numbers if privacy is not provided. Opponents, such as Rep. Oberstar, allege that there is a measurable impact.

In this debate, one of the difficulties is in finding comparable populations to that of the United States, especially among the nations most often cited by proponents of removing privacy as models: Australia, Israel, New Zealand and the United Kingdom. Of those four countries, only one has a substantial population, the United Kingdom. But there are no reasonably reliable adoption data for the entire UK. The data that exist are for England and Wales only. The data show a 93 percent decline in adoption after adoption privacy is eliminated.

William L. Pierce, *Adoption Factbook III*. Washington, DC: National Council for Adoption, 1999.
Copyright © 1999 by the National Council for Adoption. All rights reserved. Reproduced by permission.

The Picture from England and Wales

The people who make up the population of England and Wales and those who make up the population of the United States are similar in many ways: culture, language, diversity of ethnic groups, and political systems. For this reason, comparisons between the two populations, adjusted for the difference in numbers, may yield insights that will be helpful to policy makers. In particular, a look at the numbers of adoptions in the two populations may inform the debate over whether or not removing privacy has any impact on numbers of adoptions.

The population of England and Wales, as of the [1991] Census, was about 49 million, close to 20 percent of the population of the United States. All things being equal, one would expect adoptions in the U.S. to be five times larger than those in England and Wales. This was the case in the 1970s. For the US, the adoption data from

> *"The data show a 93 percent decline in adoption [in England and Wales] after adoption privacy is eliminated."*

the National Council For Adoption [NCFA] are widely acknowledged to be reliable and to be derived by using standard statistical methods. For England and Wales, the data are from Her Majesty's Stationery Office. The US Department of Health and Human Services (HHS), was directed by Congress to have a system in place by 1991 to report all adoption and foster care numbers, but nine years later no efforts had been made to collect data from the private sector, which is responsible for most adoptive placements in America.

Here is the picture from England and Wales, as reported by Patricia Morgan, a sociologist and Senior Research Fellow for the Institute of Economic Affairs, in London. Morgan, writing in *Adoption and the Care of Children: The British and American Experience*, said ". . . there were only 5,797 adoptions in England and Wales . . ." in 1995. Morgan says the numbers are down dramatically, ". . . less than a third of the 21,299 of 20 years before, and about half of these were step-parent adoptions, in which one partner (usually the husband) in a marriage formally adopts the other partner's existing children.". . .

Those who wish to end adoption privacy in America claim that in England, where records were opened in 1975, the decline was "only" 39 percent over eight years. But in the U.S., there was no such decline at all: unrelated domestic adoptions were 47,700 in 1975, 50,720 in 1982, and 54,492 in 1966. The correct data to cite . . . are from Morgan's Table 1:1, where she shows that adoptions of children under 1 year [in England and Wales] went from 4,548 in 1975 to 322 in 1995, a 93 percent decline.

Morgan continues with information about those adoptions most relevant to the debate over privacy, "baby adoptions." It is, after all, not a matter of parental choice for most of the children who are older and are in the foster care systems of either the UK or the US. These children's parents have had their legal rights terminated. The matter of privacy and choice affects those parents who are pregnant and often unmarried and are confronted with the options of abortion, adoption or parenting.

"The number of baby adoptions in 1995," Morgan writes, "was 322, a relic of the 4,548 for 1975, or even of the 969 for 1990 (out of 6,533 adoptions). The proportional increase in older child adoptions disguises the way that their numbers have been relatively static. Even then, the totals include the small but growing numbers of intercountry adoptions."

One can only speculate why those who wish to end privacy in American adoptions and who claim more women would choose adoption if privacy were to end would not provide accurate and complete data about the 93 percent decline in England and Wales after adoption privacy was eliminated. . . .

A hypohetical comparison can be made between the 322 infant adoptions in England and Wales and the 23,537 US unrelated domestic adoptions. Given the fivefold difference in population, we would expect over 4,500 infant adoptions in England and Wales in the 1990s, not the 322 observed. Or, put another way, had the US rate been that of England and Wales, there would have been only 1,610 infant adoptions in the US! The remaining 22,000 US babies would most likely have ended up being patented by unmarried, single women or would have been aborted.

No one knows for certain what all the factors are that come to bear in the complex equation of a woman's choice for adoption. NCFA speculates that there are several factors at play in England in addition to privacy; the lack of a vigorous national advocacy organization; a group of voluntary adoption agencies that have largely given up on domestic infant adoption and have no competition pushing them to renew or rebuild their services; a constituency of prospective adoptive parents that is timid, unorganized and therefore unable to advocate for change.

> *"When women do not have privacy, they do not choose adoption."*

One thing is certain; in England and Wales in the 1990s, the policy of lack of privacy in baby adoptions is unnecessary and professionally unsound. In the US, by contrast, baby adoptions have not gone into a steep decline, despite segments of the social work profession that are convinced that privacy is unnecessary.

A Negative Impact

Rep. Oberstar contends, as Dr. John Willke did in his testimony before the Ohio legislature on March 17, 1982, that a lack of privacy discourages adoption and encourages abortion. Dr. Willke quoted an English woman, Mrs. Neula Scarisbrook, who heads an organization of more than 150 outpatient [crisis pregnancy and counseling centers] and 50 homes for women, as follows: "What is relatively new here is that about five years ago [in 1975] Parliament passed a bill completely opening all adoption birth records. We have had quite a change since that time. Adoption now, as we did know it, simply no longer exists. Adoption is rare. What we have now in Britain can probably best be described as long-term foster care, with no permanent commitment. Most of the women now simply get abortions. You see, Dr. Willke, with an abortion they have a lifetime of privacy and no one will ever know. That used to always be true of adoption. But when it changed, being no longer able to have lifetime confidentiality, a significant percentage of these girls now abort."

The data strongly suggest that a lack of privacy has a negative impact on adoption. And the statistics are confirmed by the experts in dealing with pregnant women, who assert that when women do not have privacy, they do not choose adoption.

A Voluntary Registry System Is Preferable to Open Records Laws

by Naomi Cahn

About the author: *Naomi Cahn is a law professor at George Washington University Law School.*

Editor's note: The following is taken from testimony before Congress in 1998 regarding proposed legislation to establish a national voluntary adoption reunion registry. Although the Senate passed the legislation in 1997, the bill died in the House of Representatives.

My name is Naomi Cahn, and I teach Family Law at George Washington University Law School, where I am an Associate Professor of Law. I have taught Family Law at George Washington University for the past five years; prior to that, I was a Visiting Professor at Georgetown University Law Center, where I taught in a domestic violence clinic. In my work in college, law school and afterwards, I have continually focused on family-related issues. I have written extensively in the family law area, including articles concerning adoption.

Personal Adoption Experiences

In addition to my professional experiences within the adoption system, and to my academic experiences teaching about adoption, I have relevant personal experiences: my husband was adopted as an infant into a warm, loving, and wonderful family. He recently searched for his biological parents, and we will soon be attending (and helping to organize) the 90th birthday party of his biological grandmother.

My husband had maintained for the first thirteen years that he and I knew each other that he had no interest in finding out about his biological parents. He loves his family, and felt no need to find out more about his past. Then, when I

Naomi Cahn, testimony before the Subcommittee on Human Resources of the House Committee on Ways and Means, June 11, 1998.

was pregnant with our first child, he found part of his biological family. He found out the name of his birth mother, Dorothy Louise Simpson; but he also found out that she had died of a brain tumor while searching for him. She had registered with one organization's registry, but, of course, since my husband had not registered, they never found each other. She had also written to the agency which had handled the adoption, but, again, had received no information about my husband. My husband was stunned to discover that his birth mother had searched unsuccessfully for him.

My husband did find his birth grandmother. He found her, at the age of 85, in a small, rural East Texas town called Toledo Village. They have made each other so happy! There is an article in a recent *Guidepost* magazine authored by his grandmother which describes their joyous reunion. My husband, and our children, are her only surviving direct descendants. She has given us a quilt which now hangs in our house; she had begun stitching the quilt squares in 1930, when her daughter was born, and she had completed the quilt shortly before her first great-grandchild was born in 1994. Finding his birth grandmother has changed my husband's life in the most wonderful way. He firmly believes in the importance of allowing adult adoptees, when and if they are ready to do so, to contact their biological parents.

The remainder of my testimony in support of the federal registry will focus on several areas: (1) the general need for adoption registries because of the importance of facilitating contact between biological parents and adopted children and siblings; (2) the reasons for a specifically federal—as opposed to state—mutual voluntary adoption registry that would facilitate reunions; and (3) how the Senate bill serves to protect the confidentiality of adoption records.[1]

(1) The Need

First, as you know, when a child is adopted, he or she receives a new birth certificate that does not contain the name of the biological parents. No party to the adoption can have access to any information about the adoption. When an adopted child reaches adulthood and seeks information about her biological past, she is unable—in most states—to get much information. Or, when a biological parent wants to know whether the child she gave up for adoption is still alive, she cannot get any information. Even if both the adult child and the biological parent

> *"My husband was stunned to discover that his birth mother had searched unsuccessfully for him."*

are looking at the exact same moment, they may never meet each other. If they do meet, it is generally only after what will probably be a great expense, many frustrations, and many years of waiting, or worse, too late (as happened with

1. S. 1487, a law creating a national registry, was passed by the Senate in 1997 but ultimately died in the House of Representatives.

my husband). A federal mutual voluntary adoption registry, as authorized by the Senate legislation, allows biological parents and siblings to make contact with each other—but *only after they have each independently and voluntarily filed with the registry.* Because the registry is both voluntary and mutual, it creates the opportunity for a meeting only when both parties want contact.

The need for contact between the unknown members of the adoption triangle is very strong. When you read stories by biological parents, and stories by their adopted children, you feel an enormous sense of pain that they cannot contact each other. When anthropologist Judith Modell, who is an adoptive parent, interviewed birth parents, she found that "Birthparents . . . insisted that a birth bond could not be severed no matter what happened to a birth certificate." Modell found that the birth parents were completely unable to forget the birth of their child, contrary to the advice they had received from adoption experts. She also found, however, that birth parents generally do not want to disrupt the adoptive family, nor do they desire to regain a direct parental role in the child's life; rather, birth parents simply want to know whether the child was placed in an adoptive home, how he or she is developing and whether or not he or she is alive. They want to be available, if the biological child, as an adult, wants to contact them. Many birth mothers say they would rather have a mutually-desired reunion, rather than an approach desired only by one party; they do not want to disrupt the adoptive family. Even at the time of placement, most birth mothers and birth fathers agree to have their identities disclosed if their adult children want to know who they are.

Psychologist Betty Jean Lifton is an adoptee who has written several best-selling books about the complex feelings of adopted children, and has explored their quite desperate searches for their biological parents. She believes that the best interests of the adopted child will only be served when she is recognized as someone who has two distinct sets of parents that provide her with her identity.

When adopted children find their biological parents, they describe a feeling of relief. One reporter for the *Cincinnati Enquirer* . . . began the story of his search for his biological family as follows: "For the first time in my life, I delivered two Mother's Day cards this year."

For adoptive parents, who care passionately about the emotional health of their children, acceptance of their children's search is important. All of the adoptive parents with whom I have discussed this issue recognize that their children may someday want to know more about the parents who placed them for adoption, and all of the adoptive parents have said that they would help their children, just as they have always helped their children. Indeed, many have already done so. They understand that finding a biological past may be significant to their children, but also that their children do not seek to replace them.

A Historical Digression

I want to digress for a minute and talk about the history of adoption, in order to put the mutual voluntary consent registries into perspective. The first "modern" adoption statutes were enacted around the middle part of the nineteenth century. They were "modern" because they focussed on providing what was in the best interest of the child, rather than merely providing heirs for the adoptive parents. The first state law that required a home investigation on the appropriateness of the adoptive household was actually enacted in Minnesota in 1917. This law also restricted access to adoption court files to the "parties in interest and their attorneys and representatives of the State board of control." While many states soon followed Minnesota in requiring home investigations, few of them enacted the confidentiality restrictions. The purpose of the confidentiality restrictions was not, by the way, to prevent those involved in the adoption from having access to information; it was to protect against the public's seeking access to these files to determine whether a child was born outside of marriage. The statutes made court files confidential, but they did not prevent members of the adoption triad from having access to social service files. Until 1970, adoptees and biological parents could generally use a variety of sources for access to information about each other. Only recently, then, has the confidentiality of adoption information prevented adult adoptees from gaining knowledge about their biological pasts.

I want to be clear—mutual voluntary adoption registries have absolutely nothing to do with court or agency adoption files. But this very brief history of adoption shows that it was not the purpose of adoption reformers to prevent adult adoptees and biological parents from contacting each other. Indeed, the proposed federal Mutual Voluntary Adoption Registry is entirely consistent with the history of adoption, which has focussed on the child's best interests, and letting the adult adoptee, when ready, find out about her biological parents and siblings.

> *"The need for contact between unknown members of the adoption triangle is very strong."*

(2) The Federal Role

Today [June 1998], according to information provided by the federal National Adoption Information Clearinghouse, more than half of all states have established a "passive and voluntary registry," that is, a registry which allows individuals to register with an agency and then wait for a match to result from another registrant. The registry does not reveal any information until at least two people to the same adoption have filed with it indicating that they are seeking contact. In addition, there are various other passive registries available through the Internet and other media.

While the existence of these various registries is a start in helping biological parents and their adult children meet each other, there are logistical difficulties with their use that could be prevented through the existence of the federal registry. First, there is no communication between states with respect to people in their registries. For example, a child may have been raised in Colorado and the

District of Columbia; a biological parent may live in Pennsylvania; a biological sibling may live in Colorado. Unless the child, birth parent, and sibling each register in the same state registry, there will be no matches made, and they will be unable to find each other. A federal registry overcomes this problem, because it allows people to register only once. They need not know the state in which any other party to the adoption lives; they need not register with every state registry. They need only go through the process once. Even if states establish procedures to share information, as proposed by the Uniform Adoption Act, it would not solve the problem; states would not collect information uniformly, and might establish inconsistent procedures concerning when information can be released. For example, for an adopted child to register in New York, not only must she have been born there, but she must also have been adopted in that state. Other states require counselling when someone registers, something which may be a physical impossibility. Consequently, these state registries may be unable to perform matches that could be facilitated through a federal registry that had uniform standards for collecting information. Moreover, state registries are often overwhelmed by the number of intrastate requests that they receive; interstate cooperation could delay the matching process even further.

Second, registration with many state and other types of registries may be expensive. For people with few financial resources, finding out about and then registering with different registries may be extremely difficult. Not everyone has access to the Internet, for example, which closes off many possible registries to those people. The existence of state registries is often not adequately publicized, much less the existence of registries in other states. Moreover, even for someone with access to all of the information, the sheer number of registries may be daunting as someone begins to search, without enough of a basis to choose among the different ones. And, as a [June 1, 1998] *Washington Post* article pointed out, while private registries such as those available on the Internet can be extremely helpful, "the Net also is a mecca for con artists and private investigators." The establishment of a federal Mutual Voluntary Adoption Registry would solve these problems by providing one centralized, well-organized location for searches.

While some may be concerned about the need for a federal registry in the traditionally state-based area of family law, the federal registry does not encroach on state autonomy at all. Unlike other legislation in the adoption area, or in other areas of family law, it places no obligations on states, nor does it require states to change their adoption practices in any way. A mutual voluntary federal registry simply serves as a resource for adult adoptees and their siblings and birth parents who want to contact one another.

> *"The proposed federal Mutual Voluntary Adoption Registry is entirely consistent with the history of adoption."*

(3) Preserving the Confidentiality of the Adoption Process

Let me emphasize that the information that would be available to a registry, and through a registry, would not violate state laws on the secrecy of adoption records. First of all, the Senate legislation itself provides that it would not preempt states' laws on the confidentiality of adoption records. Thus, states would not be required to release any information that is sealed and confidential. The secrecy of adoption files remains entirely unaffected by this Senate legislation. We are all familiar

> *"Information that would be available to a registry . . . would not violate state laws on the secrecy of adoption records."*

with the very few stories in which adoptees or birth parents are contacted and told information that they do not want to hear. But these stories are entirely unrelated to legislation concerning the establishment of a federal mutual voluntary adoption registry which would only allow contact when two individuals independently and voluntarily file with the registry, and which would also impose penalties for the unauthorized release of information provided to the registry.

Personal Information

Second, the information provided to a federal Mutual Voluntary Adoption Registry would be information personal to the adoptees, their siblings, and their biological parents. For example, my husband might send in the following information: "I weighed 7 pounds, six ounces, and I was born in Good Samaritan Hospital in Cincinnati, Ohio, on April 3, 1956 at 7:00 a.m.; I was adopted in Cincinnati through Catholic Charities later that same month." This is information that he knows, and that he is constitutionally able to reveal, regardless of the existence of sealed records which also contain these facts. Not to allow him to do this could be a violation of his First Amendment rights to freedom of speech. This information, when sent to a federal Mutual Voluntary Adoption Registry, would almost certainly allow the registry to match him with a biological parent who had also registered and provided comparable information.

Third, a federal Mutual Voluntary Adoption Registry provides a legitimate method for facilitating contact, rather than the current system in which adoptees, birth parents and siblings may seek to circumvent state laws on adoption by trying (and frequently succeeding) in finding information without the consent of the other party. The information provided to the registry would be comparatively minimal, especially in light of all of the information already provided to the federal government as a result of other Congressional legislation, such as that involved in the child support area. For example, as a result of recent legislation, employers must provide the names and social security numbers as well as other information to the federal government for all new hires.

There are some who think that the only information that should be available through an adoption registry is medical information because this will provide the most protection to the integrity of the adoption process. That, however, denies the strong psychological need for contact between parent, adult adoptee, or siblings that I talked about earlier in my testimony. While the release of medical information is undoubtedly helpful to the adoptive parents and child, the goal of the federal Mutual Voluntary Adoption Registry is to allow the members of the biological family to find each other.

Mr. Chairman, and members of the Subcommittee, I have discussed the proposed legislation authorizing the creation of the federal Mutual Voluntary Adoption Registry with many people throughout the country, some of whom are involved in adoption issues, but most of whom are not. They cannot believe that there could be any controversy in allowing adult adoptees to contact biological parents or siblings who have indicated that they, too, want contact. What the Senate legislation would authorize is, simply, a mutual *and* voluntary registry at no cost to the federal government, and available only to adults. This can be done, but only if there is the will to do it.

Chapter 4

Should Adoptions by Gays and Lesbians Be Permitted?

Changing Policies Toward Gay Adoption: An Overview

by Heather Salerno

About the author: *Heather Salerno is a reporter for the* Journal News, *a newspaper serving New York.*

In the airy living room of her family's Croton-on-Hudson bungalow [in New York], Jian Gallo-Kohn settles between her parents with a Dragon Tales coloring book. A brick-red crayon in hand, the 6-year-old squirms on the cream-colored sofa. A tiny frown wrinkles her forehead.

"I need a lot of books piled up, so I don't have to bend down," Jian announces softly, and Jean Gallo gathers a stack from the coffee table. Jian fiddles a bit and decides that this solution isn't working. Before anyone can stop her, she wrestles an ottoman cushion to the floor, and sits on it cross-legged.

She smiles and nods. "Much better."

"Oh my goodness!" exclaims Gallo.

"Good job," says Gallo's partner, Amy Kohn.

The couple might be surprised by their daughter's sudden movements, but they're not shocked by her problem-solving skills. Jian displays the same quiet independence when curious classmates ask her why she has two mommies.

"Usually she says nothing, but that's her nature. There's not an aggressive bone in her body," says Kohn. "Or she'll say, 'Every family is different.'"

Nontraditional American families have become more visible in recent years. There are children who have single or divorced parents; children living with stepparents; and girls and boys raised by grandmothers, aunts or foster parents.

Among these emerging families are six to 10 million gay parents who are mothers and fathers to an estimated six to 14 million children, according to the Lambda Legal Defense and Education Fund, a national gay-rights organization.

Most of those households are step or blended families, in which a parent liv-

Heather Salerno, "Gay and Lesbian Adoption," *The Journal News*, November 17, 2002. Copyright © 2002 by *The Journal News*, a Gannett Co. Inc. Reproduced by permission.

ing with a same-sex partner has a biological child from a heterosexual relationship or marriage. In other instances, gay couples are having children together by taking advantage of sperm donors, surrogate mothers and other reproductive technologies.

And adoption is an increasingly popular way for gays and lesbians to build their families.

Gay Adoptions

There are no national figures on gay adoptions; one reason is that few states allow joint—or simultaneous—adoptions by same-sex couples. And many social workers don't ask about a single applicant's sexual orientation.

"Agencies have not really been tracking this," says Ada White, director of adoption services at the Child Welfare League of America. "I think agencies are looking for adoptive parents to provide a child with safety, stability and a sense of belonging, and less at sexual preference."

A growing number of child-welfare groups and medical associations have come out in support of adoption by gay men and lesbians, including the Child Welfare League, the American Academy of Pediatrics, the American Academy of Family Physicians, the American Psychological Association and the North American Council on Adoptable Children.

In 1995, the psychological association surveyed available research on gay parenting. After looking at 43 studies, the group concluded that "the results of existing research comparing gay and lesbian parents to heterosexual parents, and children of gay or lesbian parents to children of heterosexual parents are quite uniform: common stereotypes are not supported by the data."

The most outspoken critics claim such studies are biased. Among them is the Family Research Council, an organization that champions families with heterosexual, married parents, which contends that children raised in homosexual households are at greater risk for emotional, social and sexual-identity problems.

In a written statement posted on the group's Web site, its president, Ken Connor, says: "The sad fact is that promiscuity, domestic violence, and other problems endemic to the homosexual lifestyle make these relationships inherently unstable, and thus unsuitable for the raising of children."

The public appears split on the issue. In an ABC News poll conducted earlier this year [2002], supporters of gay adoption outnumbered opponents

> *"Adoption is an increasingly popular way for gays and lesbians to build their families."*

for the first time—but by a slender margin. Forty-seven percent of 1,031 adults surveyed thought gay couples should be legally permitted to adopt, compared with 35 percent four years ago and 28 percent in 1994.

There is no better illustration of this conflict than a Florida lawsuit that seeks to overturn a state law banning gay adoption. (In Florida, adoption applicants must indicate their sexual orientation.)

Two of the plaintiffs, Steve Lofton and Roger Croteau, were thrown into the national spotlight in March [2002] after Rosie O'Donnell spoke publicly about their plight. Because of the law, the couple aren't able to adopt Bert, one of their five foster children, whom they've raised since he was nine weeks old.

O'Donnell herself was prohibited from adopting her young foster daughter, Mia, who was later adopted by a married couple.

In an interview with Diane Sawyer, during which O'Donnell discussed her own sexuality, the former talk-show host said: "You have to really want to save a child who others have deemed unsavable. And for the state of Florida to tell anyone who's willing, capable and able to do that, that they're unworthy, is wrong."

Amy Kohn, 47, the chief executive officer of the YWCA of White Plains and Central Westchester, and Gallo, 56, a facilities director at Westchester Jewish Community Services, faced few legal obstacles when adopting Jian. Still, the Florida case reminds them of the discrimination that gay parents across the country face every day.

"It's mind-boggling," says Gallo.

The women look proudly at Jian, who has quietly abandoned her artwork for an after-dinner snack of canned peaches.

> *"The Family Research Council . . . contends that children raised in homosexual households are at greater risk for emotional . . . problems."*

"I don't think the three of us could be better off under any circumstances," says Kohn. "I just wouldn't change a thing."

A Tough Decision

One of the toughest parental decisions for Kohn and Gallo emerged before they met their daughter.

As they applied to a California agency specializing in Chinese adoptions in 1996, they knew that the country did not welcome gay adoptive parents. They didn't hide their relationship during a home study (a social worker's evaluation of potential parents), but Kohn was named as a single parent on all Chinese paperwork.

"It did list Jean as an occupant at our address, but made no mention of our relationship," she says. "It was really left as benign as that."

"I guess it was like, don't ask, don't tell."

So when the couple got a call about Jian 15 months later, they agreed that Kohn should go overseas with one of Gallo's longtime friends, Elvira Macri, who is now Jian's godmother.

"It just wasn't a comfortable situation for us to go to China together, largely because we didn't want to lie," says Kohn. "We didn't want to pretend that one of us wasn't the parent."

That meant Gallo wouldn't be there to comfort an 11-month-old Jian when she cried at the orphanage in Guangzhou. Nor would she be there to change Jian's diaper for the first time.

Instead, Gallo helped Kohn pack bags filled with antibiotics, cortisone cream and other prescriptions that the couple's pediatrician recommended in case Jian had an immediate health problem. They withdrew thousands of dollars to pay the balance of the adoption costs, which totaled $17,000 with travel.

> *"Prospective adoptive parents need to tread carefully . . . when it comes to disclosing their homosexuality."*

Kohn and Macri embarked on a whirlwind six-day trip to China, and Gallo stayed behind to baby-proof the house (they then lived in Carmel). She put up safety gates, locked cabinets and plugged electrical outlets. She assembled a crib, and stocked up on baby food.

Despite the separation, the couple believe that they made the right decision.

"We interact in a certain way—it comes off clearly that we're a couple, and we would have been hypervigilant about it," says Kohn. "We always had this thing that the beginning of a beautiful life shouldn't be based on a lie."

Prospective adoptive parents need to tread carefully, though, when it comes to disclosing their homosexuality. According to the National Adoption Information Clearinghouse, it is legal to omit information about one's sexual orientation during the adoption process. But if applicants lie when asked directly, they are committing fraud.

Other adoption professionals, like the Child Welfare League's Ada White, take issue with this interpretation of the law.

"It would be fraud, wouldn't it, if you didn't tell the whole truth," says White. "Leaving things out is sometimes wrongful adoption."

Since Kohn and Gallo adopted Jian, China has tightened loopholes that allowed adoption by gays and lesbians. Now applicants must sign statements that they are unmarried and not homosexual.

This policy saddens both women, and Kohn worries that many Chinese children might now languish in orphanages: "We actually have friends who were about to go (to China), and they switched their plans to Guatemala."

China isn't the only country with such restrictions. Panama, too, bans homosexuals from adopting. Korea and Thailand do not allow unmarried people to adopt, which eliminates same-sex couples along with single parents.

As Cindy Freidmutter, executive director of the Evan B. Donaldson Adoption Institute, says, "Other cultures are very different from ours, and we have to respect that they set the rules."

Confusing Rules

In this country, supporters and detractors have been engaged in a head-spinning legislative tug-of-war that makes it challenging for gays and lesbians to determine exactly where they can adopt.

Gay adoptions have been granted in nearly half the states, but even in those, outcomes of cases are hard to predict. "It can be easier or harder, depending on where you live," notes Ed Sedarbaum, former executive director of the LOFT in White Plains, the largest community-based gay organization in the region.

Indeed, unless a statewide law or court ruling has been put into effect, decisions can hinge on the county in which a gay applicant resides, what judge hears a case and whether someone is adopting as an individual or as part of a same-sex couple.

New Jersey and New York are among the more progressive states when it comes to gay and lesbian parenting rights. In 1997, New Jersey became the first state to allow a joint adoption by a same-sex couple. The New Jersey Supreme Court also issued a landmark decision in 2000, ruling that a lesbian who helped raise her then-partner's children was a "psychological parent," and granted visitation rights.

New York was one of the first states to recognize second-parent adoption, a court proceeding that allows a same-sex co-parent to legally adopt his or her partner's child. (Data compiled by the National Gay and Lesbian Task Force shows that second-parent adoptions have been granted in the District of Columbia and 22 other states.)

Once Kohn returned home and re-adopted Jian—something that many parents adopting a child from overseas do to secure their relationship under U.S. law— Gallo had no trouble obtaining a second-parent adoption in a Putnam County court.

Gay rights advocates saw the New York and New Jersey rulings as a move toward equality, particularly since they came on the heels of another triumph: In 1999, New Hampshire repealed an 11-year-old statute that prohibited homosexuals from adopting or becoming foster parents.

> *"China has tightened loopholes that allowed adoption by gays and lesbians."*

Kate Kendell, executive director of the San Francisco-based National Center for Lesbian Rights, says these actions provided "a brief, bright window where it appeared that rationality and objectivity and fairness were finally going to be fundamental principals in dealing with lesbians and gay men and adoption."

Yet as Kendell notes, these victories were short-lived. Laws considered unfavorable to gay and lesbian families were soon introduced in nine other states. Arkansas's Child Welfare Agency Review Board passed a state regulation in 1999 that prohibited agencies from placing children with foster parents who are gay or who share a household with someone who has engaged in same-sex sexual behavior. Lawyers for the American Civil Liberties Union . . . point out that this policy affects prospective foster parents who are gay and straight: One heterosexual married man was ineligible because his gay son lives at home.

Currently [November 2002], there are laws that explicitly ban gay adoption in Florida, Utah and Mississippi.

The Florida law, which dates to 1977 and is being challenged in a Miami appeals court,[1] blocks all homosexuals from adopting—whether applying as an individual or with a partner. In March 2000, Utah enacted legislation that bars unmarried, cohabitating couples from becoming adoptive or foster parents. Two months later, adoption by same-sex couples was outlawed in Mississippi.

According to Kendell of the lesbian-rights center, more legislative activity on this topic has taken place in the last two years [2000–2002] than in the entire preceding decade.

"From my perspective, it appeared that many folks realized for the first time that we were adopting," she says. "It was as if it finally hit the radar screens of the radical right and fundamentalist conservative organizations."

Other Obstacles

These laws are the most overt obstacles facing gay adoptive parents, but some activists claim that there are less obvious hindrances, too.

Private adoption agencies can issue eligibility requirements used to accept or reject an applicant. Such restrictions may address sexual orientation, but they just as often discriminate based on age, marital status, income, health or the number of children already present in a household.

"There are laws that explicitly ban gay adoption in Florida, Utah and Mississippi."

Adoption professionals can also let their own prejudices—whether conscious or unconscious—affect final judgments about gay adoptive parents.

"You never know what kinds of considerations your particular agency or individual social worker brings to the job," says attorney Jennifer Middleton of the Lambda Legal Defense and Education Fund.

Even if an agency makes it a practice to support gay or lesbian parents, birth parents are not always as open-minded. In many domestic adoptions, birth mothers choose a family from a long list of waiting parents who have provided albums filled with photographs and detailed biographical information.

"We feel it's our obligation and responsibility to give (birth parents) the widest range of options," says Gretchen Viederman, director of domestic adoption programs at Spence-Chapin Services to Families and Children, a private adoption agency based in Manhattan. "But they can choose anyone they want."

Some gay and lesbian adopters are troubled, too, by a sense that there is an unspoken agency ranking that places white, married upper-class couples in the

---

1. Arguments were held before a federal appeals court in March 2003; no decision had been reached as of October 2003.

top slot—particularly when considering the placement of a healthy white infant, the most sought-after child.

Critics say gays and lesbians are sometimes offered only hard-to-place children, which includes older children, and babies with complex medical or psychiatric needs. At Family Focus Adoption Services, a Little Neck, N.Y., agency that places mostly foster care children, executive director Maris Blechner says this hierarchy, if true, might stem partly from the gay community's history of caring for the ill and disabled.

> *"Critics say gays and lesbians are sometimes only offered hard-to-place children."*

"They stepped forward to take care of babies with AIDS in the late 1980s when no one else would touch them, and people found out that they made wonderful parents," she says.

Blechner agrees that gays and lesbians can be wonderful resources for hard-to-place kids, but she says the most important criterion for parents willing to adopt children with emotional or physical disabilities is whether they can provide a loving, stable environment.

"We feel many different kinds of people make good parents to many different kinds of children," she says. "Gay applicants should be treated exactly the same way as straight applicants. Children need a solid, sensitive, open-minded family who can relate to what they've been through."

Jian is only a first-grader at Carrie E. Tompkins Elementary School, but her mothers are already preparing her for taunts from classmates and strangers. To pre-empt any misunderstandings when Jian started school in September, they wrote a heartfelt introductory letter that explained her background.

"I was really proud of us putting it all out there, in anticipation of any problems," says Kohn. "The response we've gotten has been just astonishing, really wonderful."

Harassment Concerns

So far Jian hasn't heard a single harsh word about having gay parents. Other children's comments have been mostly inquisitive. Jian's teacher gave Kohn and Gallo several books about adoption, some of which feature two moms.

Yet the couple knows the day will come when Jian must confront a hostile remark or attitude. To prepare her, they've talked to her about how she can respond.

Gallo jokes that if Jian were a boy, she'd tell her to react by "clocking 'em!"

"We're going to worry about her the way any other parent worries about any potential hurt that their child is going to go through, whatever that child's vulnerabilities are," says Kohn.

The women can't believe that Jian will suffer long-term harm if she's teased or harassed. Besides, they add, bullies could choose Jian as a target for reasons that have nothing to do with her parents' sexual orientation.

"It could be because she looks different, or wasn't as smart, or wasn't as beautiful," says Kohn. "It could be anything, whether she's tall or short. Whatever she's going to go through, she's going to be stronger for it, and so are we."

Harassment is just one concern voiced by those arguing against gay adoption. They also fear that these youngsters will develop an impaired sense of sexual identity or become gay; that they'll be more vulnerable to mental breakdowns, behavioral problems and psychological troubles; and that they're more likely to be sexually abused by their parents' friends.

Contradictory Research Findings

With the increase in gay and lesbian parenting, researchers are taking a harder look at these worries.

Not surprisingly, research findings have been contradictory.

Groups like the American Psychological Association and the American Academy of Pediatrics have said that the bulk of evidence shows that children with gay parents suffered no significant detrimental effects, and that they are no different from their counterparts with heterosexual parents. Foes insist that these studies are distorted because the researchers themselves are gay or defend gay rights, or that the medical associations have overlooked or twisted data to come to faulty conclusions.

Focus on the Family, a national organization in Colorado Springs, maintains that children do better with a married mother and father. Bill Maier, the group's vice president and psychologist-in-residence, points to past studies that suggest that gay men and lesbians are at a higher risk for suicide, depression and substance abuse.

"If we know that the research is telling us that children raised by homosexuals are more likely to have problems, are we being responsible by advocating gay adoption as broad social policy?" says Maier.

Clinton Anderson, the lesbian, gay and bisexual concerns officer at the American Psychological Association, notes that research on gay parenting is slim. Yet the information available is consistent, he says, and there is no indication that people should be discriminated against as parents because of their sexual orientation.

Anderson acknowledges that those who engage in same-sex behavior may have disproportionate rates of depression and other psychological difficulties. However, he says, this

"So far, Jian hasn't heard a single harsh word about having gay parents."

finding shouldn't exclude all gay men and lesbians as potential parents.

"We don't make decisions like that in this country based on those kinds of things," he says. "We don't look at whole groups of people and say something like, 'You are susceptible to getting cancer, therefore, you don't deserve to have children.'"

One research paper garnering a great deal of attention was conducted by University of Southern California sociology professors Judith Stacey and Timothy J. Biblarz, whose work was published in the American Sociological Review last year [2001]. Stacey and Biblarz analyzed 21 studies that claimed to find no difference in developmental outcomes when comparing children raised by gay men or lesbians with children raised by heterosexuals.

The authors found that the data suggested some contrast in gender behavior and sexual preferences. But, the two stressed, these differences should not be considered deficits.

Stacey and Biblarz discovered that children of gay parents showed no variation in levels of self-esteem, anxiety, depression, behaviorial problems, emotional difficulty and cognitive functioning, but that they were more affectionate, responsive and concerned about younger children.

These youngsters were also less likely to be stereotyped by gender. Daughters with lesbian mothers, for example, showed less interest in typical feminine dress and more interest in activities that involved participation of both sexes. They were also more likely to aspire to nontraditional female occupations such as engineer or astronaut.

One of the more controversial conclusions in the Stacey and Biblarz study is that these children were "significantly" more likely to experience homosexual attraction and relationships. Maier uses this point to chip away at support for gay parenting: "In this day and age, where homosexual experimentation can lead to death from AIDS, it would seem to me that that's taking a big risk."

Stacey and Biblarz, though, add that the majority of these young people identified themselves as heterosexual, even if they had engaged in a same-sex relationship.

Regarding harassment that might be inflicted on children because of their parents' homosexuality, the authors write, "Granting legal rights and respect to gay parents and their children should lessen the stigma that they now suffer."

Today, Jian's more interested in the Olsen twins (Mary-Kate and Ashley, of course) than in why she has two mothers.

Kohn and Gallo are surprised that she hasn't asked more questions. When she does ask about their relationship, they plan to be as honest about it as they have been about her adoption.

"She's known her China story. We've been telling it to her since she was a baby," says Kohn.

"Even before she could understand it," adds Gallo.

But maybe, in Jian's mind, having two mothers doesn't make her different.

"Jean and I were out to a great extent for many years. But when you have a child, it's a whole other level of being out," says Kohn. "You're out at the cleaners, because she turns to both of you and says 'Mom.' You're out at restaurants, at the drugstore."

To Jian, Gallo is just Mom. Kohn is simply Mommy.

Sexual Orientation Should Not Be a Barrier to Adoption

by Jeffrey G. Gibson

About the author: *Jeffrey G. Gibson, a trial lawyer, served for six years on the American Bar Associaton's (ABA) Committee on the Rights of Lesbians and Gay Men.*

There are many children in the United States in need of the stability of a permanent home with good parents, including large numbers of foster children. Despite this growing need, many prospective parents who are identified as gay or lesbian have been refused as candidates for adopting children solely on the basis of their sexual orientation. The American Bar Association (ABA) has an interest in the laws and policies that will promote the increased permanent placement of children in stable homes with good parents. It also has long been a leader in efforts to eradicate bigotry and prejudice against, among other groups, gay and lesbian Americans. In 1995, the ABA extended policy developments regarding nondiscrimination on the basis of sexual orientation to the field of family law by adopting a policy supporting legislative measures to ensure that child custody or visitation is not denied or restricted on the basis of sexual orientation.

On February 8, 1999, the Association adopted a Resolution sponsored by the Section of Individual Rights and Responsibilities, the Section of Family Law, the Steering Committee on the Unmet Legal Needs of Children, and the National Gay and Lesbian Law Association, which provides:

> RESOLVED, that the American Bar Association supports the enactment of laws and implementation of public policy that provide that sexual orientation shall not be a bar to adoption when the adoption is determined to be in the best interest of the child.

On November 19, 1997, President [Bill] Clinton signed the Adoption and

Jeffrey G. Gibson, "Lesbian and Gay Prospective Adoptive Parents: The Legal Battle," *Human Rights*, vol. 26, Spring 1999, pp. 7–11. Copyright © 1999 by the American Bar Association. Reproduced by permission.

Safe Families Act into law, which was intended to promote adoption or other permanent arrangements for foster children who are unable to return home and to make general improvements in the nation's child welfare system. The legislation responded to concerns that children were remaining in foster care unnecessarily long, that their adoption rate continued to be low, and that additional safeguards were needed to ensure their safety. In response to this federal legislation, states have begun to revisit their adoption laws. Unfortunately, conservative organizations have made this state review an opportunity to introduce legislation that would prohibit gay or lesbian prospective parents from being eligible to adopt, even though the adoption may be in the best interest of the child. . . . Hopefully, this newly adopted ABA resolution will provide guidance to courts, legislatures, and legal practitioners who will require guidance on these issues in drafting and reviewing draft laws for the various states.

Children of Lesbian and Gay Parent Families

Barriers faced in preserving and protecting family relationships. Many children are being raised in lesbian and gay parent families in which both partners have parented the child since the child's infancy or birth, and have undertaken all the obligations and responsibilities of equal parenthood. For the great majority of these families, second parent or joint adoptions are the *only* legal avenue through which both parents can establish a legal parental relationship to the couple's child. In jurisdictions where these forms of adoption are not available, lesbian and gay parents attempt to protect their relationship with their children through a variety of privately executed documents: wills, guardianship agreements, authorization to consent to emergency medical treatments, and the like. While lesbian and gay parents willingly assume these obligations, these documents do not create a legally recognized parental relationship, and they are vastly inferior to the security and protection of legal recognition through adoption. In the absence of a legally protected parental relationship, the child has no right to financial support or inheritance from the second parent, cannot receive Social Security benefits or state workers' compensation benefits if the second parent dies or becomes incapacitated, and cannot

> *"Conservative organizations have . . . [introduced] legislation that would prohibit gay or lesbian prospective parents from being eligible to adopt."*

receive health insurance or other insurance benefits from the second parent's employer in the majority of cases. The second parent may not be eligible for leave to care for a seriously ill child under the Family and Medical Leave Act. In the event of an emergency in which the legal parent is unavailable, the second parent may be unable to consent to medical treatment for the child—or even to visit the child in a hospital emergency room.

If the parents separate, adoption is critical to protect the child's right to financial support and to maintain a relationship with the second parent. Courts in family law situations generally attempt to ensure ongoing contact between a child and both of his or her parents, even when the family unit is no longer intact. This is based on the recognition that ongoing contact with the parents is almost invariably in the best interest of the children because "children generally will sustain serious emotional harm when deprived of emotional benefits flowing from a true parent-child relationship." In the absence of a legally defined parent-child relationship, children of lesbian and gay parents are routinely deprived of this right.

Similarly, if the legal parent dies or is incapacitated, the child may become a ward of the state or be placed in foster care or with relatives of the legal parent with whom the child has no bond. The nomination of the second parent in the legal parent's will as the child's guardian is merely that—a nomination. Courts are not required to approve the guardianship nomination. Moreover, there is always a risk that relatives of the legal parent can and will challenge such a guardianship nomination. Even if the surviving partner ultimately prevails, the nomination does not prevent expensive and time-consuming litigation, and the concomitant trauma and injury to the child during the intervening period of uncertainty.

The . . . case of Victoria Lane demonstrates the critical difference that second parent adoptions can and do make in protecting children in lesbian and gay parent families. Victoria Lane was granted a second parent adoption of Laura Solomon's biolog-

> *"Social science research has confirmed . . . that a person's sexual orientation has no bearing on his or her capacity to be a good parent."*

ical child, Tessa, and Laura Solomon was granted a second parent adoption of Victoria's biological child, Maya, by a District of Columbia trial court. Two years later, Victoria Lane was killed in an automobile accident. Due to the second parent adoption, Laura, as the surviving parent, had no need to undergo any court action to protect her relationship with her deceased partner's child. Both children were eligible for Social Security survivor benefits, and both were permitted to file an action for wrongful death. If a second parent adoption had not been in place, both children's financial stability would have been seriously impaired, and Maya might well have undergone the additional trauma of being legally separated from her surviving parent.

Sexual orientation's irrelevance to parental ability. Social science research has confirmed what experience and common sense have already demonstrated: that a person's sexual orientation has no bearing on his or her capacity to be a good parent. In fact, [social scientist Beverly Hoeffer writes that] studies have found "a remarkable absence of distinguishing features between the lifestyles, childrearing practices, and general demographic data" of lesbian and gay parents and those who are not gay. The American Psychological Association

(APA) reports that "not a single study has found children of gay or lesbian parents to be disadvantaged in any significant respect relative to children of heterosexual parents. Indeed, the evidence to date suggests that home environments provided by gay and lesbian parents are as likely as those provided by heterosexual parents to support and enable children's psychosocial growth." In all respects, lesbians and gay men have proven to be just as committed to the parental role and just as capable of being good parents as their heterosexual counterparts.

> *"Courts should evaluate all prospective adoptive parents on the basis of their individual character and ability to parent, not merely on their sexual orientation."*

Given this overwhelming evidence, numerous professional organizations have condemned discrimination against lesbian and gay parents. In 1976, the APA affirmed that "[t]he sex, gender identity [transgender], or sexual orientation of natural, or prospective adoptive or foster parents should not be the sole or primary variable considered in custody or placement cases." The National Association of Social Workers (NASW) has long affirmed that gay men and lesbians are capable parents. The NASW policy statement on lesbian and gay issues deplores the fact that lesbians and gay men have been denied custody of children and the right to provide foster and adoptive care. The policy holds that NASW shall work for the adoption of policies and legislation to end all forms of discrimination on the basis of sexual orientation. The code of ethics adopted by the NASW Delegate Assembly further states that "the social worker should not practice, condone, facilitate or collaborate with any form of discrimination on the basis of . . . sexual orientation.". . .

Types of Adoption

The growing visibility of lesbian and gay parent families has contributed to a dramatic decrease in antigay discrimination on the part of adoption agencies and courts. Despite much progress, however, significant obstacles to equal treatment remain, including efforts to pass new state laws that would categorically prohibit lesbians and gay men from being eligible to adopt.

The following is a brief description of the different types of adoption that are available to lesbian and gay parents. . . .

Individual adoptions. Every state permits unmarried individuals to adopt. Individual adoptions—sometimes called "stranger" adoptions—are adoptions in which a single (i.e., unmarried) person adopts a child who has been placed for adoption by his or her biological parent or parents, who have agreed to give up all of their parental rights. Individual adoptions may take place through (1) a state child welfare or public adoption agency; (2) a private, state-authorized adoption agency; or (3) consensual arrangements between private parties, including everything from the adoption of the child of a relative, acquaintance, or friend to the adoption of an orphan situated abroad and brought into the United States. Like all adoptions, individual adoptions must be reviewed and approved by a court and almost always include a home investigation by the state's child welfare agency. . . .

Second parent adoptions. "Second parent adoption" is a legal term of art used to describe an adoption in which a lesbian, gay man, or unmarried heterosexual person adopts his or her partner's child, as a means of ensuring that both parents have a legally recognized parental relationship to the child. The concept of second parent adoption was originated by the National Center for Lesbian Rights (formerly the Lesbian Rights Project) in the mid-1980s, when the first such adoptions were granted in San Francisco. Since that time, a number of high-profile and high-level cases in other states have begun to establish second parent adoption as a formal legal protection for same-sex parent families. . . .

Joint adoptions. Joint adoption refers to an adoption in which both partners in a couple *simultaneously* adopt a child who, at least in the usual case, has no biological or preexisting adoptive relationship to either party. Joint adoption is especially important for gay male couples, for whom adopting a child is often the only viable route to becoming parents. Until very recently, joint adoptions have been restricted to married couples, with the exception of a steady stream of cases granted by lower courts in the San Francisco Bay Area from the mid-1980s to the present.

On December 21, 1997, however, New Jersey became the focus of national media attention when it announced a formal statewide policy permitting lesbian, gay, and other unmarried couples to jointly adopt. New Jersey adopted the policy in a consent agreement reached in a class action suit brought by the American Civil Liberties Union on behalf of more than 200 lesbian and gay couples, including Jon Holden and Michael Galluccio, the named plaintiffs in the suit, who sought to adopt the two-year-old foster child who had been living with them since he was three months old. Under the terms of the agreement, the New Jersey Division of Youth and Family Services must apply the same standards to all prospective adoptive parents, without regard to marital status or sexual orientation.

A Final Thought

Every child deserves a permanent home and all the love and care that good parents can provide. Each child is entitled to the emotional and financial security that follows from legal recognition of his or her family relationships. For these reasons, courts should evaluate all prospective adoptive parents on the basis of their individual character and ability to parent, not merely on their sexual orientation. In addition, courts should also grant second parent and joint adoptions when they are determined to be in a child's best interest.

Restrictions on Gay and Lesbian Adoptions Are Unconstitutional

by the Lesbian & Gay Rights Project

About the author: *The American Civil Liberties Union (ACLU) is the nation's oldest and largest civil liberties organization. Its Lesbian & Gay Rights Project, started in 1986, handles litigation and education work on behalf of gays and lesbians.*

Most states in the country consider adoption applications on a case-by-case basis and have no blanket ban on adoption by lesbians and gay men. Nevertheless, sometimes judges deny adoption applications either explicitly because a prospective parent is gay, or under circumstances which make it fairly easy to conclude that was the reason (to have any chance of successfully attacking an order which is not explicit, the anti-gay motive has to be pretty obvious).

One way to attack these orders is to say that they are not allowed under state law. Since state laws usually require a case-by-case evaluation, it can be argued with considerable force that state law simply does not allow decisions to be based on one aspect of a person's identity. More importantly, since most state laws require that decisions be based on the "best interests of the child," arguably no factor should even be used against a prospective parent (much less be the basis for a disqualification) unless it is actually shown to be harmful or damaging to children.

A few states do have laws which restrict gay adoption. This section outlines some of the constitutional arguments that can be used to challenge those restrictions (and which can also be used to challenge an individual judge's decision to deny an adoption because a prospective parent is gay). And of course, these are also the constitutional concerns that will inevitably arise in any legislation aimed at excluding lesbians and gay men from being able to adopt.

The restrictions on adoption by lesbians and gay men that currently exist [in

Lesbian & Gay Rights Project, *Too High a Price: The Case Against Restricting Gay Parenting*. New York: American Civil Liberties Union, 2002. Copyright © 2002 by the American Civil Liberties Union. All rights reserved. Reproduced by permission.

2002] take several forms . . . Florida bans adoption by all gay people. Mississippi bans adoption by lesbian or gay couples, but has no ban on adoption by single people, even if they are lesbian or gay. Utah restricts adoption to married couples, which of course effectively excludes lesbians and gay men, who cannot marry (and are exactly who that law was targeting when it passed). Finally, Arkansas and Nebraska do not ban adoption by lesbians and gay men but do prohibit them from becoming foster parents.

The Fourteenth Amendment

The primary weapon against restrictions on adoption by lesbians and gay men is the U.S. Constitution. The Fourteenth Amendment to the Constitution mandates that all citizens are entitled to equal protection under the law. The courts say this means that the government may not treat one group of people differently from others unless it can fairly say that it is treating them differently to achieve some legitimate policy goal. Except when the group singled out for unfavorable treatment is one that has historically been the target of prejudice, the courts give government tremendous leeway in deciding if it is fair to treat a group differently. So most of the time, the courts say that the different treatment must simply have a "rational relationship" to a "legitimate state interest." That means, the courts say, that if anyone could rationally think that treating the group in question differently would help bring about a legitimate policy goal, the government can do it. The focus is on what someone could (legitimately) think about what different treatment would accomplish, not whether, in the end, they are right or wrong about what it does.

So far, most courts have not been willing to say that lesbians and gay men have historically been victims of prejudice. So the analysis which gives the government so much leeway is usually the one used to evaluate bans on adoption by gay people. Even so, the bans should not survive.

First, states often admit that the purportedly "legitimate state interest" of a restriction on adoption is some version of expressing disapproval of lesbians and gay men. But disadvantaging any group of people, including lesbians and gay men, simply to say that you don't like them is not a "legitimate" state purpose. As the U.S. Supreme Court has made clear, "if the constitutional conception of 'equal protection of the laws' means anything, it must at the very least mean that a bare congressional purpose to harm a politically unpopular group cannot constitute a *legitimate* governmental interest." *U.S. Dep't of Agric. v. Moreno*, 413 U.S. 528, 534 (1973). Illegitimate "disapproval" does not become "legitimate" simply because the state says that its disapproval is based in morality. Virtually every time a state has said that it wanted to discriminate against a group because it disap-

> *"The primary weapon against restrictions on adoption by lesbians and gay men is the U.S. Constitution."*

proved of them, that disapproval has been wrapped in "morality." Some states tried to ban interracial relationships, keep women out of the workplace, and even sterilize the mentally disabled, all in the name of morality. The equal protection clause does not allow discrimination against any group just because those in power don't like them, and it doesn't matter if the dislike can be couched in high-minded terms like "morality" or not. Discrimination based on dislike is simply discrimination for its own sake, which is precisely what the equal protection clause forbids.

The Best Interests of Children

Second, states may argue that restrictions on adoption by lesbians and gay men are designed to advance the best interests of children. While this interest looks legitimate at first blush, the equal protection clause still requires that there be a plausible connection between the adoption restriction and the state's goal of ensuring that children are well off. That connection is lacking in most if not all adoption restrictions aimed at lesbians and gay men. For example, if the state's goal is to place as many children as possible with married two-parent families, excluding lesbians and gay men will simply do nothing to further that goal, since the exclusion will not create more married two-parent households willing to adopt. Further, if in fact the state cannot place all of the children in its care in married two-parent families, or even with single parents who are willing to adopt, but instead leaves many children in foster care, the exclusion of lesbians and gay men from the pool of people eligible to adopt simply does not further the state's goal.

> *"What a state does often undercuts its own explanations for restricting adoption by lesbians and gay men."*

What a state does often undercuts its own explanations for restricting adoption by lesbians and gay men. It is not unusual, for example, for a state to place children in long-term foster care with lesbians and gay men, which in effect amounts to permanent placement. Moreover, it is virtually impossible to credibly explain banning adoption by lesbians and gay men, while evaluating all other adoption applicants on a case-by-case basis. . . . There is no credible scientific evidence that heterosexuals make better parents than lesbians and gay men do. So the best the state can offer is speculation.

While at first that might seem to be enough to get past the "rational relationship" standard, the state has a further problem. There is plenty of evidence that people with some character traits generally do make poorer parents. This is true of people with a history of substance abuse, and people with a history of child abuse, as well as people who have abandoned children in the past, and people who have failed to keep up child support in the past. Even far less negative characteristics, like relative poverty, relative lack of education, and having had parents who were abusive or negligent, are said by some to be traits of individuals who will have a harder time becoming good parents. So the formidable task the state faces is explaining why it makes sense to absolutely prohibit gay people from adopting, in the absence of evidence of harm, while all these other groups are permitted to apply and be individually evaluated despite real, concrete evidence of harm.

> *"It seems very clear that gay adoption bans are based on nothing but prejudice."*

If the state cannot explain why it draws the line of blanket exclusion at lesbians and gay men, but allows applications from those whom it knows to pose a significant risk to children, it violates the Constitution's equal protection guarantees.

Denying Equal Protection to Children Raised by Gay Foster Parents

Discriminating against lesbians and gay men in adoption also denies equal protection to children who are being raised by lesbian and gay foster parents, guardians, and other care givers who are otherwise willing and able to adopt them. Unlike their peers who have the potential to be adopted by their heterosexual care givers, and thus, get all of the emotional and tangible benefits associated with being adopted, children raised by lesbians and gay men are shut out of the possibility of being adopted, and instead, left vulnerable to being separated from their families. And for all the reasons detailed above, the equal protection clause does not permit this kind of discrimination against children based on their parents' status.

Restrictions on joint adoption by same-sex couples in states which allow married people to adopt jointly are subject to very similar constitutional objections.

Until 1996, most lower courts assumed that the U.S. Supreme Court would not strike down any law which discriminated against gay people. Particularly in a 1986 case which upheld Georgia's sodomy law, the court displayed considerable hostility to civil rights claims made on behalf of lesbians and gay men. That assumption began to change after the Supreme Court struck down a section of the Colorado constitution that said neither cities nor the state could pass civil rights laws protecting gay people. But attitudes change slowly, and litigation takes time. So while it seems very clear that gay adoption bans are based on nothing but prejudice, it may take some time before the courts strike them down.

Restrictions on Gay and Lesbian Adoptions Harm Children in Need

by Albert R. Hunt

About the author: *Albert R. Hunt is a columnist for the* Wall Street Journal.

Imagine breaking up families and sentencing thousands of kids to perpetual foster care. Yet, under the guise of family values, that's exactly what some social conservatives would do.

Groups like the Family Research Council, and the Traditional Values Coalition, headed by renowned hate monger Lou Sheldon, want to deny gays and lesbians the right to adopt children. Unfortunately this put-these-kids-last posture has the backing of both President George W. Bush and his brother, Florida Governor Jeb Bush.

In a perfect world, each of the more than 100,000 kids waiting to be adopted would be taken in by a caring, responsible husband and wife. But, as Adam Pertman, author of "Adoption Nation: How the Adoption Revolution is Transforming America," notes: "It's far from a perfect world when it comes to adoption." Most kids who can't fit into that perfect world are better off with single parents or gay and lesbian parents.

The issue crystallized when a federal judge upheld a mean-spirited quarter-century-old Florida law that bans adoption by gays or lesbians. There are only two other states, Mississippi and Utah, that prohibit adoptions by gay couples, but there are efforts to make it more difficult elsewhere.

This is hypocrisy writ large. Gay and lesbian couples in Florida can adopt a child in most other states, so it's the kids who are hurt. Moreover, while the social right insists on the sanctity of married couple adoptions, one out of four Florida adoptions is by a single parent.

With the work of Bill Clinton, America's most pro-adoption president, and

Albert R. Hunt, "Blocking Gay Adoption Hurts Kids," *Wall Street Journal*, March 21, 2002. Copyright © 2002 by Dow Jones & Company, Inc. All rights reserved. Reproduced by permission.

sympathetic GOP congressional leaders, adoption is on the upswing. There are more generous tax breaks, states are rewarded for moving kids more expeditiously out of foster care, and transracial barriers are eroding. In 2000 the number of kids adopted from the public foster-care system doubled from five years earlier to 50,000.

Still, the supply outstrips the demand. There were 134,000 children waiting to be adopted in 2000. These aren't babies. On average they are over eight years of age and have been waiting for more than three years.

Gay Parents

The American Academy of Pediatricians recently supported gay adoptions or, more precisely, second-parent adoptions in same-sex couples: "Children who grow up with one or two gay or lesbian parents fare as well in emotional, cognitive, social and sexual functioning as do children whose parents are heterosexual," the pediatricians reported.

"We looked at a lot of data and there is no support for a commonly held belief that these kids are at special risk or do poorly," says Dr. Joseph Hagan, a Burlington, V.T., pediatrician who chaired the committee that directed the study.

Other medical associations and prominent adoption advocates, such as the Dave Thomas Center for Adoption, support this view. But the homophobic right went ballistic. Lou Sheldon labeled the pediatricians a "homosexual" group that wanted to tear down the American family. The Family Research Council insisted data showed this is "incontrovertibly inconsistent" with raising healthy kids. Foes of gay and lesbian adoptions, frequently cite a study by two University of Southern California academics published in the *American Sociological Review*, which they claim proves harmful effects of gay and lesbian parenting.

"That is totally false," replies sociologist Judith Stacey, one of the authors of that study. "They use phony research and then egregiously distort real research."

Professor Stacey's study, actually a review of all the surveys on the subject, paralleled the pediatricians' conclusions. There was one very small British study involving about 50 children which showed kids with a gay or lesbian parent are more inclined to have a homosexual experience. But, she says, that's not conclusive.

It also is largely irrelevant to current realities. Hard data on adoption is remarkably elusive—the census

> *"There's considerable anecdotal evidence suggesting gays and lesbians disproportionately are willing to take these hard-to-adopt kids."*

asked an adoption question for the first time in 2000—but the very reliable Evan B. Donaldson Institute estimates that 30% to 40% of kids in foster care are physically disabled, and as many as 60% have some sort of psychological disorder. There's considerable anecdotal evidence suggesting gays and lesbians disproportionately are willing to take these hard-to-adopt kids.

The Florida Case

In the Florida case,[1] two gay men wanted to adopt a 10-year-old, HIV-positive boy they'd cared for since he was an infant. Gov. Bush's administration also is fighting the efforts of another gay man to adopt a 9-year-old boy he's cared for ever since he was abandoned by his parents.

There are an estimated 3,400 foster-care kids in Florida waiting for adoption. Many, like these two children, suffer special disadvantages. If gays or lesbians aren't permitted to adopt these kids, there is only one recourse: they'll stay in foster care. So when Ken Connor, the president of the Family Research Council, says there's no justification for adoption by a gay or lesbian couple, he sends a simple message to these children: Let them rot.

> *"If gays and lesbians aren't permitted to adopt these kids, there is only one recourse: they'll stay in foster care."*

"We're not talking about kids where there's a long line around the block to adopt," notes Mr. Pertman. "Many of these are the hardest kids to get anybody to take. How anyone justifies putting a child in the ninth foster home in seven years rather than be adopted by someone who wants them is beyond me."

The Analogy to Transracial Adoption

The situation is analogous to the fight over transracial adoption. African-American social workers long argued that to allow whites to adopt black children amounted to "racial genocide." Since there weren't enough prospective African-American adoptive parents, this meant relegating these minority kids to perpetual foster care.

But Bill Clinton backed an effort spearheaded by liberal Democratic Sen. Howard Metzenbaum to break down this barrier. It's okay to give an African-American preference in adopting a baby of the same race. But if that's not possible, it's no longer permissible to block a transracial adoption. This is precisely what ought to be done with gay or lesbian adoptions in Florida and elsewhere.

Enhancing adoption in America is putting kids first. Bill Clinton was right to take on one of his constituencies, black social workers, to further this goal. It will be instructive to see whether Jeb and George W. Bush likewise care more about these kids who need homes, or are more interested in pandering to one of their constituencies, the homophobic right.

---

1. A lawsuit challenging Florida's gay adoption ban was heard in a federal appeals court in March 2003. No decision has been announced as of October 2003.

Legalizing Gay Adoptions Will Strengthen and Stabilize Families

by E.J. Graff

About the author: *E.J. Graff is an author and journalist who has written extensively on same-sex marriage and related issues.*

Imagine waking up one morning to the news that because of a recent court decision, you may no longer be your child's legal parent. Forget all those times you've read *Goodnight Moon*, those long nights you spent in a steam-filled bathroom trying to keep your sick child breathing. In the eyes of the law, you may suddenly be just a kind stranger. No emergency room, insurance plan, schoolteacher, tax man, or judge will count you as essential to your child.

Sound like one of Kafka's nightmares? It's what happened to thousands of California parents last October [2001], when a San Diego court struck down the procedure by which, for 15 years, lesbian co-mothers—parents who helped to imagine, create, feed, clothe, and raise a child, but who didn't give birth—had legally adopted their children. Many California lawyers' phones rang nonstop until the decision was erased from the books while it went up on appeal.[1]

Welcome to the world of lesbian and gay parents, where you can be a parent one day and not the next; in one state but not another; when you're straight but not when you're gay. At any moment, your heterosexual ex might find a judge willing to yank the kids after you come out. Or you might hear your parental fitness debated by strangers—on radio, on TV, and in newspapers—using language that makes your children wake up at night from dreams that the government has taken you away.

Yes, the climate for lesbian and gay parents has improved dramatically in the

1. The California Supreme Court reversed the lower court's decision in August 2003, affirming the validity of second-parent adoptions.

E.J. Graff, "The Other Marriage War," *American Prospect*, vol. 13, April 8, 2002. Copyright © 2002 by *American Prospect*, 5 Broad Street, Boston, MA 02109. Reproduced by permission.

past 20 years. There can't be an American left who hasn't heard about Heather and her two mommies. And though the children's book by that name kicked off an antigay uproar in the early 1990s, by the end of the decade the mainstream media were covering [famous lesbians] Melissa Etheridge and Julie Cypher's two babies without a blink. . . . The lesbian baby boom began in Boston and San Francisco in the mid-1980s. In both cities, after mainstream doctors refused to offer donor insemination (DI) services to unmarried women, lesbians started their own sperm banks and DI clinics. Since then, two-mom families have popped up everywhere from Maine to Utah, from Alaska to Florida. In smaller numbers, gay dads have followed, taking in foster children, hiring surrogates, or adopting (as individuals, if necessary) whenever they could find birth moms, local authorities, or judges who'd help. And that's only the latest incarnation of gay and lesbian parenting. Lesbians and gay men have long become parents the conventional way: through heterosexual marriage.

But law is lagging badly behind this social transformation. Although many [people]. . . may know two-mom or two-dad families, they probably do not know about the daily legal insecurity, the extra level of anxiety and effort, and the occasional shocking injustices those families face. Society is still profoundly ambivalent about lesbians and gay men—and about the unfamiliar, sometimes queasy-making idea of queers raising kids. As a result, unpredictable legal decisions about lesbian and gay parents too often leave their children in limbo.

The Kids Are All Right

Is there any reason to worry about how these kids are raised? No. More than 20 studies have been done on about 300 children of lesbians and gay men. Some compare children of divorced lesbian moms or gay dads with children of divorced heterosexual moms or dads; others compare two-mom families with mom-and-pop families that used the same DI clinic. The results are quite clear: Children of lesbian or gay parents turn out just fine on every conceivable measure of emotional and social development: attachment, self-esteem, moral judgment, behavior, intelligence, likability, popularity, gender identity, family warmth, and all sorts of obscure psychological concepts. Whatever the scale, children with lesbian or gay parents and children with heterosexual parents turn out equally well—and grow up to be heterosexual in the same overwhelming proportions.

Not surprisingly, antigay pundits challenge this conclusion. Brigham Young University law professor Lynn Wardle and his followers argue that the population samples in these studies have been exceedingly small, haven't been "randomly" chosen, and don't accurately represent lesbian and gay parents as a whole. All these charges are accurate, as far as they go. But the conclusion drawn by Wardle and company—that the results are therefore meaningless—is not. Here's the problem: No one can ever get a "random" sample of lesbians or gay men, much less of lesbian or gay *parents*, so long as there's any stigma to being gay—and any realistic fear that the children might be taken away. For the most part, researchers have had to make do with samples of lesbian or gay parents who will consent to being studied and match them with groups of heterosexual parents. Does that limitation invalidate these studies? Maybe it would if results varied dramatically, but because they are remarkably consistent, the vast majority of social scientists and physicians accept them. Social science deals with people, not elements on the periodic table. Like doctors, they must always make informed decisions based on the best and latest evidence.

That's why organizations such as the American Psychological Association, the National Association of Social Workers, the American Academy of Child and Adolescent Psychiatry, and the American Counseling Association have released statements in support of lesbian and gay parents. This February [2002], for instance, the American Academy of Pediatrics came out with a report that had been vetted by an unprecedented number of committees and had taken four years to wend its way toward the academy's full approval. Its conclusion: "No data have pointed to any risk to children as a result of growing up in a family with one or more gay parents." Nor, the AAP found, is parents' sexual orientation an important variable in how kids turn out.

> *"Children with lesbian or gay parents and children with heterosexual parents turn out equally well."*

So what is? If basics like food, shelter, clothing, and health care are covered, what matters to kids is the happiness and satisfaction of the parents. Are the parents happily mated and content with the way household responsibilities are shared? Or are they miserable and sniping at each other, whether together or separated? You can guess which type of household will produce happier and more confident kids. Harmony helps children; conflict and disruption hurt. Despite the yammering of the conservative marriage movement, *how* households are run matters more than *who* (read: which sex or sexual orientation) runs them.

There's another right-wing line of challenge to these studies: shouting about statistical blips. Occasionally, intriguing differences do show up between the children of lesbian moms and those of heterosexual moms. Here, conservatives want it both ways: They want to throw out the common findings because of methodological suspicions while making a big deal about onetime results. But in every case, these variations are differences, not deficits. For instance, in one study of kids with divorced moms, the lesbians' daughters were more comfortable than the heterosexual women's daughters in "rough-and-tumble" play, more likely to play with trucks and guns—although the sons were no more likely to play with tea sets or Barbies. More controversially, a British study found that more of the divorced lesbians' children said that they had imagined or tried a same-sex romance; but as adults, they still called themselves straight or gay in the same proportions as the straight moms' kids. Is it good, bad, or neutral that lesbians might raise their children to feel free to try out all sides of themselves in gender and sexuality? Or are these results too small to be generalized? The answers depend on your political point of view. And in a pluralist society, that must be taken as an argument for freedom of choice in child-rearing.

Judge Not

So what do these children need from society? The same thing all children need: clear and enforceable ties to their parents. Child psychologist Anna Freud once wrote that children "can handle almost anything better than instability." Not coincidentally, trying to shore up a family's stability is the goal of much marriage-and-family law.

Except if your parents are gay. . . . If a map were to be drawn of the legal situation for lesbian and gay parents, it would look kaleidoscopic . . . with the colors constantly shifting. The answers to some questions may be predictable by geography. On others, even in the supposedly liberal states, how well you're treated depends on your judge. . . .

Things are even iffier for two-mom families than for divorced parents who come out. Most judges just don't know what to do with these families. Adoption laws, written by state legislatures in the late nineteenth century, cover two situations: a couple adopting an orphan or a remarried parent who wants legally to link the child to the stepparent. A mother can add a father; a father can add a mother. But can a mother add *another* mother? Most judges say no, with attitudes ranging from uncertainty to outright antagonism; one Illinois judge, Susan McDunn, went so far as to appoint the Family Research Council [a conservative Christian advocacy group] as *guardian ad litem*[2] for the children. Judges in up to half the states have allowed what's called "second-parent adoption," but in only seven states and the District of Columbia is this a statewide policy. Elsewhere, you're playing roulette: In Michigan, for instance, an Ann Arbor judge might grant one, while a Grand Rapids judge might say no. And advocates try not to appeal—because of the risk that the appeals court might flatly rule out second-parent adoptions, as has happened in the Wisconsin supreme court and in five other states' appellate courts. . . .

No biggie, some people think: Just write a will and some health care proxies, appoint a guardian, and you're all set. It's not that simple. The biomom better be the breadwinner, because the co-mom won't be able to list the child on her taxes or health insurance; nor can she pass on her Social Security benefits or pension. If the biomom dies, the biological grandparents can challenge the co-mom's guardianship and legally kidnap the child. And if the moms break up, cross your fingers for that child.

2. A *guardian ad litem* is a special guardian appointed by the court to represent the child's interests in a particular litigation.

Custody Battle Nightmares

Many—one hopes most—divorcing couples put aside their anger to do what's best for their children. Not everyone does. We all know how hideous people can be when fighting over custody: They play dirty, cheat, lie, even kidnap, always persuading themselves that they're doing it for the kids. When lesbian couples have such no-holds-barred breakups, a spiteful biomom can pull legal rank. If the facts won't let her eviscerate her ex's right to custody or visitation, she may insist that the co-mom was never a parent at all, but just a babysitter, a visitor, a pretender, a stalker. (Because gay men don't give birth, they more often start out on an equal legal footing and can't use this trick.) A biomom and her attorney may exploit a judge's discomfort with homosexuality or cite the state's Defense of Marriage Act to blowtorch any legal link between the co-mom and the child. And if the biomom wins, it leaves tortuous and cruel case law on the state's books that can hurt other lesbian and gay families for decades.

> *"Coherent laws and public policies are desperately needed to help gay and lesbian parents order their families' lives."*

These cases can be heartbreaking. There's the video of the moms' wedding, there's the co-mom's last name as the child's middle name, there's the Olan Mills picture of the three together—and there's the biomom in court saying, "Keep that dyke away from my child." How gratuitously nasty—and legally dangerous—can it be? After getting a legal second-parent adoption in Illinois, one couple moved to Florida to take care of the biomom's dying mother. There the pair broke up. Florida has the dubious distinction of hosting the nation's most draconian ban on adoptions by lesbians and gay men. And so in court, the biomom is now arguing that Florida should refuse to recognize her ex's "foreign" adoption of the child. If this biomom wins, every other two-mom or two-dad family will have to think thrice about visiting Key West or Disney World: What if a Florida emergency room or police station refused to recognize their adoption?

Similar cases are percolating in Nebraska and North Carolina. If these biomoms win, the map of the United States could become a checkerboard of states where two-mom and two-dad families don't dare travel. Can you imagine having your parenthood dissolve when you hit the interstate? You might never leave home again.

"This is a level of damage," says Kendell of the National Center for Lesbian Rights, "that [conservatives] Jerry Falwell and Pat Robertson and Lou Sheldon and all their ilk can only dream of."

What Children Need

Coherent laws and public policies are desperately needed to help gay and lesbian parents order their families' lives. Fortunately, history's heading in the right direction. More and more state courts are coming up with guidelines that refuse to let a biomom shut out her ex, or a co-mom skip out on child support, if the pair together planned for and reared their child. The public and the media are sympathetic. Most policy makers are open to persuasion, understanding that even if they wouldn't want to be gay themselves, kids whose parents are gay deserve the most security possible.

Unfortunately, lesbian-gay-bisexual-transgender advocacy organizations can't change the legal landscape alone. Both in the courts and in public opinion, gay folks are too often cast as biased, the mirror image of the radical right. As a result, liberals and progressives—especially heterosexuals—can make an enormous difference in the lives of these families.

"Children who are born to or adopted by one member of a same-sex couple deserve the security of two legally recognized parents," reads the February [2002] report from the American Academy of Pediatrics. Originally written to be an amicus brief for co-moms or co-dads trying to sway a judge into waving the parent-making wand, the AAP report did much more: It gave editorial writers and talk shows across the country an excuse to agree. And aside from *The Washington Times* and press-release attacks from the usual suspects, agree they did, in an astonishing array of news outlets ranging from local radio shows to *USA Today* to *The Columbus Dispatch*.

So what, besides social tolerance, should the forces of good be working for? Policies and laws that tie these kids firmly to their real, daily parents. These children need strong statutes that let co-moms and co-dads adopt—preferably without the intrusive home study, the thousands of dollars in legal fees, and the reference letters from colleagues and friends that are now required. They need decisive guidelines saying that an adoption in one state is an adoption in every state. And they need marriage rights for their parents. Much of marriage law is designed to help spouses rear families, letting them make a single shelter from their combined incomes, assets, benefits, pensions, habits, strengths, weaknesses, and knowledge. Today, when a heterosexual married couple uses DI, the man is automatically the legal father (as long as he has consented in writing) without having to adopt; if any marriage (or even some lesser system of recognition, like civil unions or registered partnership) were possible, the same could and should be true for lesbians.

By taking up this banner, liberals and progressives can prove that they have a practical commitment to real families and real children. As an Ontario judge wrote in 1995: "When one reflects on the seemingly limitless parade of neglected, abandoned and abused children who appear before our courts in protection cases daily, all of whom have been in the care of heterosexual parents in a 'traditional' family structure, the suggestion that it might not ever be in the best interests of these children to be raised by loving, caring, and committed parents who might happen to be lesbian or gay, is nothing short of ludicrous."

Restrictions on Gay and Lesbian Adoption Are Not Unconstitutional

by Lynn Wardle

About the author: *Lynn Wardle is professor of law at Brigham Young University J. Reuben Clark Law School, and has written extensively on family law issues.*

The benefits to children in need of adoption of being raised by a mother and father who are married to each other are tremendous. The "marriage factor" in terms of the welfare of children justifies adoption rules that discriminate against nonmarital couples including gay couples and partners.

Some advocates of gay rights assert that it is unconstitutional for states and state adoption agencies to prohibit or restrict adoption by homosexual couples (herein "gay couple adoption"). Most of these claims fall into two categories: (1) that homosexual couples have a constitutional right or liberty to adopt, or (2) that refusal to allow homosexual couples to adopt violates the Equal Protection Clause of the Fourteenth Amendment.

Both claims are flawed. There is no fundamental constitutional right to adopt. While adoption has very deep historical roots, it is not deeply rooted in the history and traditions of this Nation or of the common law. It is a totally statutory creation and since it always has been closely regulated by the state, the claim that a person or couple has a right to adopt independent of strict state regulation has never been accepted. Some have argued that a right to adopt is embodied in the constitutional right of intimate association. However, only traditional family relationships have been found to be intimate family associations protected by the Constitution, and no court has found that the Constitution protects the creation of an adoptive relationship.

Even if married couples might be able to assert a constitutional right to adopt, it would not extend to homosexual couples. It could not be said that gay couple adoption is deeply rooted in the history and traditions of this Nation. No court

Lynn Wardle, presentation at the Marriage, Adoption, and the Best Interests of the Child Symposium, November 1, 2002. Copyright © 2002 by Lynn Wardle. Reproduced by permission.

has ever held that homosexual couples have a fundamental constitutional right to adopt. Gay couple adoption does not come within the ambit of traditional family relations.

Equal protection analysis depends upon infringement of a fundamental right or suspect classification. For the reasons reviewed above, laws that disallow gay couple adoption do not violate a fundamental right.

Some argue that refusal to allow gay couples to adopt discriminates on the basis of a suspect classification. Most courts have rejected the claim that sexual orientation is a suspect classification. While a few courts have held that sexual orientation alone may constitute a suspect classification, no court has held that homosexual coupling is a suspect classification. No court has held that it violates equal protection to deny gay couple adoption.

Even if heightened judicial scrutiny were appropriate (either because a fundamental right or suspect classification were infringed) in the context of adoption, there is compelling justification for allowing married couples but not homosexual couples to adopt, and laws restricting or forbidding gay couple adoption could be written in a proper constitutional way.

The marriage factor is the critical distinction. The value and benefit to children in need of adoption of being raised by a mother and father who are married to each other justifies strong preference for married couple adoption. There are powerful reasons to prefer and promote adoption by married (husband-wife) couples. Thus, as a general rule, preference for married couple adoption is clearly constitutional. Adoption by a stepparent—the new spouse of a biological parent—also comes within the marriage preference. As to all children that could be adopted by a married couple or by some other prospective adopter(s), a rule that allows only married couples to adopt is clearly proper and correct.

But adoption law must face practical realities as well as conceptual principles. Even after married prospective adopters adopt, some parentless children may remain in need of adoption. As to those children, the constitutionality of a rule against gay couple adoption may depend upon the alternatives available. A rule against nonmarital couples adopting is constitutional because of the marriage factor.

Some adoptions involve children abandoned by one parent living with the other biological parent who is cohabiting with a nonmarital partner, either same-sex or heterosexual. A law that allows stepparent adoption but does not allow gay partner adoption does not violate Equal Protection because of the marriage factor. If nonmarital partners generally are treated alike (both heterosexual and same-sex) there are compelling justifications for a law that generally disallows adoption by nonmarital couples including gay partners.

Potential risks as well as potential advantages must be considered with comparing alternatives for children. Adoptions by unmarried single persons are distinguishable because of the heightened risks to children of being raised in an environment of nonmarital cohabitation.

Permitting Gay and Lesbian Adoptions May Put Children at Risk

by Paul Cameron

About the author: *Paul Cameron, a research psychologist, is chairman of the Family Research Institute and author of* The Gay 90s: What the Empirical Evidence Reveals About Homosexuality.

On Feb. 4, 2000, the American Academy of Pediatrics (AAP) recommended "legal and legislative efforts" to allow children "born to or adopted by one member of a gay or lesbian couple" to be adopted by the homosexual partner. Such a law effectively would eliminate the possibility of adoption by other family members following the death of the parent. It also would cause problems for numerous children.

The AAP, like many other professional organizations, apparently was too caught up in promoting identity politics to address all the evidence relevant to homosexual adoption. In its report, the organization offered only positive evidence about gays and lesbians as parents. "In fact," the report concluded, "growing up with parents who are lesbian or gay may confer some advantages to children." Really?

There are three sets of information on the issue: clinical reports of psychiatric disturbance of children with homosexual parents, testimonies of children with homosexual parents concerning their situation and studies that have compared the children of homosexuals with the children of nonhomosexuals. The AAP ignored the first two sets and had to cherry-pick the comparative studies to arrive at the claim that "[n]o data have pointed to any risk to children as a result of growing up in a family with one or more gay parents."

A number of clinical reports detail "acting-out behavior," homosexual seduction, elective muteness and the desire for a mother by children with homosexual

Paul Cameron, "Yes: The Conclusions of the American Academy of Pediatrics Are Not to Be Believed," *Insight on the News*, vol. 18, April 22, 2002, p. 40. Copyright © 2002 by News World Communications, Inc. All rights reserved. Reprinted by permission.

parents. I am unaware of a single child being disturbed because his mother and father were married.

The AAP also ignored the testimonies of children with homosexual parents—probably the best evidence since these kids had to "live with it" rather than deal with a theory. More than 150 children with homosexual parents have provided, in extensive interviews, detailed evidence of the difficulties they encountered as a result. A study Paul and Kirk Cameron published this year [2002] in *Psychological Reports* analyzed the content of 57 life-story narratives by children with homosexual parents assembled by lesbian researchers Louise Rafkin (United States) and Lisa Saffron (Britain).

Disturbing Stories

In these narratives, children in 48 of the 52 families (92 percent) mentioned one or more "problems." Of the 213 problems which were scored—including hypersexuality, instability, molestation, domestic violence—children attributed 201 (94 percent) to their homosexual parent(s).

Here are four sample excerpts:

• One 9-year-old girl said: "My biological mother is S. and my other mother is L. We've lived together for a year. Before that L. lived across the street. . . . My mom met L.; L. had just broken up with someone. We moved in together because it got complicated going back and forth every night. All of a sudden I felt like I was a different person because my mom was a lesbian. . . . I get angry because I can't tell anybody about my mom. The kids at school would laugh. . . . They say awful things about lesbians . . . then they make fun of me. Having lesbian mothers is nothing to laugh about. . . . I have told my [mother] that she has made my life difficult."

• A 12-year-old boy in the United Kingdom said: "Mum . . . has had several girlfriends in my lifetime. . . . I don't go around saying that I've got two mums. . . . If we are sitting in a restaurant eating, she'll say, 'I want you to know about all these sex things.' And she'll go on about everything, just shouting it out. . . . Sometimes when mum embarrasses me, I think, 'I wish I had a dad.' . . . Been to every gay pride march. Last year, while attending, we went up to a field . . . when two men came up to us. One of them started touching me. I didn't want to go this year because of that."

• According to a 39-year-old woman: "In my memories, I'm always looking for my mother and finding her with a woman doing things I don't understand. . . . Sometimes they blame me for opening a door that wasn't even locked. . . . [At about the age of 10], I noticed a door that I hadn't yet opened. Inside I saw a big bed. My mother sat up suddenly and stared at me. She was with B. . . . and then B. shouted, 'You f***ing sneaking brat!' My mother never said a word. [Then came N.] I came to hate N. because of the way she and my mother fought every night. They screamed and bickered and whined and pouted over everything. N. closed my mother's hand in the car door. . . . She and N. hadn't made love in seven years."

• According to a 19-year-old man: "When I was about 7, my mother told me that this woman, D., was going to stay with us for a while—and she never left! I didn't think anything much about it until I was about 10. . . . It just became obvious because she and my mother were sleeping together. A few months after D. left, my mother started to see another woman, but that didn't last. Then she got involved with a different woman . . . ; she'd be violent toward my mother. . . . After that she started to go on marches and to women's groups. . . . There were some women in these groups who objected to men altogether, and I couldn't cope with that."

All 57 narratives can be found at www.familyresearchinst.org. Anyone who believes that living with homosexual parents confers "some advantages to children" should read these accounts.

Studies Were Ignored

The AAP ignored every comparative study of children that showed those with homosexual parents experiencing more problems. These include the largest comparative study, reported in 1996 by Sotirios Sarantakos in the journal, *Children Australia*, of 58 elementary schoolchildren raised by coupled homosexual parents who were closely matched (by age, sex, grade in school, social class) with 58 children of cohabiting heterosexual parents and 58 raised by married parents. Teachers reported that the married couples' children scored best at math and language but somewhat lower in social studies, experienced the highest level of parental involvement at school as well as at home and had parents with the highest expectations for them. The children of homosexuals scored lowest in math and language and somewhat higher in social studies, were the least popular, experienced the lowest level of parental involvement at school and at home, had parents with the lowest expectations for them and least frequently expressed higher educational and career expectations.

Yet the AAP said that studies have "failed to document any differences between such groups on . . . academic success." The organization's report also ignored the only empirical study based upon a random sample that reported on 17 adults (out of a sample of 5,182) with homosexual parents. Detailed by Cameron and Cameron in the journal *Adolescence* in 1996, the 17 were disproportionately apt to report sexual relations with their parents, more apt to report a less than exclusively heterosexual orientation, more frequently reported gender dissatisfaction and were more apt to report that their first sexual experience was homosexual.

> *"A number of clinical reports detail 'acting-out behavior,' homosexual seduction, elective muteness, and a desire for a mother by children with homosexual parents."*

The AAP report also seemingly ignored a 1998 *Psychological Reports* study by Cameron and Cameron that included the largest number of children with homosexual parents. That study compared 73 children of homosexuals with 105 children of heterosexuals. Of the 66 problems cited by panels of judges who extensively reviewed the living conditions and psychological reactions of children of homosexuals undergoing a divorce from heterosexuals, 64 (97 percent) were attributed to the homosexual parent.

> *"The AAP ignored every comparative study of children that showed those with homosexual parents experiencing more problems."*

Finally, while ignoring studies that contradicted its own conclusions, the AAP misrepresented numerous findings from the limited literature it cited. Thus, Sharon Huggins compared 18 children of 16 volunteer/lesbian mothers with 18 children of 16 volunteer/heterosexual/divorced mothers on self-esteem. Huggins reported statistically nonsignificant differences between the 19 children of mothers who were not living with a lover versus the 17 children of mothers who were living with a lover; and, further, that [the four] "adolescent daughters with high self-esteem had been told of their mother's lesbianism at a mean age of 6.0 years. In contrast, [the five] adolescent daughters with low self-esteem had been told at a mean age of 9.6 years" and "three of four of the mothers with high self-esteem daughters were currently living with lesbian lovers, but only one of four of the lesbian mothers with low self-esteem daughters was currently living with a lesbian lover."

The AAP cited Huggins as proving that "children's self-esteem has been shown to be higher among adolescents whose mothers (of any sexual orientation) were in a new partnered relationship after divorce, compared with those whose mother remained single, and among those who found out at a younger age that their parent was homosexual, compared with those who found out when they were older," thus transforming statistical nonevents based on niggling numbers of volunteers into important differences—twice in one sentence!

We have examined more than 10,000 obituaries of homosexuals: The median age of death for lesbians was in the 40s to 50s; for homosexuals it was in the 40s. Most Americans live into their 70s. Yet in the 1996 U.S. government sex survey the oldest lesbian was 49 years old and the oldest gay 54.

Children with homosexual parents are considerably more apt to lose a parent to death. Indeed, a homosexual couple in their 30s is roughly equivalent to a nonhomosexual couple in their late 40s or 50s. Adoption agencies will seldom permit a couple in their late 40s or 50s to adopt a child because of the risk of parental death, and the consequent social and psychological difficulty for the child. The AAP did not address this fact—one with profound implications for any child legally related to a homosexual.

As usual, the media picked up on the AAP report as authoritative, assuming that it represented the consensus of a large and highly educated membership.

Not so. As in other professional organizations, the vast majority of members pay their dues, read the journal and never engage in professional politics. As a consequence, a small but active minority of members gains control and uses the organization to promote its agenda. Too often, the result is ideological literature that misrepresents the true state of knowledge.

Gay-rights activists have been particularly adept at manipulating research and reports to their own ends. For years the media reported that all studies revealed that 10 percent of the population was homosexual. In fact, few if any studies ever came to that conclusion. For the next few years we will have to live with the repeated generalization that all studies prove homosexual parents are as good for children as heterosexual parents, and perhaps even better. What little literature exists on the subject proves no such thing. Indeed, translated into the language of accounting, the AAP report could be described as "cooking the books."

Adoption Workers Are Wrongly Biased in Favor of Gays and Lesbians

by Candi Cushman

About the author: *Candi Cushman is a writer for the* Citizen, *a publication of Focus on the Family, a conservative Christian organization.*

Laurie Ellinger still remembers the moment she first cradled Adam,* a chubby-cheeked black newborn with twinkling eyes and a budding crop of curly hair. Barely a month old, Adam was suffering a painful withdrawal from the drugs that had been pumped into his bloodstream before he was born.

So for the next several months, Ellinger, an emergency foster mom in Alameda County, Calif., rocked Adam to sleep in her arms as tremors quaked his tiny frame.

"He wanted to be a happy baby," Ellinger fondly recalled. "When he wasn't in pain, he was so sweet. He would smile and respond."

Through Ellinger's persistent care, though, the tremors subsided and Adam became a vigorous 1-year-old with a grin and giggle that easily charmed adults. So it was no surprise when two married Christian couples who regularly visited Adam fell in love with him and tried to adopt him. Jimmie and The'ssa McCoy, black parents who have cared for foster children since 1997; and Susan and Gary Hartman, a white couple state-licensed to provide baby-sitting services for Ellinger, had cared for Adam since his birth.

The couples had high hopes one of them would become new parents. Especially The'ssa McCoy, who had recently adopted another baby (Isaiah) cared for by Ellinger and said she had been told by social workers that her home also had been approved for Adam's possible placement. But in February 2000, the county shocked everyone by instead placing Adam with two white, homosexual men who eventually adopted him.

---

* Names have been changed to protect children's identities.

Candi Cushman, "He Has No Mama Now," *Citizen*, January 2003. Copyright © 2003 by Focus on the Family. All rights reserved. Reproduced by permission.

The decision was unprecedented, said Ellinger, because social workers are trained to choose a home that involves the least disruptive change for the baby. Instead, they moved Adam out of his own county into a "nontraditional" home of different ethnicity—and passed up not one, but two heterosexual, married couples who knew him personally.

"It made no sense," she said, adding that she still grieves for the now 4-year-old Adam. "The only word he was saying [at that time] was 'mama.' And he has no mama now."

Threats for Faith

Little-noticed cases like Adam's are popping up across the nation as homosexual activists intensify their quest to win government sanctioning of their lifestyle. And adoption represents one of the last hurdles standing in the way of that prize.

"The new millennium will see the battle for GLBT [gay, lesbian, bisexual, transgender] civil rights won," said a Web site for the Adoption Family Center, an agency for "nontraditional" families. "As we have come out in record numbers for same-sex marriage . . . gays and lesbians have also demanded our right to be parents."

Since only three states specifically forbid homosexual adoption—Florida, Mississippi and Utah—the resulting legal vacuum has enabled gay couples to gain adoption privileges on a county-by-county basis. And the foster care system provides a convenient back door for that approach, since most states give adoption preference to state-licensed foster parents. As a result, ground zero in the battle to normalize homosexuality has moved into the nation's courtrooms, where custody cases are deciding the fate of hundreds of children.

In Alameda County Juvenile Court, for instance, Adam's natural father vigorously protested his son's placement with a homosexual couple, begging the judge to place him with a black, married couple like the McCoys. But the judge ignored his pleas, giving social workers control over who adopted the baby.

"The interesting thing was," Ellinger later told *Citizen*, "I could not cut Adam's hair without permission from his parents. But he could be placed in

> *"Ground zero in the battle to normalize homosexuality has moved into the nation's courtrooms, where custody cases are deciding the fate of hundreds of children."*

a homosexual home, which both of his parents were violently opposed to."

Asked why the state passed up two married couples before placing Adam with two gay men, Carol Collins, assistant director for the county social services department, told *Citizen*, "I'm really not in a position to respond to that."

Risking their own foster care licenses, the McCoys, Hartmans and Ellingers joined forces to protect Adam, writing letters to their representatives, telling their story to local media and attending the baby's placement trial.

"The McCoy family before you, and mine, are not in competition for Adam, but rather come together before you as two good choices," wrote Susan Hartman to a juvenile court commissioner. "Please do not refuse him the basic development, social and psychological need for a mother. . . . Please, your honor, Adam has already had a rough start."

But theirs was a lonely battle. In court, the Christian moms huddled together on one side of the room while the homosexual couple and lawyers from the San Francisco–based National Center for Lesbian Rights consorted on the other. "They had managers and a supervisor and three caseworkers and an attorney for them, and they also had a psychologist," remembered The'ssa McCoy. "We were like, 'Wow, they're bringing in the big guns.'"

Ironically, as homosexual activists complained in national media that they were being denied a "fundamental right" to have kids, the Christian families fighting for Adam in Alameda suddenly found themselves the target of behind-the-scenes intimidation.

One day after the trial, McCoy received a disturbing phone call from a social worker. "She told me that we have nothing to do with Adam, and we need to stop fighting and stop coming to the courts," McCoy told *Citizen*. "Then she said, 'How would you feel if I came and removed Isaiah from your care and you wouldn't be able to adopt him?'"

Since all that was needed to complete Isaiah's two-year adoption process was the signature of that same social worker, McCoy saw the comment as a veiled threat. Isaiah's adoption was eventually finalized, but pro-gay activists succeeded in prohibiting McCoy & Co. from attending the last part of Adam's trial.

Ellinger also suffered the consequences of protesting a homosexual adoption. She was temporarily suspended from sheltering foster children after social workers accused her of breaching confidentiality laws by making public Adam's intended placement with a gay couple (an event which garnered front-page news).

But Ellinger, who has cared for some 60 foster children over the last 22 years and was quickly reinstated after the controversy, believes the real issue was her refusal to bow to a political agenda:

"I told them [during the suspension meeting] that I felt a child should be placed with a mom and a dad. They asked how I can do my job if that was the way I felt. And I said, 'Because I take care of babies. That's what my job is.' And [the social worker] said, 'But how can you put . . . your feelings, your strong convictions, aside?'

"The whole thing was a power play," she said. "They wanted me to know their eye was on me."

But instead of backing down, the three families fought back harder. McCoy recruited the help of her church, Shiloh Christian Fellowship, which launched a letter-writing campaign to county officials, arguing that placing a black baby with two white, gay men was not in the child's best interest. Parishioners also held a prayer walk around the courthouse.

Though they ultimately lost the custody battle for Adam, the Alameda Christian community learned some valuable lessons, said McCoy: like the myth behind the claim that homosexual couples are getting children because nobody else wants them, the reality of prejudice against Christians within the foster care system and, most importantly, the need for the church to step forward.

"At that point we weren't just fighting for Adam," she said. "We were fighting for all children. . . . The realization came to us that if this was happening to one child, how many times had it happened in the past and how many times will it happen in the future?"

Whose Best Interests?

Apparently, it's happening a lot. Courts in at least 20 states have granted same-sex adoptions. And gay activists have used emotional arguments to defeat homosexual-adoption bans elsewhere by claiming that since they take the foster children no one else wants—those suffering from AIDS, sexual abuse and severe mental disabilities—to prevent them from adopting is nothing short of cruelty to children.

Former TV talk-show host and foster parent Rosie O'Donnell put a popular face on that agenda last March [2002] when she "came out" as a lesbian opposed to Florida's homosexual-adoption ban.

"I think as long as the place is safe, [children] don't care what the parents do in the bedroom," she told Diane Sawyer on ABC's *Primetime Thursday*, adding that the gay men suing to overturn Florida's homosexual-adoption ban "should be held up and heralded as the perfect family, not as one that needs to be pulled apart because of hatred."

But is compassion for children really what's motivating the push for homosexual adoption? Less publicized comments from the gay community reveal a different agenda, one that caters to the whims of adults. A fact sheet posted by the Adoption Family Center, for example, said gays and lesbians "are troubled by the feeling that adoption agencies offer them the children who are the most difficult to place: those with physical, mental, or emotional disabilities; those who are older; children of color."

Equally revealing is the Florida lawsuit touted by O'Donnell, which bases homosexual adoption on a supposed constitutional "right" to be parents. However, the lawsuit leaves "unchallenged" the "assertion that the best interest of the child is to be raised by a married family," wrote U.S. District Court Judge James Lawrence King, who upheld Florida's law last August [2002]. (Homosexual activists have appealed the decision.)[1]

But in the public limelight, at least, gays and lesbians have successfully

---

1. A federal appeals court heard arguments in March 2003; no decision had been reached as of October 2003.

painted themselves as a victimized group being denied the right to help impoverished children. Problem is, nobody seems to be worrying about the real-life babies becoming pawns in this latest political skirmish, those like Adam whose right to have a married mommy and daddy is forgotten.

Research completed over the last 30 years clearly shows that children need both a mother and a father to have the healthiest upbringing, according to Glenn T. Stanton, Focus on the Family's marriage and sexuality analyst. At the same time, there is no evidence that gay parenting actually benefits children.

"It is unwise to embark on a historically unprecedented and unproven social experiment with our children fueled by adult desire," said Stanton.

California isn't the only state where wisdom is lacking, as the plight of another baby, Stephen*, illustrates.

Like Adam, Stephen was born in 1997 with drugs in his system. But he had one thing going for him: his uncle, Eugene Helm, who won an award from President [Bill] Clinton for putting aside his own career aspirations to raise five nieces and nephews (two are Stephen's sisters). Helm's heroic actions were featured on *The Oprah Winfrey Show* and NBC's *Today*.

Despite those qualifications, when Helm learned social workers had taken Stephen from a younger sister because of her drug and legal problems, he found himself mysteriously cut out of the process. State officials didn't return his phone calls requesting information about the baby and, without notifying him, began the process of placing Stephen for adoption with a lesbian couple, according to Dallas attorney Kyle Basinger, who successfully fought for Helm's right to gain custody.

"All this was expedited without ever involving the one relative that wanted to take the child," Basinger told *Citizen*. "They wanted to place the child with a lesbian couple. I can't think of any other reason, because of the way it was all conducted in secret and shoved through."

Baby Stephen's case has disturbing similarities to the Alameda case in that those who tried to oppose the homosexual adoption were quietly punished.

> *"There is no evidence gay parenting actually benefits children."*

Texas social worker Rebecca Bledsoe, for instance, sacrificed her career to defend Stephen's right to have a traditional family. Arguing that the "right" of homosexual adults to adopt shouldn't outweigh the *need* of children to have a mommy and a daddy, she removed then 3-month-old Stephen from the lesbian household.

"My professional view is that putting a child in any situation where there is admitted criminal activity of a sexual nature is wrong," said Bledsoe at the time, referring to Texas' sodomy law, which prohibits homosexual conduct. But even if the law didn't exist, she said, "In this situation, you are making a decision to guarantee that child will never have a father."

Despite her spotless work record during the previous 10 years, though, Bledsoe was demoted from her position as a supervisor for "failure to follow procedure" when removing Stephen. At least in Texas, she will never regain the tenure she spent 13 years obtaining.

"Which Children Will It Be?"

Bledsoe, and other social workers interviewed by *Citizen* over the last five months, said the small percentage of homosexuals wanting to adopt isn't large enough to solve a real or perceived foster parent shortage—and for that reason, isn't enough to justify subjecting some children to taxpayer-funded experiments on homosexual parenting.

"There's probably not more than half a dozen licensed homosexual households in Texas," said Bledsoe. "It's not a significant enough number to risk some children.

"Which children will it be who are not going to have the opportunity of having a mother and a father?"

Still, homosexual-adoption proponents point out that some 580,000 children annually languish in the foster care system, asking "Why should they languish when gay parents are willing to adopt?"

But what they don't acknowledge is that in fiscal year 2000 only about 11 percent—or 64,000—of those 580,000 had their parental rights terminated, making them eligible for

> *"Rather than opening the system up to . . . homosexuals, a more logical . . . solution would be to reduce the red tape preventing married couples from obtaining children."*

adoption. And data from the U.S. Department of Health and Human Services show that, in 1999, married couples accounted for 66 percent of adoptions, while unmarried couples accounted for only 1 percent (397).

What's more, studies from the Centers for Disease Control and Prevention (CDC) show there is a vast untapped pool of adoption seekers. More than a quarter of "ever-married" women have considered adoption (9.9 million). And according to the CDC, two of the strongest factors affecting which of those women take steps toward adopting are "being currently married" and "having ever used infertility services."

So rather than opening the system up to a small number of homosexuals, a more logical and far-reaching solution would be to reduce the red tape preventing married couples from obtaining children, according to Ken Connor, who served on the Governor's Partnership for Adoption in Florida and is now [2003] president of the D.C.-based Family Research Council.

"These children are languishing in foster care not because . . . people aren't willing necessarily to adopt them, but because the appropriate steps have not been taken to make those children adoption-eligible," he said.

An adoptive parent himself, Connor added that data show "homosexuals have higher incidences of drug abuse, domestic abuse, depression, suicide. . . . We know that foster care is not the ideal situation for a child, but rather than reverting to an alternative that is fraught with risk . . . let's cut through barriers and make it easier for people to adopt."

The Silent Prejudice

County governments' subtle antagonism toward religious and conservative families also aggravates the backlog of homeless children, according to social workers like Larry Phillips, who recently won a lawsuit against the Missouri government after being fired for refusing to place children with homosexuals because of his religious beliefs.

Formerly responsible for licensing and recruiting foster parents, Phillips said his county "had a shortage because they created a philosophy that limited who they would select."

Phillips recalled how a Baptist father who applied to become a foster parent made the mistake of admitting he was a strong Christian whose family regularly attended church. Privately, foster care supervisors expressed concerns about the man being a "right-wing fundamentalist," said Phillips, but they were too smart to discriminate in writing, so they "created secondary reasons":

"For example, with [the Baptist], they indicated he didn't have enough 'diversified social interests.' . . . A lot of what he did revolved around his church activities; they felt he was too narrow in his perspective.

"I spoke up, but I was outnumbered. We generally voted by consensus. . . . And I was just a lone voice. But there were many instances like this.

"The challenge is not . . . availability of homes," he summarized. "If we change the selection and screening process for traditional Christian families, we would have all the foster parents we need."

Some foster care divisions have gone so far as to create nondiscrimination policies that, in practice, place homosexual couples on equal or better footing than married couples—automatically putting religious families at a disadvantage.

> *"County governments' subtle antagonism toward religious and conservative families also aggravates the backlog of homeless children."*

"They'll take . . . a gay or lesbian couple who want children and they'll give them preference in the evaluative process in hopes of being diverse," Dale Billeter, a 15-year social services investigator for Alameda County (Baby Adam's hometown), told *Citizen.* "They'll put what I see as good religious families with good values on the bottom of the pile."

Christian families often are phased out through heavier screening processes and regulations, he said: "If you're going to be religious, then they are going to hold you to a greater weight of certain rules. Like where the bed's located. . . . Do they have their own separate bedrooms? . . . there's 100 different questions." Billeter also expressed concern that "we lost five of the best [religious] homes in the county" because of that bias.

Meanwhile, homosexual activists seem to have no trouble accessing the system. Paul Welander, a senior social worker for California's Santa Barbara County, told *Citizen* he and other co-workers were required to attend a gay-rights seminar in 2002.

During the seminar, speakers from a local gay activist group called the Pacific Pride Foundation announced they were actively recruiting more gay and lesbian foster parents and told social workers to place children struggling with their sexual identity in those homes.

That frustrated Welander, who said social workers have a hard enough time finding a home for any child:

"We are out here trying to do our job, and that is to place kids with the most loving families available. . . . So anybody coming in and saying, 'We demand this right' is an irritant to us.

"I don't think I'm being unduly nasty against this certain group," he added. "I'm more against the principle of the thing, of somebody trying to dictate to us . . . to mix and match just to their specific agenda."

Staring Down the State

But where individual foster parents and social workers have failed to change the system, Christians who pool their resources have conquered political pressure.

Take what happened to Kentucky Baptist Homes for Children (KBHC)—the state's largest private foster care provider, which has found homes for more than 1,200 children over the last five years.

Despite the home's vital role in alleviating that state's foster care backlog, in 1998 some 200 Louisville-area social workers signed a statement refusing to place children with KBHC. At issue was the home's refusal to hire avowed homosexuals to work with children, which the statement claimed violated the National Association of Social Workers' nondiscrimination policy.

For the next two months, KBHC saw its state referrals cut in half. Then the state social services department turned up the heat by requiring the home to sign a contract promising to abide by the association's code.

Not signing meant "we were going to have to go from a 22-million-dollar agency to about a 6-million-dollar agency," Bill Smithwick, KBHC's director, told *Citizen*. "The sad part was that all those kids we were helping were going to have to go somewhere else."

But thanks to the backing of hundreds of Christian foster parents, Smithwick and his board of directors stared down the state, choosing to lose government money (80 percent of the home's budget) rather than their biblical principles.

"There's a great satisfaction in doing what's right . . . in knowing we are not promoting a lifestyle that is so damaging to young people," Smithwick said. In the end, the reality that the state had nowhere else to send hundreds of homeless children forced the hand of the governor, who overruled the contract change and sent a letter to social workers informing them they could refuse to place kids at KBHC if it violated their conscience.

Homosexual activists have since reignited their attack with a federal lawsuit challenging KBHC's government funding, not seeming to mind that they might eliminate hundreds of good homes from the Kentucky foster care system. But Smithwick remained confident that Christians working together could resist future attacks:

"This is an issue that America has got to wake up to. The homosexual agenda is a beast. [It] wants our kids. . . . And the only thing that's standing between them and that agenda . . . are those of us who believe in the Judeo-Christian values of this country."

Organizations to Contact

The editors have compiled the following list of organizations concerned with the issues presented in this book. The descriptions are derived from materials provided by the organizations. All have publications or information available for interested readers. The list was compiled on the date of publication of the present volume; the information provided here may change. Be aware that many organizations take several weeks or longer to respond to inquiries, so allow as much time as possible.

Abolish Adoption
PO Box 401, Palm Desert, CA 92261
e-mail: info@abolishadoption.com • website: www.abolishadoption.com

Abolish Adoption is an organization that petitions to end the practice of adoption. It believes that adoption is not in the child's best interests and violates human rights. Abolish Adoption also campaigns for open adoption record laws. Its publications include *The Ultimate Search Book Worldwide Adoption, Genealogy & Other Search Secrets.*

American Adoption Congress (AAC)
PO Box 42730, Washington, DC 20015
(202) 483-3399
website: www.americanadoptioncongress.org

AAC is an educational network that promotes openness and honesty in adoption. It advocates adoption reform, including the opening of records, and seeks to develop plans for alternative models for adoption. It directs attention to the needs of adult adoptees who are searching for their birth families. AAC publishes articles and position statements on its website.

Bastard Nation (BN)
PO Box 271672, Houston, TX 77277-1672
(415) 704-3166
e-mail: bn@bastards.org • website: www.bastards.org

Bastard Nation is an adoptee's rights organization that campaigns to legalize adopted adults' access to records that pertain to his or her historical, genetic, and legal identity. It publishes the newsletter *Bastard Quarterly.*

Concerned United Birthparents (CUB)
PO Box 230457, Encinitas, CA 92023
(800) 822-2777 • fax: (760) 929-1879
e-mail: group@cubirthparents.org • website: www.cubirthparents.org

CUB provides assistance to birth parents, works to open adoption records, and seeks to develop alternatives to the current adoption system. It helps women considering the placement of a child for adoption make an informed choice and seeks to prevent unnecessary separation of families by adoption. CUB publishes the newsletter *Cub Communicator* and the booklet *What You Should KNOW If You're Considering Adoption for Your Baby.*

David Thomas Foundation for Adoption
(800) 275-3832 • fax: (614) 766-3871
e-mail: adoption@wendys.com • website: www.davethomasfoundationforadoption.org

The organization works to promote adoption of the children in America's foster care system. Its publications include *A Child Is Waiting . . . A Beginner's Guide to Adoption.*

Evan B. Donaldson Adoption Institute
120 Wall St., 20th Floor, New York, NY 10005
(212) 269-5080 • fax: (212) 269-1962
e-mail: geninfo@adoptioninstitute.org • website: www.adoptioninstitute.org

The Evan B. Donaldson Adoption Institute, founded in 1996, is a national not-for-profit organization devoted to improving adoption policy and practice. It provides information on adoption and advocates ethical adoption practices. It publishes reports on adoption including *Analysis of Child Outcomes: Wednesday's Child Program*, which can be downloaded from its website.

Family Research Council (FRC)
801 G St. NW, Washington, DC 20001
(202) 393-2100 • fax: (202) 393-2134
website: www.frc.org

The council is a research and educational organization that promotes the traditional family, which the council defines as a group of people bound by marriage, blood, or adoption. The council opposes gay marriage and adoption rights. It publishes numerous reports from a conservative perspective on issues affecting the family, including *Free to Be Family*. Among its publications are the monthly newsletter *Washington Watch* and the bimonthly journal *Family Policy*.

Institute for Adoption Information (IAI)
PO Box 4405, Bennington, VT 05201-4405
e-mail: info@adoptioninformationinstitute.org
website: www.adoptioninformationinstitute.org

The institute is a nonprofit organization of adoptees, birth parents, adoptive parents, adoption professionals, and others who have united to enhance public understanding of adoption. It develops tools used to educate others about adoption and to dispel the myths and stereotypes surrounding adoption. It publishes and distributes *An Educator's Guide to Adoption* and other writings.

National Adoption Information Clearinghouse (NAIC)
330 C St. SW, Washington, DC 20447
(703) 352-3488 • fax: (703) 385-3206
e-mail: naic@calib.com • website: www.calib.com/naic

Part of the U.S. Department of Health and Human Services, NAIC distributes publications on all aspects of adoption, including infant and international adoption, the adoption of children with special needs, and pertinent state and federal laws. For research, it provides a computerized information database containing titles and abstracts of books, articles, and program reports on adoption.

National Association of Black Social Workers (NABSW)
8436 W. McNichols, Detroit, MI 48221
(313) 862-6700 • fax: (313) 862-6998
website: http://ssw.unc.edu/professional/NABSW.html

NABSW seeks to support, develop, and sponsor programs and projects serving the interests of black communities. It is committed to a policy of same-race adoptions, promoting adoption of black children by black adoptive parents. NABSW publishes the annual *Black Caucus.*

National Council for Adoption (NCFA)
225 N. Washington St., Alexandria, VA 22314-2561
(703) 299-6633 • fax: (703) 299-6004
e-mail: ncfa@adoptioncouncil.org • website: www.ncfa-usa.org

Representing volunteer agencies, adoptive parents, adoptees, and birth parents, NCFA works to protect the institution of adoption and to ensure the confidentiality of all involved in the adoption process. It strives for adoption regulations that will ensure the protection of birth parents, children, and adoptive parents. Its biweekly newsletter, *Memo*, provides updates on state and federal legislative and regulatory changes affecting adoption. It also publishes and distributes *Adoption Factbook III*, a reference volume.

National Organization for Birthfathers and Adoption Reform (NOBAR)
3821 Tamiami Trail, #301, Port Charlotte, FL 33752
(941) 637-7477

NOBAR acts as an advocate for men affected by adoption, including birth fathers of adoptees, divorced fathers whose children are or may be adopted by stepfathers, single fathers, and adoptive fathers. The organization promotes social policies and laws that protect the individual rights of those involved; it also works for the unrestricted opening of adoption records for birth parents and adoptees. NOBAR publishes *Birthfathers' Advocate*, a monthly newsletter.

North American Council on Adoptable Children (NACAC)
970 Raymond Ave., Suite 106, St. Paul, MN 55114-1149
(651)644-3036 • fax: (651) 644-9848
e-mail: info@nacac.org • website: www.nacac.org

NACAC, an adoption advocacy organization, is composed of parents, groups, and individuals. It emphasizes special needs adoption, keeps track of adoption activities in each state, and promotes reform in adoption policies. NACAC publishes *Adoptalk*, a quarterly newsletter, and other papers and articles on adoption.

Internet Resources

Adoption.com
http://adoption.com

Adoption.com is a web-based network of adoption organizations. It features profiles of prospective adoptive parents and adoptable children and addresses adoption issues such as unplanned pregnancy, international adoption, and adoption reunions.

Adoptivefamilies.com
www.adoptivefamilies.com

The website of *Adoptive Families* magazine features current and archived articles from the award-winning publication aimed at families before, during, and after adoption.

Mothers in Exile
www.exiledmothers.com

This website, created by a group of birth mothers who regret their decision to relinquish their children, includes stories and articles on the negative effects of adoption on mothers and children.

Bibliography

Books

Salman Akhtar and Selma Kramer, eds.	*Thicker Than Blood: Bonds of Fantasy and Reality in Adoption.* Northvale, NJ: Jason Aronson, 2000.
L. Anne Babb	*Ethics in American Adoption.* Westport, CT: Greenwood, 1999.
Elizabeth Bartholet	*Nobody's Children: Abuse and Neglect, Foster Drift, and the Adoption Alternative.* Boston: Beacon Press, 1999.
Carolyn Campbell	*Together Again: True Stories of Birth Parents and Adopted Children United.* New York: Berkley, 1999.
E. Wayne Carp	*Family Matters: Secrecy and Disclosure in the History of Adoption.* Cambridge, MA: Harvard University Press, 2000.
Sherrie Eldridge	*Twenty Things Adopted Kids Wish Their Adoptive Parents Knew.* New York: Dell, 1999.
Leslie Foge and Gail Mosconi	*The Third Choice: A Woman's Guide to Placing a Child for Adoption.* Berkeley, CA: Creative Arts, 1999.
Hawley Fogg-Davis	*The Ethics of Transracial Adoption.* Syracuse, NY: Cornell University Press, January 2002.
Lynn C. Franklin	*May the Circle Be Unbroken: An Intimate Journey into the Heart of Adoption.* New York: Three Rivers Press, 1997.
Stephen Hicks and Jane McDermott, eds.	*Lesbian and Gay Fostering and Adoption: Extraordinary Yet Ordinary.* Philadelphia: Jessica Kingsley, 1998.
Randall Kennedy	*Sex, Marriage, Identity, and Adoption.* New York: Pantheon, 2003.
Betty Jean Lifton	*Journey of the Adopted Self.* New York: Basic Books, 2000.
Ron Nydam	*Adoptees Come of Age: Living Within Two Families.* Louisville, KY: John Knox Press, 1999.
Sandra Patton	*Birthmarks: Transracial Adoption in Contemporary America.* New York: NYU Press, 2000.
Joyce Maguire Pavao	*The Family of Adoption.* Boston: Beacon Press, 1999.

Bibliography

Adam Pertman
Adoption Nation: How the Adoption Revolution Is Transforming America. New York: Basic Books, 2000.

William L. Pierce, ed.
The Adoption Factbook III. Washington, DC: National Council for Adoption, 1999.

Bruce M. Rappaport.
The Open Adoption Book: A Guide for Adoption Without Tears. New York: Hungry Minds, 1998.

Evelyn Burns Robinson
Adoption and Loss: The Hidden Grief. Christies Beach, Australia: Clova, 2000.

Dan Savage
The Kid: What Happened After My Boyfriend and I Decided to Go Get Pregnant—An Adoption Story. New York: Dutton, 1999.

Jayne E. Schooler and Betsie L. Norris
Journeys After Adoption: Understanding Lifelong Issues. Westport, CT: Bergin & Garvey, 2002.

Rita J. Simon and Howard Altstein
Adoption Across Borders: Serving the Children in Transracial and Intercountry Adoptions. Lanham, MD: Rowman and Littlefield, 2000.

Rickie Solinger
Beggars and Choosers: How the Politics of Choice Shapes Adoption, Abortion and Welfare in the United States. New York: Hill & Wang, 2001.

Gail Steinberg and Beth Hall
Inside Transracial Adoption. Indianapolis, IN: Perspectives Press, 2000.

Amal Treacher and Ilan Katz
The Dynamics of Adoption. Philadelphia: Jessica Kingsley, 2000.

Susan Wadia-Ellis
The Adoption Reader: Birthmothers, Adoptive Mothers, and Adopted Daughters Tell Their Stories. Seattle, WA: Seal Press, 1995.

Katarina Wegar
Adoption, Identity, and Kinship: The Debate Over Sealed Birth Records. New Haven, CT: Yale University Press, 1997.

Periodicals

Janet Albrechtsen
"Restoring Adoption," *Quadrant*, January/ February 2002.

David Andrusko
"Raising Consciousness About Adoption," *National Right to Life News*, November 2001.

Paula Bernstein
"Why I Don't Want to Find My Birth Mother," *Redbook*, March 2000.

Devon Brooks, Sigrid James, and Richard P. Barth
"Preferred Characteristics of Children in Need of Adoption: Is There a Demand for Available Foster Children?" *Social Service Review*, December 2002.

Christian Science Monitor
"A Law Changes, A Birth Mother Worries," April 17, 2000.

Issues in Adoption

Amy Dickinson
: "Bicultural Kids: Parents Who Adopt Children of a Different Ethnicity Are Enjoying the Best of Both Worlds," *Time*, August 26, 2002.

Anne Taylor Fleming
: "A Baby and Two Mothers," *Glamour*, July 1998.

Nancy Hanner
: "Demystifying the Adoption Option," *Newsweek*, February 10, 2003.

Ellen Herman
: "The Paradoxical Rationalization of Modern Adoption," *Journal of Social History*, Winter 2002.

Leslie Doty Hollingsworth
: "Promoting Same-Race Adoption for Children of Color," *Social Work*, vol. 43, no. 2, 1998.

Martine Jacot
: "Adoption: For Love or Money?" *UNESCO Courier*, February 1999.

Gay Jervey
: "Priceless: That's How Adoptive Parents Describe Their Children. But Adoption Is Also a Financial Transaction. A Look at the Intersection of Money and Miracles," *Money*, April 1, 2003.

Andrew Katz
: "Bastard Nation," *POZ*, January 1998.

Anne Adams Lang
: "When Parents Adopt a Child and a Whole Other Culture," *New York Times*, March 8, 2000.

Irving G. Leon
: "Adoption Losses: Naturally Occurring or Socially Constructed?" *Child Development*, March/April 2002.

Tara Mack
: "The Export of American Babies," *Ladies' Home Journal*, October 2000.

K. Mahler
: "Young Mothers Who Choose Adoption May Be Regretful, But Not Usually Depressed," *Family Planning Perspectives*. May/June 1997.

Marvin Olasky
: "Forgotten Choice: Adoption Is a Rebuke to Abortion and Single-Parenting, and the Liberal Media Will Have None of It," *National Review*, March 10, 1997.

Pediatrics
: "Coparent or Second-Parent Adoption by Same-Sex Parents," February 2002.

Katha Pollitt
: "Adoption Fantasy," *Nation*, July 8, 1996.

Dan Savage
: "Is No Adoption Really Better Than a Gay Adoption," *New York Times*, September 8, 2001.

Scott Sherman
: "If Our Son Is Happy, What Else Matters?" *Newsweek*, September 16, 2002.

Christopher Tkaczyk
: "A Waiting Game (Adoption)," *Advocate*, April 15, 2003.

USA Today
: "Adoption More Open for Gays and Lesbians," April 2003.

Jennifer Wilson
: "Blessed by Adoption: More Americans Are Adopting than Ever Before. Their Stories Are Heartwarming Sagas of Hope, Faith, and Love," *Better Homes and Gardens*, February 2003.

Index